Subversives and Mavericks in the Muslim Mediterranean

Subversives and Mavericks in the Muslim Mediterranean

A Subaltern History

EDITED BY ODILE MOREAU AND STUART SCHAAR
PREFACE BY EDMUND BURKE III

University of Texas Press ⟨⟩ *Austin*

Requests for permission to reproduce material from this work should be sent to:
Permissions
University of Texas Press
P.O. Box 7819
Austin, TX 78713-7819
http://utpress.utexas.edu/index.php/rp-form

⊗ The paper used in this book meets the minimum requirements of
ANSI/NISO Z39.48-1992 (R1997) (Permanence of Paper).

Library of Congress Cataloging-in-Publication Data

Names: Moreau, Odile, editor. Schaar, Stuart, editor.
Title: Subversives and mavericks in the Muslim Mediterranean : a subaltern
    history / edited by Odile Moreau and Stuart Schaar ; preface by Edmund
    Burke III.
Description: First edition. Austin : University of Texas Press, 2016. Includes
    bibliographical references and index.
Identifiers: LCCN 2016023594 (print) LCCN 2016024708 (ebook)
    ISBN 9781477319956 (paperback)
    ISBN 9781477310915 (cloth : alk. paper)
    ISBN 9781477310922 (library e-book)
    ISBN 9781477310939 (non-library e-book)
Subjects: LCSH: Muslims—Mediterranean Region—History. Subversive
    activities—Mediterranean Region—History. Mediterranean Region—
    History—19th century. Mediterranean Region—History—20th century.
    Dissenters—Mediterranean Region—History—19th century. Dissenters—
    Mediterranean Region—History—20th century. Individualism—Social
    aspects—Mediterranean Region—History.
Classification: LCC DS37.7 .S83 2016 (print) | LCC DS37.7 (ebook)
DDC   305.6/9709221822—dc23
LC record available at https://lccn.loc.gov/2016023594

doi:10.7560/ 310915

Contents

Preface

EDMUND BURKE III

Subversives and Mavericks in the Muslim Mediterranean represents an important intervention in the historical writing about the Middle East. Since the 1980s and 1990s, historians have explored the history of women, workers, and minorities, utilizing new sources and research strategies. The result has been a revolution in the writing of the history of the Middle East. In the new social history of the 1960s and 1970s, the focus had been upon social categories (class, occupational groups), rather than individuals. But under the inspiration of works like Carlo Ginzburg's *The Cheese and the Worms* and Emmanuel Le Roy Ladurie's *Montaillou*, attention moved to individuals, especially women, workers, and minorities.[1] Inspired by these works, my *Struggle and Survival in the Modern Middle East* introduced this approach to the study of the Middle East.[2] Another source of inspiration was the subaltern school of South Asian historians, who sought to study nonelite persons in the context of the British Empire. Claiming to read sources "against the grain," the subalterns and micro-historians staked claims to a new historical subject, history from below. Among the recent flowering of social biographies of Middle Eastern men and women one might mention Fanny Colonna's *Récits de la province égyptienne* and Baya Gacemi's *Moi, Nadia, Femme d'un émir du GIA*.[3] Odile Moreau's and Stuart Schaar's *Subversives and Mavericks in the Muslim Mediterranean* represents the next step in opening up the history of the Middle East and North Africa to voices from below.

The lives recounted in this book take place in a new cultural-geographical space, the Muslim Mediterranean. This invented space serves as a kind of shorthand for the Ottoman Empire and the Maghreb, and has proved a helpful generalization for this generation of historians.

Taken together with a second important generalization—the circulation of goods, persons, and ideas throughout the Inner Sea—it expands the comparative historical game board, and puts it in motion. Previously, Middle Eastern histories were conceived as occurring in national or regional contexts. The comparative and interactional dimension was largely absent. In particular thanks to Julia Clancy-Smith, whose extraordinary *Mediterraneans: North Africa and Europe in an Age of Migration, c. 1800–1900* draws our attention to the ways in which poor and powerless individuals (as well as elites) spilled over the boundaries between states, we have learned how important it is to understand the kinetic effect of Mediterranean migration stories. Ian Coller's *Arab France: Islam and the Making of Modern Europe, 1798–1831* is another work that crosses borders. In the process it launches an exciting new subject: the histories of Arabs in France, which has great potential to shatter generations of stereotypes.[4]

Finally, the chapters in this book also stand astride the division between the precolonial and colonial histories of Middle Eastern history. Here too *Subversives and Mavericks in the Mediterranean Muslim World* reflects a new historiographical trend that denies the significance of this supposed transition. Whether explicitly acknowledged or not, this approach takes its origins in Timothy Mitchell's *Colonizing Egypt*[5]—a Foucauldian attempt to see the modern history of the region through the discursive lens of modernity. In this telling, Ottoman modernization represented the imposition of Western modernity, either indirectly via its importation in the Ottoman reforms known as the *tanzimat* or directly under the auspices of European colonial powers.

One way of describing the attraction of this volume is to note how the broad angle lens to individual stories opens new perspectives on the pre–World War I Middle Eastern past. Emblems of the modern, officers like the Albanian Ottoman Aref Taher Bey (Odile Moreau), the Moroccan ex-slave and officer Qa'id al-Raha al-Najim al-Akhsassi (Wilfrid Rollman), and Enver Pasha, a leader of the Young Turk movement (Şuhnaz Yilmaz), all link cosmopolitanism, anticolonial resistance, and the dispersal of the modern military toolkit.

Another group of essays in this book introduces the perspectives of Middle Eastern women of both elite and nonelite status and the role of women's networks and the struggle for survival in a patriarchal culture. Education is key. Leïla Blili's study of three Ottoman elite women's lives (Nazli Hanem, Kmar Bayya, and Khiriya Bin Ayyad) showcases how elite women were transformed by modern education and how they worked for social change in their societies. Julia Clancy-Smith's chapter focuses on the lives of two North African women of different generational, social, and cultural backgrounds: Tawhida Ben Shaykh and Fadhma Amrouche. In Clancy-Smith's telling, each was able to fashion for herself a significant public life—and thereby reveal some of the opportunities available to and limits imposed on strong-minded women.

The role of the individual in the social and political struggles of the Middle Eastern region in the late nineteenth and early twentieth centuries provides a third category of contributions to this volume. Some individuals, like Boubeker El-Ghanjaoui, whose portrait is limned by Khalid Ben-Srhir, saw the end of *ancien regime* Morocco and the dawn of the French protectorate as an opportunity for self-enrichment. Others sought in diverse ways to oppose the onset of colonialism with all their force. Stuart Schaar, who has written about the Tunisian labor movement of the early twentieth century, provides an illuminating picture of Mukhtar Al-Ayari. Wilfrid Rollman's social biography of Qa'id al-Najim al-Akhsassi affords us a glimpse of a little-known but important Moroccan activist. Finally, Sanaa Makhlouf's chapter on the Islamist roots of al-Kawakibi's important *Umm al-Qura* considers the cultural background of the author of a key text in the development of fin de siècle Arab modernism.

Life histories such as those conveyed in this book provide a series of perspectives that allow us to grasp the significance of the personal, the political, and the accidental in the unfolding of the lives of individuals. They also provide a view of the history of the pre–World War I era in motion, as individuals coped with the First World War and the onset of colonialism in the transformation of the history of the Middle Eastern region in a key period.

Notes

1. Carlo Ginzburg, *The Cheese and the Worms: The Cosmos of a Sixteenth-Century Miller* (Baltimore: Johns Hopkins University Press, 1980); Emmanuel Le Roy Ladurie, *Montaillou: The Promised Land of Error* (New York: George Brazillier, 1979).

2. Edmund Burke III, *Struggle and Survival in the Modern Middle East* (Berkeley: University of California Press, 1993), 2nd ed. Co-edited with David Yaghoubian, 2005.

3. Fanny Colonna, *Récits de la province égyptienne: Une ethnographie sud/sud*

(Paris: Sindbad, 2004), and Baya Gacemi, *Moi, Nadia, Femme d'un émir du GIA* (Paris: Seuil, 1998). Eng. tr. *I, Nadia, Wife of a Terrorist* (Lincoln: University of Nebraska Press, 2006).

4. Ian Coller, *Arab France: Islam and the Making of Modern Europe, 1798–1831* (Berkeley: University of California Press, 2011).

5. Timothy Mitchell, *Colonizing Egypt* (Cambridge: Cambridge University Press, 1988), paperback ed. (Berkeley: University of California Press, 1991).

Subversives and Mavericks in the Muslim Mediterranean

Map of the Greater Middle East. Courtesy of Styx, Wikimedia Commons.

Trajectories of Subversives and Mavericks in the Muslim Mediterranean

ODILE MOREAU

We have organized this collection in order to demonstrate how non-conformists in the Mediterranean Muslim world in the late nineteenth and early twentieth centuries influenced those around them and fostered positive changes in their societies. Throughout history mavericks and subversives have disturbed the social order, created new ways of doing things, and have seen the world through different lenses than their contemporaries. Their nonconformity often shocked bourgeois and aristocratic smugness and sometimes forced those who came in contact with them to rethink basic values and mores. This book presents key moments from the lives of several such people in the Muslim Mediterranean world at the turn of nineteenth to the twentieth centuries. Some, such as Enver Pasha (chapter 6), were well known and in the limelight throughout their adult lives. Others, such as the Tunisian worker and labor union leader, Mukhtar Al-Ayari (chapter 8), have long been forgotten even in the country where they flourished and made their mark. Three aristocratic women (chapter 3) broke with the traditions of domesticity, set up or participated in intellectual salons, and mixed freely with male intellectuals. Another two women (chapter 7) used modern education to break free of social conformity and constraints. In another case, a freed black slave (chapter 4) liberated himself of social stigmas by allying himself with a foreign diplomat and became his intermediary with the sultan of Morocco.

This book examines such people in order to determine their contributions to local and Mediterranean history and their long-term impact on their societies. For the famous among them, we have chosen moments of their life when they acted out of the limelight, sometimes illegally, underground, or subversively. For those unknown, our contributors have reconstructed parts of their lives where records exist in order to reveal how useful subaltern history can be to illuminate larger trends or periods when we know little about the course of events beyond narrow elite circles.

In this book we feature people who broke norms, including aristocratic women who established salons in Cairo and Tunis, where political leaders sharpened their discourse and gained confidence to oppose their oppressors. As Leïla Blili shows in chapter 3, aristocratic women such as Nazli Hanem (1853–1913), the granddaughter of Mohamed Ali (r. 1805–1848), the ruler of Egypt at the beginning of the nineteenth century, set up salons in Cairo and Tunis where men and women interacted and polished their arguments in favor of liberation. After marrying a Tunisian, Nazli moved to the suburbs of Tunis in La Marsa near the beylical palace and became close friends with Kmar Bayya (1866–1943), who periodically left the confines of the princely harem to participate in Nazli's nearby salon. Kmar, very intelligent and a striking beauty, married several beys and had great influence over Nasir Bey, her husband, and Moncef Bey, her stepson, who both challenged the legitimacy of the French protectorate. She also began educating the young girls living in the royal harem and followed the Turkish press, organizing discussions in the palace on current events. She also had her agents within the Old Destour Party, who she subsidized and encouraged to resist colonialism. Her actions helped politicize the ruling elite circles of Tunisia. Both she and Nazli were mavericks and subversives, challenging the status quo.

So did Khiriya Bin Ayyad, who was the daughter of a tax farmer who absconded with a fortune belonging to the beylical state of Tunis. Taking refuge in the capital of the Ottoman Empire, Khiriya's father, Mahmoud Bin Ayyad, made sure that she received an excellent education. She delivered a lecture in Vienna about the condition of women in the harem, of which she had firsthand experience. It was one of the few texts published by an Ottoman woman in the early twentieth century, and in it she denounced in public the slave trade even though her father engaged in that trade.

The presentation of these aristocrats' itineraries follows a thematic approach: Professor Blili analyzes the weight of these women's fathers and family experiences in both private and public space. Long-term connections were forged between Istanbul, Cairo, and Tunis in the private sphere and especially matrimonial alliances. These women's central roles manifest themselves in informal networks parallel to official diplomacy, such as private circles and connections to local notables—all to evade colonial police controls.

Thanks to groundbreaking feminist research at the end of the twentieth century, we now understand better the nature of harems in which upper class women were raised. When these began breaking up at the end of the nineteenth century, women took with them the skills they had learned in these complex organizations and applied them in other settings, transferring those skills from private to public space. When the Tunisian princess, Kmar Bayya, left the palace grounds to join Hanem's salon, she already had spent years reading the Ottoman press and discussing current events with visitors and some of the harem women. Her worldliness, developed within the confines of the palace walls, had prepared her to participate in the high-powered discussions that took place in Mohamed Ali's granddaughter's nearby home.

Both mavericks and subversives are nonconformists. Under colonial regimes those who opposed European domination refused to abide by rules laid down by the Europeans for collaborators. Instead they defied the status quo and actively organized new forms of resistance either against the European protectors or the traditional society in which they lived.

The Term Maverick

Mavericks are independent people who do not abide by conventions and rules. Their unorthodox tactics often get results and foster change. The term first surfaced in the West (Texas) of the United States when Samuel A. Maverick (1803–1870) refused to brand his cattle and let them roam free. He went against the grain but did not lose any of his livestock. He was a large landowner in the San Antonio region and was more interested in amassing large ranches than in putting livestock on his holdings. His cattle were known as Mavericks, named after him.[1]

Several books have been written about maverick business leaders who follow their instincts and break with accepted patterns, innovate, and succeed in their affairs.[2] Not too many books exist describing historical figures as mavericks, breaking rules, following their own instincts, innovating, and influencing their environments positively. Our own volume presents eleven historical figures who broke rules, went their own ways, and pushed for changes, which sometimes took hold and in some cases produced dramatic results.[3]

Nationalists as Subversives

In the same vein, almost by definition, nationalist leaders opposed to colonialism had to be subversive to escape police surveillance and imprisonment. A subworld existed out of view of the police, their spies, and snitches, which operated out of range of European dominators. The colonial system gave little choice to opponents other than being subversive. The idea was to stay out of range of the police and their informants, which meant that parallel worlds existed that Europeans scarcely knew about but which functioned at the highest levels of the native society. Subversion became the norm for any colonial who challenged the status quo. A cogent example of a subversive character is presented in chapter 8 by Stuart Schaar, Mukhtar Al-Ayari, a populist Tunisian leader in the 1920s, who also served in the French army during the First World War and was often imprisoned for insubordination. On returning to Tunis after the war, he joined the nascent Communist Party, and then worked to form a new indigenous labor union, the UGTT.[4] Al-Ayari was followed continuously by police spies who reported on his many public appearances. An unsung hero on the Left, Al-Ayari ended his days in forced exile far from his native Tunisia.

Alternatively, nonconformists, especially in North Africa, took advantage of European officials and the Catholic Church and mobilized them for their own liberation and to protect themselves from family members who wanted to constrain their actions. Convents would shelter nonconformists and schools set up by nuns would educate them as well, preparing some North Africans to study in France and converting a few to Catholicism. Doing so represented a significant break with the Muslim society, accentuating the gulf between such mavericks and the majority of the Muslim population.

Julia Clancy-Smith, in chapter 7, demonstrates how two North African women, Fadhma Amrouche (1882–1967) and Tawhida Ben Shaykh (1909–2010), broke away from social constraints and liberated themselves through their French education. Fadhma's widowed mother transgressed by having her third child while unmarried. Normally the Kabyle patrilineal society would have punished her severely, most likely killing her, but she escaped their wrath by mobilizing French administrators to protect her, also linking up with French missionary nuns (the White Sisters), who provided her daughter with an education and a place to live. Fadhma subverted the society where she grew up by also seeking French protection and ultimately by becoming a Catholic. In this way, she exploited the contradictions of the colonial situation to maximize her freedom. She married another converted Kabyle and lived with him and eight children in a town with other converted Kabyles before ultimately moving to Tunis, where she lived for forty years, and then France as a French citizen. Two of their children, Jean Amrouche (1906–1962) and Marie-Louise-Taos Amrouche (1913–1976), a poet, singer, and novelist, became major cultural icons of the Franco-Algerian experience, and Fadhma wrote her memoirs, leaving a record of her life, which were published posthumously.[5]

Tawhida Ben Shaykh, a privileged member of a leading Tunisian family, the Ben Ammars, was a true pioneer, being the first Tunisian women to receive a French baccalaureate and then in 1937, the first Arab women to become a medical doctor, having studied in Paris. Supported by the regime of President Habib Bourguiba, she championed birth control while serving the needs of ill Tunisian women. In her life and career she broke down barriers and helped pave the way for other Tunisian women to receive modern educations. Her mother, Halima Ben Ammar, encouraged her and protected her from relatives who wanted Tawhida to follow the traditional route of marriage and establish a foyer instead of heading for Paris for her advanced education. Tawhida later married a dentist in Paris and set up a medical practice in Tunis. Because of the racist nature of the French colonial system, she was shut out of practicing in Tunisian hospitals until after independence in 1956.

Aref Taher Bey and Morocco

In chapter 2 Odile Moreau presents the narratives of an Ottoman military instructor in the Muslim Mediterranean world in the early twentieth century. Born in the Ottoman territory of Albania, Aref Taher Bey held the rank of a captain of operations staff in the Ottoman army. After the Young Turk Revolution of 1908, and more exactly the tentative counterrevolution of March 1909, he was dismissed from the Ottoman army and sought exile in Egypt. From this period until the end of World

War I, he served in various regions of the Muslim Mediterranean. Exiled to Egypt, he heard about the request made to the Egyptian Khedive Abbas Hilmi Pasha asking for Ottoman officers willing to serve in Morocco. From 1909 to 1910 Aref Taher Bey led an unofficial "Ottoman military mission" to Morocco involved in the anticolonial struggle.

His subversive position prior to the French and Spanish conquest of Morocco in 1912 made his status tenuous since France would not tolerate foreign military advisers in Morocco, which they viewed as their sphere of influence. After being expelled from Morocco under the pressure of the French authorities, he returned to Egypt where he continued networking with an Egyptian secret society, al-Ittihad al-Maghrabî [Maghreb Unity], involved in anticolonial fighting in Morocco. He was on several fronts, involved in guerrilla warfare as a regular staff officer, recruiting and directing irregulars and volunteers, involved in special services and networking, and doing press propaganda and writing articles for Ottoman newspapers including *al-Muayyad* in Egypt. During World War I, he was based in Madrid at the Ottoman Embassy, working on a German-Ottoman subversive program in Morocco. During the summer of 1918, he returned to Istanbul where he became aide-de-camp of the new sultan Vahidettin, soon to be deposed by Mustafa Kemal. Afterward, he had to again seek exile in Europe with the sultan's retinue, not allowed to return to the Republic of Turkey. Finally, he returned to his home country, Albania, where he served as a general and lived the rest of his life.

Taher Bey seems to have reveled in his subversive life, first in the Ottoman Empire, then in Egypt, Morocco, and then in Tripolitania. As a maverick who opposed the new regime installed by the Committee of Union and Progress, he naturally gravitated toward military adventures. Sure of himself, because of his excellent training in modern war methods, he had the necessary technical skills to make him valuable to several states. When the Moroccans employed him as the head of an informal military mission to the kingdom, he and his team clashed with the French who were establishing a dominant position in Morocco. The Gauls would not tolerate his and his men's presence in the kingdom as France was consolidating its power and preparing the country for Protectorate status. Even when chased out of the Sharifian kingdom due to French pressure, he kept one foot in the anticolonial struggle there and worked through underground organizations to have influence on events in that country.

His technical skills allowed him to enter the Tripolitanian front on the side of the Ottomans under Enver Pasha's direction. Those skills, in short supply in North Africa, made him an acceptable player despite his apparent insubordination within Ottoman ranks. Necessity made him indispensable and his wayward ways were temporarily and conveniently forgotten. Military needs trumped insubordination and he flourished because he possessed rare skills which were desperately needed. Once the First World War ended, his outsider and oppositional status drew him close to the powerless reigning Caliph/Sultan and for a few years he found a role at the royal palace and in exile as the deposed sultan's aide de camp. By siding with the losing side, in the face of Ataturk's growing popularity and invincibility, Taher Bey found himself without a role in the new Turkish state. Ever the imposing military technician, he then found a post as an important military officer in his native Albania where he moved toward the end of his life. His remarkable trajectory illustrates the importance of modern military technical knowledge in keeping astute mavericks employed and employable.

Ex-Slave, Boubeker al-Ghanjaoui

In chapter 1, Khalid Ben-Srhir presents the very rapid rise of Boubeker al-Ghanjaoui, a humble trader, a cameleer in caravans between Marrakech and the Atlantic ports of El Jadida and Essaouira, who became an important go-between in charge of delivering secret mail and messages between the Moroccan sultan and the British Legation in Tangier for more than twenty years. This dark skinned man from an unknown background with a poor education and near illiteracy succeeded in establishing important relations with key figures in the makhzen while simultaneously working with the British Legation. Becoming an important wealthy and notable, working as a mediator, he enjoyed a unique status of double protégé, first with the sultan and second with the head of the British Legation in Tangier. This self-made man built an efficient network of informers from different social milieus, most of whom were in the Moroccan high administration. Being the wealthiest man in Marrakech, he was accused, falsely it seems, by the British journalist Budgett Meakin of participating in the slave trade and being the owner of houses of ill repute in the town.

Qaʾid al-Raha al-Najim al-Akhsassi, Berber ex-Slave

Wilfrid Rollman in chapter 4 presents a study based on Qaʾid al-Raha al-Najim al-Akhsassi's autobiography, given orally to the historian Muhammad Mukhtar al-Susi and published in his *Maʾsul*. Qaʾid al-Najim was a subaltern figure, who served the state from a largely oral tradition in Tashalhit, the Amazigh language of the Shleu of the Moroccan south, and colloquial Arabic. His parents were second-generation freed slaves. His father seems to have made the transition from slave to a respected independent person in the southeast of Tiznit. Qaʾid al-Najim received an education in a Quranic school [*kuttab*], but because of his poor skills in Arabic and because he was a black descendant of slaves, he was treated very harshly. For all these reasons he fled and never returned. First, he worked in a household and then as a merchant. Due to his capable military and political performances, he was appointed to the *Askar Nizam*, regular troops patterned after European models. He was rapidly promoted as a leader of a battalion (*tabor*) of more than five hundred officers and men (*qaʾid al-raha*), volunteers raised at his own initiative mostly from his native region. After 1900, he participated in all the makhzen's military campaigns. He was working for Sultan Moulay ʾAbd al-Hafidh. As he rose in the ranks of the new army, Qaʾid al-Najim was at the center of the struggle by the state and society to confront the interventions imposed on them by the European powers seeking to control Morocco. Qaʾid al-Najim's struggle was at the same time personal and professional. His commitment to resistance was consistent all of his life, on the level of practice as well as on the symbolic level. As a pious Muslim, for religious reasons he rejected the notion of soldiers wearing European uniforms. He felt obliged to live by the prescriptions of Islamic Shariʾa, and was also involved in the jihad (holy war) to defend his community of Muslims while under attack. He abandoned his position in the army when he became aware that in a French system he would again be subjected to a new form of servitude. He continued as a combatant in the resistance to French and Spanish expansion in Morocco. He was a transitional figure, an individual who bridged cultures while being involved in personal struggles for professional respect and success. His narrative of his own experience mixed analytical and literary genres.

Abd al-Rahman al-Kawakibi: Syrian Novelist

In chapter 5, Sanaa Makhlouf presents the trajectory of the Syrian Kurd-ish writer Abd al-Rahman al-Kawakibi (1855–1902), a subversive, viru-lent critic of despotism and propagator of an Arab-based Muslim revival through an analysis of one of his major works, the semiautobiographical novel *Umm al-Qura*. Abd al-Rahman al-Kawakibi was born in Aleppo to a Persian father and a Kurdish mother. However, most of his biogra-phers present him as an Arab. His real identity is still mysterious. Flu-ent in three languages, Arabic, Turkish, and Persian, he first worked in Aleppo as a lawyer and as a journalist, publishing two newspapers. Due to his political activities he got in trouble with the Ottoman administra-tion. For these reasons, he escaped to Egypt in 1898–1899 to join Mu-hammad Abduh's political circle and was introduced to the Egyptian Khedive Abbas Hilmi Pasha. A copy of the manuscript of this semiauto-biographical novel was presented to the khedive who approved its publi-cation and offered his patronage to its author. This novel, a new genre, was published in Egypt in 1899 and then serialized in the Egyptian newspaper *al-Manar*, directed by Rashid Rida, which had a wide read-ership. Through the description of twelve meetings of a secret political organization, the book presents the three corrupting factors, the ulama, the Ottoman administration, and the Sufi shaykhs with whom he had to fight during all of his life. As a dangerous subversive, Abd al-Rahman al-Kawakibi's life was all the time in danger, and he escaped two assas-sination attempts in Aleppo. Four years after his arrival in Cairo, al-Kawakibi was poisoned in a café where he had met Rashid Rida and Shaykh Ali Yusuf, the head of *al-Muayyad* newspaper.

Enver Pasha in post–World War I Central Asia

In chapter 6, Şuhnaz Yilmaz presents one of the most controversial fig-ures in Turkish history, Enver Pasha. She examines the narratives of his-tory concerning Enver Pasha and the networks he operated in after the First World War. Was he a subversive, a hero, a maverick, or all of these? This top figure became one of the "heroes of freedom" after the Young Turk Revolution of 1908. He rose very quickly in the military ranks. In the autumn of 1911, he volunteered to fight in the Libyan War against the Italians, where he successfully organized local Arab tribes in resis-tance. In early 1914, he became Minister of War and due to his networking with Germany, he was influential in forging an alliance with Germany in World War I. At the end of the war, he had to escape abroad.

The chapter shows the activities of Enver Pasha during his little studied émigré years (1918–1922), especially shining light on the intricate web of networks that he formed, from Anatolia to the Caucasus and Central Asia. He had several allegiances. After an attempt to collaborate with the Bolsheviks, he attempted to resume a leading role in the national resistance in Anatolia, but failed, and joined the Basmatchi movement in Central Asia. The chapter provides a critical analysis of Enver's motives, role, and impact in/on an intricate web of networks in the eventful final chapter of his life.

Difficulties of Writing Subaltern Biographies

Most of these chapters make use of written materials. However, it is especially difficult to find data about most ordinary people such as some of those included in this book. Biographies of individuals had to be compiled from various scattered documents, especially when our authors lacked narratives, diaries, or memoirs of their subjects' lives. This represents most of the cases in this book. By using a comparative approach these biographies and microhistories can help us rethink narratives in modern Middle Eastern and North African studies. Although based on individual and local perspectives, this book, we hope, will reveal new hitherto unrecognized translocal connections across the Muslim world. Our authors explore the itineraries of both well-known and unknown personalities.

That poses two very different sets of problems. For known people, we hoped to discover the networks in which they moved as well as how they affected those they worked with and how they left their mark on other individuals and their times. This has entailed writing history at a macro level, placing our well-known personalities in new contexts, and allowing us to view well-explored events in a new light. For those of our personalities whom historians have ignored, we needed to establish their importance as guideposts to understand the times in which they lived.

Our approach uses microhistory and subaltern studies.[6] Oftentimes we have had to depend on broader social history[7] and contextual analysis of the times in which our subjects lived and worked, since important documents, memoirs, narratives, and life experiences in many cases may have been lacking to construct classical biographies. Such an approach has allowed us to look at old material and known events in a new light, to illuminate new aspects of Muslim history.[8]

Biographical Geography

Our biographical approach has its limits, since our contributors have little interest in relating the total lives of our subjects. In the chapters that follow our authors have chosen to present a number of moments, or some parts of the itinerary of an individual and not all of his/her life. Our authors' relationships to the individuals they have chosen to study were not always very clear. Neither was it always easy to establish definitive accounts of people's lives because of lacunes in the available data, inevitable mysteries regarding individuals, and the lack of any professionally generated psychological profiles.

The individuals presented in this collective edition have been chosen due to the important role they played in others' lives. They are not ordinary people because they asserted themselves and influenced others while not necessarily becoming well known or famous, but at the least they scored numerous achievements. In addition, some of them were from modest origins, such as El-Ghanjaoui, and later moved up in the society.

We have various forms of narratives in this book based on real-life experiences. Some are linear, following some semblance of a chronological order and others show different thematic facets illuminating a character's complexity.

We have particular difficulties hearing women's voices because, during this period, few of them wrote about themselves. Official archives do contain references to many women, but male historians have often neglected to report on their activities because they often considered what they did and accomplished unimportant or marginal. Women historians, with fresh insights into the past, often have had to rediscover the roles of other women in historical events.

Social "Bio"itineraries

Reconstructing individuals' trajectories may allow us to shed light on individual strategies and experiences. In fact, we need to understand how individuals were connected with institutions, intellectual trends, and media forms. To accomplish our task we need to contextualize itineraries and their connections with existing networks[9] to avoid what Pierre Bourdieu named biographic illusion.[10] This notion of "overlapping" implies various pieces fitting together: temporal, spatial, and various circles, such as familial, professional, or political friendships. In cases where these did not exist, we need to know how our actors created the necessary networks in which they functioned. Deciphering a plurality of networks and understanding how they worked therefore will be one way to help us understand how individuals navigated in unfamiliar territory and cultures, as an outcome of a complex set of historical interactions.

Mediterranean Stories?

Could we depict these itineraries, these "stories" as Mediterranean life stories? This "Mediterranean" term appears at the same time very general and very specific. From the early nineteenth century, the Mediterranean world was from a very long time in contact with other world configurations such as the Atlantic and the Indian Oceans.[11] What constitutes community/communities in and across the Muslim Mediterranean world? How did local individuals define the communities? Is there a sense, a feeling of Mediterranean-ness among the communities?[12] What are the characteristics of various kinds of connections that were created and eventually cut off in the Muslim Mediterranean world?

Women's lives and experiences are most of the time not included in history books, and it is particularly the case in history books dealing with the Muslim Mediterranean world. However, as these five female itineraries will show, certain women succeeded in becoming prominent individuals and realized achievements not only in their private lives but also in their public lives and had impacts on people within their related networks, be they familial, professional, or social.

People on the Move in the Mediterranean World

We will present trajectories of people on the move who influenced an assortment of people in various places, and most of them had an impact on the circuits of thought and action in their environments. In fact, they introduced different worldviews, manners, and categories of thinking and ways of life. The communication in the Mediterranean world changed radically, due to time-space compressions. These case studies highlight cross-border connections in the Mediterranean World. How are the networks and paths through the Mediterranean forged, created, opened/closed, and reopened? What are the effects of such processes on individual lives?

Freedom

The question of slavery appears directly or indirectly in several chapters. After the abolition of slavery, new kinds of relationships between individuals changed the ways of living during the nineteenth century. For example, Qa'id al-Najim, who was the son of freed slaves, had done all he could to protect his freedom. In fact, he avoided several attempts to enslave him. Avoiding this discrimination against him, the Moroccan new army gave him new opportunities to become a respected professional person.

Networks

Networks are not always easy to identify. Often, in order to protect themselves from the rapacity of states, they were organized secretly and remained secret. Such were the Masons, who spread rapidly throughout the Mediterranean zone. For example, Italians created the first Masonic lodge in Tunis in 1830. Movements of youth, giving themselves the titles of Young Turks, Young Tunisians, and so forth, or "pan-Islamic movements," always under intensive European police surveillance, had to remain largely underground or out of view of the old regimes—as was the case in the Ottoman Empire—or the colonial regime's secret police and informants. These movements, sometimes bringing reform and modernity in their wake, have had important impacts intellectually and institutionally on the countries within the Mediterranean basin and often held the seeds for later nationalist movements. At times animated by ideas coming from the French Revolution, they have carried along with them demands for constitutions and parliaments.

Every individual presented in this book was involved in struggles against very difficult circumstances, either in his/her private or public life against power, be they local or colonial. All these individuals had dynamic personalities, carrying out tireless activities, and were very courageous men and women.

In constructing the microhistories of little-known people, our contributors have had to conduct interviews and search widely in an assortment of archives, private papers, diaries, memoirs, and police reports. Often the colonial, Ottoman, and Arab police followed our protagonists and reported on their activities, political or otherwise. Such records are as good as the observers' ability to decipher events and contexts. Much was hidden from snooping eyes and ears, so that unconventional records in local languages often had to be consulted to divulge the secret sides to our protagonist's lives, which they hid from the authorities. Eccentrics and mavericks engaging in subversive activities usually had more to hide than most people, making the reconstruction of parts of their lives ever more difficult.

Getting to these sources often required great digging and resourcefulness beyond the normal research conducted on famous people who lived in the light of day. Of course, all people have their private lives, which outsiders find difficult or impossible to decipher. In addition, most archives have reserved files that only librarians, or privileged individuals, may see in order to protect people and their families. It can take decades and even generations for those files to be opened, so that a more complete story often remains impossible to reconstruct. The reserved files deal with scandals, private and often illegal land transactions, brushes with the law, and so forth. They often supply the missing pieces that make given events intelligible. Without them, and even with them, biographies are often incomplete and deficient. Knowing this should keep historians and biographers humble about the possibility of constructing a full history of anyone's life. In addition, some people are inveterate liars, others brag, while still others hide the salacious parts of their life, if such parts exist. In this sense, we have to keep in mind that reconstructing people's lives is often akin to writing a novel, since you may approximate truth without being certain of reality in its full dimensions.

Then why do it? Approximate lives are better than not knowing at all and may give us clues into larger social or political trends that we may otherwise ignore. Likewise, the characters in this book travelled widely and formed or came in contact with large networks, often across the Mediterranean and beyond, to facilitate their work. Comprehending how those networks operated can guide us to see history in a new light and understand the weight of these individuals in helping to create a new world different than the one into which they were born.

Likewise, the development of native theater companies in Tunis in the early years of the twentieth century created new public spaces for artists to meet and socialize and become politicized. Their highly censored theatrical productions performed for the bourgeoisie as well as students and workers, who flocked to plays and filled cheap balcony seats, infused the audiences with nationalism when actors spoke off script, and added their own politicized dialogues. We do not know the connections between the small salons that developed in many Arab countries at the turn of the nineteenth century and the new cultural clubs that cropped up as nascent nationalist movements emerging before and after the First World War. Much research still has to be done to connect the dots and make sense of emerging civil society as it developed across the Mediterranean.

Recent theoretical work on twenty-first century movements and what Asef Bayat calls "non-movement movements" leading to the Arab citizens' revolts, beginning in Tunisia in December 2010, gives us a greater appreciation of public space where street politics plays itself out. New forces coalesced in the early twentieth century and today continue to shape events. Women's movements formed to extend rights for themselves and all citizens. Labor unions organized workers to improve the quality of their lives. Their demonstrations, strikes, and other actions heightened consciousness and pressured the liberal colonial state to become interventionary in order to improve conditions of life and work. Mosques served as points of organization for the nationalist movements as they did in recent revolts, just as outdoor markets did, for they are/were the places where people congregated, forming the hubs of communication then and now. Of course, the Internet did not exist, but networking did. Just as the Internet has produced instant and complex networks for organizing mass movements in recent years, their existence sensitizes us to the importance of networks of all kinds and forces us to pay attention to how networks developed and worked at the turn of the nineteenth to twentieth century.

Social Biographies and the Question of Lacunes

Social context becomes extremely important in elucidating most of the case studies that we present. By the same token, the narrative benefits from analysis of individuals and enriches our knowledge of the society and the networks in which they moved. We follow the way shown by Edmund Burke III and David Hagopian in their illuminating edited volume, *Struggle and Survival in the Modern Middle East*,[13] where the authors contributing to their volume have drawn social biographies to explore the complex ways in which individuals relate to social structures, process reality, and interact with their culture. Doing this has allowed us to shed light on individual strategies and experiences. We also needed to understand how individuals were connected with institutions, intellectual trends, and the media.

This book fits into two important new categories of comparative history. The first, modern Mediterranean Studies, began with the pioneering work of Fernand Braudel, *The Mediterranean and the Mediterranean World in the Age of Phillip II* (Vols. 1–2, 1975 and 1976). He demonstrated that by studying this region, new light can be shed on old history that historians missed by concentrating on purely national sources. S. D. Goitein in his pioneering study of Medieval Mediterranean Jewish communities as depicted in the Cairo *Geniza* (published in six volumes up until his death in 1985), reconstructed the life of Jewish traders and their society and culture across the Mediterranean and showed the networks developed by the communities within the Mediterranean that gave Jewish traders commercial advantages over their competitors. More recently, David Abulafia, who teaches Mediterranean history at Cambridge University, has published *The Mediterranean in History* (Los Angeles: J. Paul Getty Museum, 2011), which established the sea as a cogent area for study. Julia Clancy-Smith in her recent prize-winning *Mediterraneans: North Africa and Europe in the Age of Migration, c. 1800–1900* (Berkeley: University of California Press, 2012), places Tunisia within a large framework and demonstrates interrelationships between the varied peoples who settled on her shores and ultimately joined the colonial enterprise led by France in that country. Lastly, the review *Mediterraneans*, published in French and English by Kenneth Brown over the past decade, has celebrated the interactions of Mediterranean culture, seeing the region as a whole. By doing so, Brown has contributed to defining a new region of study that makes eminent sense. In early 2013 the US AP Program for high school seniors and college freshmen organized a conference in Washington, DC, attended by Edmund Burke III, Julia Clancy-Smith, the Moroccan historian Driss Maghraoui, curriculum developer Joan Brodsky Shur, and others dealing with constructing new programs for Mediterranean history in the United States. Their work will establish a new field of studies for high schools and AP classes.

Second, there is a new trend in colonial studies identifying the ways in which the unwillingly colonized, though forced to accept foreign domination, subverted the system as much as they could. The pioneering work of Hamid Irbouh, *Art in the Service of Colonialism: French Art Education in Morocco 1912–1956* (London, New York: Tauris Academic Studies, 2005), analyzes the way that young Moroccan girls willingly attended French schools, run by French women, where they learned artisanal skills, but in the process took every occasion they found to subvert their teacher's efforts to instill discipline, the work ethic, and respect for time. In so doing, the pupils learned new methods of creating old objects, but made the life of their teachers extremely miserable.

Our book likewise examines the significance of subversion and insubordination in precolonial and colonial history in the Muslim Mediterranean in an attempt to show how a new form of primary resistance to colonialism developed within the hegemonic encroaching European empires. Mavericks, such as the ones presented in our book, changed the course of history through subterfuge and noncooperation, by joining European institutions while subverting them. This new dimension of response of the colonized should be incorporated more into the analysis of the field of resistance to colonialism.

Mediterranean Stories of People on the Move

Are the "stories" we present in this book peculiarly Mediterranean? The Mediterranean world for a long time had been in contact with the Atlantic and the Indian Oceans.[14] How did Mediterranean peoples differentiate themselves from others? What constituted communities in and across the Muslim Mediterranean world? How did individuals define their communities? Was there a sense or a feeling of "Mediterraneanness" among them?[15] What characterized the connections that were created and eventually differentiated people in the Muslim Mediterranean world from others outside this region?

Until recent times women's lives and experiences in the Mediterranean Muslim world have not been included in history books. However as our five female itineraries show, certain women succeeded in emerging onto the public scene and realizing achievements in their private and public lives. They also influenced others who came in contact with them.

We present trajectories of individuals on the move who influenced an assortment of people in various places. Most of them had an impact on thought and action in their environments. In fact, they introduced different worldviews, manners, categories of thinking, and ways of life. Communication in the Mediterranean world changed radically, due to variations in perceptions of time and space as new networks and paths through the Mediterranean were forged, created, opened, and closed, and reopened. We have posed the question what were the effects of such processes on individual lives?

As mentioned previously, the question of slavery and the relationships developed after its abolition have appeared directly or indirectly in several chapters of this book. For example, Khiriya Bin Ayyad, in chapter 3, whose father Mahmoud Bin Ayyad was a slave merchant, publically denounced the trade in human beings in a lecture that she gave in Vienna.

In order to protect them from the rapacity of states, networks were organized secretly. As discussed previously, the Masons who spread rapidly throughout the Mediterranean zone were such a group. Italians created a Masonic lodge in Tunis in 1830. Youth movements such as the Young Turks and Young Tunisians and Pan-Islamic movements also faced constant European and Ottoman police surveillance and had to remain largely underground or out of view.

Notes

1. See Irving and Kathryn Sexton, *Samuel A. Maverick* (Gainesville, FL: Naylor, 1964); *Memoirs of Mary A. Maverick, A Journal of Early Texas* (first published in 1921; San Antonio, TX: Maverick Publications, 2005); Gene Fowler, *Mavericks: A Gallery of Texas Characters* (Austin: University of Texas Press, 2008).

2. See, for example, William C. Taylor and Polly G. LaBarre, *Mavericks at Work: Why the Most Original Minds in Business Win* (New York: Harper Reprint, 2008).

3. Doug Hall, *The Maverick Mindset: Finding the Courage to Journey from Fear to Freedom* (New York: Simon & Schuster, 1997).

4. See chapter 8, Stuart Schaar, "Mukhtar al-Ayari: A Radical Tunisian in the 1920s and His Place in Labor History."

5. Fadhma-Aïth-Mansour Amrouche, *Histoire de ma vie*, ed. Vincent Monteil and Kateb Yacine, 2005.

6. Giovanni Levi, "Les usages de la biographie," *Annales* ESC 44 (1989) 6: 1325–1336.

7. Edmund Burke III, "The Mediterranean before Colonialism: Fragments from the Life of 'Ali bin 'Uthman al-Hammi in the late Eighteenth and Nineteenth Centuries," in *North Africa, Islam and the Mediterranean World*, ed. Julia Clancy-Smith (London: Frank Cass Publishers, 2001).

8. Jacques Revel, "L'Histoire au ras du sol," Preface to Giovanni Levi, *Le pouvoir au village: Histoire d'un exorciste dans le Piémont au 19ème siècle* (Paris: Gallimard, 1989), 1–33.

9. Jacques Revel, ed., *Jeux d'échelle: La micro-analyse à l'expérience* (Paris: Gallimard, 1996).

10. Pierre Bourdieu, "L'illusion biographique," in *Raisons pratiques sur la théorie de l'action* (Paris: Seuil, 1994).

11. Julia Clancy-Smith, "Khayr ad-Din," in O. Moreau, *Réforme de l'État et réformismes au Maghreb* (Paris-Tunis: L'Harmattan-IRMC [Institut de Recherche sur le Maghreb Contemporain], collection "Socio-anthropologie des mondes méditerranéens," 2009), 164.

12. Julia Clancy-Smith, *Mediterraneans: North Africa and Europe in the Age of Migration, c. 1800–1900* (Berkeley: University of California Press, 2011), 347.

13. Edmund Burke III and David Yaghoubian, eds., *Struggle and Survival in the Modern Middle East*, 2nd ed. (Berkeley: University of California Press, 2005), 6.

14. Julia Clancy-Smith, "Khayr ad-Din," In O. Moreau, *Réforme de l'État et réformismes au Maghreb*, 164.

15. Julia Clancy-Smith, *Mediterraneans: North Africa and Europe in the Age of Migration, c. 1800–1900*, 347.

Bibliography

Ahmad, Eqbal, and Stuart Schaar. "M'hamed 'Ali, Tunisian Labor Organizer," in Edmund Burke III, ed., *Struggle and Survival in the Modern Middle East*, 2nd ed. Berkeley: University of California Press, 2005.

———. "Tahar al-Haddad: A Tunisian Intellectual [1920's]." *The Maghreb Review* (London) 21, no. 3–4 (1996): 240–55.

Al Sayyad, Nezar, ed. *Hybrid Urbanism: On the Identity Discourse and the Built Environment*. Westport, CT: Praeger, 2001.

Anderson, Benedict. *Imagined Communities: Reflections on the Origin and Spread of Nationalism*. London, New York: Verso, 1983.

"Biographies et récits de vie." *Alfa, Maghreb et sciences sociales*. Tunis: Institut de Recherches sur le Maghreb Contemporain, 2005.

Bourdieu, Pierre. "L'illusion biographique." In *Raisons pratiques sur la théorie de l'action*. Paris: Seuil, 1994.

Burke III, Edmund. "Pan-Islam and Moroccan Resistance to French Colonial Penetration, 1900–1912." *Journal of African History* 13 (1972): 97–118.

———. "The Mediterranean before Colonialism: Fragments from the Life of 'Ali bin 'Uthman al-Hammi in the late Eighteenth and Nineteenth Centuries." In Julia Clancy-Smith, ed., *North Africa, Islam and the Mediterranean World*, London: Frank Cass, 2001.

Burke III, Edmund, and David Hagopian, eds. *Struggle and Survival in the Modern Middle East*. 2nd ed. Berkeley: University of California Press, 2005.

Caillet, Laurence. *La maison Yamazaki: la vie exemplaire d'une paysanne japonaise devenue chef d'une entreprise de haute coiffure*. Paris: Plon, 1991.

Clancy-Smith, Julia. "Women, Gender, and Migration in the 19th-Century Mediterranean World." *Gender and History* 17 (April 2005): 1.

———. *Mediterraneans: North Africa and Europe in the Age of Migration, c. 1800–1900*. Berkeley: University of California Press, 2011.

———, ed. *North Africa, Islam and the Mediterranean World*. London: Frank Cass, 2001.

Clancy-Smith, Julia, and Frances Gouda, eds. *Domesticating the Empire: Gender, Race, and Family Life in the Dutch and French Empires*. Charlottesville, VA: University Press of Virginia, 1998.

Corbin, Alain. *Le monde retrouvé de Louis-François Pinagot. Sur les traces d'un inconnu (1798–1876)*. Paris: Flammarion, 1998.

Dosse, François. *Le pari biographique: écrire une vie*. Paris: La Découverte, 2005.

Georgeon (François). *Abdül Hamid II, le sultan calife (1876–1909)*. Paris: Fayard, 2003.

Gribaudi, Maurizio. "Les discontinuités du social: Un modèle configurationnel." In Lepetit Bernard, dir., *Les formes de l'expérience. Une autre histoire sociale*. Paris: Albin Michel, 1995, 187–225.

Gribaudi, Maurizio. "Des micro-mécanismes aux configurations globales: Causalité et temporalité historiques dans les formes d'évolution et de l'administration française au XIXième siècle." In Jürgen Schlumbohm, ed., *Mikrogeschichte-Makrogeschichte: komplementär oder inkommensurabel?* Göttingen: Wallstein Verlag, 1998, 83–128.

Heyberger Bernard, Chantal Verdeil, ed. *Hommes de l'entre-deux: Parcours individuals et portraits de groupes sur la frontière de la Méditerranée (XVIe–XXe siècles)*. Paris: Les Indes savantes, Rivages des Xantons, 2009.

al-Hajwi, Muhammad Ibn al Hassan. *Le voyage d'Europe—le périple d'un réformiste—traduction et postface de Roussillon, A et A. Saâf*. Casablanca: Afrique-Orient, 2001.

Horden, Peregrine, and Nicolas Purcell. *The Corrupting Sea: A Study of Mediterranean History*. Oxford: Blackwell, 2000.

Levi, Giovanni. "Les usages de la biographie." *Annales* ESC 44, no. 6 (1989): 1325–1336.

Le Goff, Jean. *Saint Louis*. Paris: Gallimard, 1996.

Levi, Giovanni. "The Origins of the Modern State and the Microhistorical Perspective." In Jürgen Schlumbohm, ed., *Mikrogeschichte-Makrogeschichte: komplementär oder inkommensurabel?* Göttingen: Wallstein Verlag, 1998, 53–82.

McKeown, Adam. "Global Migration, 1846–1940." *Journal of World History* 15, no. 2 (June 2004): 155–189.

Miller Gilson, Susan, and Muhammad al-Jaffar. *Disorienting Encounters: Travels of a Moroccan Scholar in France in 1845–1846; The Voyage of Muhammad al-Jaffar*. Translated and edited by Susan Gilson Miller. Berkeley: University of California Press, 1992.

Moreau, Odile, ed. *Réforme de l'Etat et réformismes au Maghreb (XIXe–XXe siècles)*. Paris: L'Harmattan, 2009.

———. *L'Empire ottoman à l'âge des réformes: Les hommes et les idées du "Nouvel Ordre" militaire (1826–1914)*. Paris: Maisonneuve et Larose, Collection passé ottoman, présent turc, 2007.

————. "Les ressources scientifiques de l'Occident au service de la modernisation de l'armée Ottomane (fin XIXe début XXe siècle)." *Revue des mondes musulmans et de la Méditerranée* (2003): 101–102, 51–67.

Moreau, Odile, and Abderrahmane El Moudden, eds. "Réforme par le haut, réforme par le bas: la modernisation de l'armée aux 19ᵉ et 20ᵉ siècles." *Quaderni di Oriente Moderno*, Rome, 30 n.s., no. 84 (2004): 5.

Passeron, Jean-Claude. "Biographies, flux, itinéraires, trajectoires." *Revue française de sociologie* 21 (1989): 3–22.

Pedani, Maria Pia. *Dalla frontiera al confine*. Rome: Herder Editrice, 2002.

Revel, Jacques. "L'Histoire au ras du sol." Préface à Giovanni Levi. *Le pouvoir au village: Histoire d'un exorciste dans le Piémont au 19ème siècle*. Paris: Gallimard, 1989, 1–33.

Revel, Jacques, ed. *Jeux d'échelle: La micro-analyse à l'expérience*. Paris: Gallimard, 1996.

Ricœur, Paul. *Soi-même comme un autre*. Paris: Le Seuil, 1990.

Sivaramakrishnan, K. "Situating the Subaltern: History and Anthropology in the Subaltern Studies Project." *Journal of Historical Sociology* 8, no. 4 (1995).

Werner, Michael, and Benedict Zimmermann. "Penser l'histoire croisée: entre empire et réflexivité." *Annales Histoire, Sciences Sociales* 1 (2003): 7–36.

PART I

Boubeker El-Ghanjaoui in Marrakech. Published for P. D. Trotter, *Our Mission to the Court of Morocco in 1880*, p. 84.

CHAPTER 1

The Life of Boubeker El-Ghanjaoui: From a Cameleer to a Wealthy Notable in Precolonial Morocco, 1870–1905

KHALID BEN-SRHIR

Through documents newly discovered and rarely used, this chapter will trace the career of Boubeker El-Ghanjaoui, an unusual and little known personality during the Moroccan precolonial period. This man, who had begun his career as a cameleer between Marrakech and the ports of El Jadida and Essaouira, became a British protégé in the service of an English trading company located in Essaouira and Marrakech. The documents gathered about this man allowed us to follow the rapid ascension of this humble trader to the point that he became one of the richest Moroccans. He had succeeded in winning the confidence of John Drummond Hay (1845–1886), the representative of Queen Victoria in Morocco, as well as the trust of the Sultan Sidi Mohamed ben Abderrahman (1859–1873) and his successor Moulay El-Hassan (1873–1894), who assigned him the mission of transmitting secretly the confidential correspondence between the makhzen (the bureaucracy surrounding the ruler) and the head of the British Legation in Tangier. This mission, which involved enormous risks, allowed Boubeker El-Ghanjaoui not only to become one of the most influential persons in the city of Marrakech because of his enormous wealth, but it made him one of the principal witnesses to a number of important political and economic events that Morocco experienced during the precolonial period in its relationships with European nations.

In 1896, the British explorer Cunninghame Graham described Boubeker Ben El-Haj Al-Bachir, nicknamed El-Ghanjaoui, as someone "known from the Atlas ranges to the Rif . . . and from the Sahara to Essaouira for being detested and feared by everyone, but was respected."[1]

El-Ghanjaoui was a flamboyant figure who played a key role in the history of Moroccan-British relations during the second half of the nineteenth century.[2] However, he remained a shadowy figure, for he received little attention and study from historians.[3] There are many reasons for such neglect. First, it was difficult to have access to documents related to his career and the missions with which he was charged within the framework of Moroccan–British relations. Second, in his close relations with key figures of the makhzen, be they sultans themselves, different ministers, 'umal (governors of towns), qa'ids (tribal governors), military men and umana (preceptors and custom functionaries), he operated in extreme secrecy. Beside this, he had ties with rich people, dignitaries, inside and outside the makhzen, and in Muslim, Jewish, and Christian circles. El-Ghanjaoui led a secret life in many fields, which were sensitive and sometimes suspicious.

Given his importance, I trace the different stages he went through from his appearance on the Moroccan scene in the 1870s up to his death in 1905. I also discuss the crucial events that marked his life, keeping in mind that fluctuations in his career were directly linked to British interests in Morocco during the same period.

El-Ghanjaoui worked for the British Legation in Tangier for more than twenty years, starting in 1873. Consular protection of El-Ghanjaoui was complicated socially, politically, and economically. We have to ask under which circumstances such protection was granted? What position did the man have in the history of Moroccan–British relations? What tasks did he undertake and what impact did they have on the makhzen, Britain, and El-Ghanjaoui himself, his entourage, and other men of his era, be they Moroccan or foreigners?

El-Ghanjaoui's Background and His Involvement with the Elite: Lack of Information about his Early Identity and Ties with Britain

We do not know for sure who the man was. We know neither when nor where he was born. Cunninghame Graham, who knew him well, said that El-Ghanjaoui was from an unknown background and was almost black.[4] When talking about himself, El-Ghanjaoui states that he started his career as a cameleer[5] in caravans, which used to carry imported and exported goods from Marrakech to the ports of El Jadida, Safi, and Essaouira. He gradually established close ties with the trader Hunot, a brother of the British vice consul in Safi who served as a general agent for Messrs Perry and Company, Liverpool, England. Their Moroccan branch dealt in various imported and exported goods, which they shipped from and to Marrakech, Safi, and Essaouira, as well as to Liverpool. The British botanist Hooker reported that El-Ghanjaoui used to work with a middleman by the name of El-Hassnaoui, for Hunot in 1871.[6]

The name El-Ghanjaoui appeared in official Moroccan documents in the early 1870s, when he worked in Marrakech in the wool trade. In 1871, English commercial representatives complained that the *muhtassib* (market inspector) forbade them from buying wool in Marrakech for eight days, and that this official raised the commodity's price twice. When the representative of Queen Victoria in Morocco and the head of the British Legation in Tangier John Drummond Hay heard the news, he complained to the sultan's *naib* (representative) Mohamed Bargach claiming that the Marrakech *qa'id* breached some terms and articles of the 1856 treaty between Britain and Morocco,[7] and he should compensate the company for losses incurred. Besides, he stressed, Bargach should let the sultan know about the disgraceful conduct of the Marrakech governor Qa'id Ibn Daoud. Drummond Hay claimed that Ibn Daoud would not have acted the way he did without the protection of the sultan's *hajib* (chamberlain) Ahmed Ben Moussa.[8] When the British botanist Hooker came to Marrakech carrying a recommendation from the Sultan Mohamed Ben Abderrahman instructing his qa'id Ibn Daoud to find a decent house where the botanist could live, the *qa'id* did not carry out the sultan's orders and made Hooker live in a house almost in ruins.[9] When the *khalifa* Sidi Hassan (viceroy, crown prince, and soon to be sultan himself) found out about this, he sent Boubeker El-Ghanjaoui to Ibn Daoud to blame and scold him for not respecting the orders of his father the sultan. Ibn Daoud then remedied the problem and put Hooker and his companions in the Ibn Idriss palace.[10]

Drummond Hay reiterated his claim to Bargach against Ibn Daoud and asked the makhzen for 750 *riyal* in compensation for the loss that he claimed the British traders incurred when they were prevented from buying wool, and also for 250 *riyal* compensation for almonds, which Ibn Daoud confiscated from a British trader, quantities of which were spoiled during that confiscation.[11]

The tension continued between Qa'id Ibn Daoud, El-Ghanjaoui, and British traders who had important commercial interests in Marrakech and its neighboring areas. More than once, the Marrakech governor was accused of intentionally obstructing their business.[12] The British merchants and their agents made their claims to Drummond Hay and produced evidence about how Ibn Daoud's conduct significantly affected their trade. The head of the British Legation reported their claims to the Sultan Mohamed Ben Abderrahman, who asked his governor about the matter, but the latter denied every accusation, which he backed up by producing notarized documents.

Not only did Bargach send such documents to Drummond Hay to support Ibn Daoud's claim of innocence, but he asked him to punish the British traders because they falsely accused the sultan's governor.[13] However, Drummond Hay was not convinced about the authenticity of the notarized documents and ordered his vice consul Hunot, who lived in Safi, to go to Marrakech and look into the matter. Hunot claimed that the investigation was difficult to carry out and accused Ibn Daoud of preventing any *qadi* (judge) or *udul* from drawing up documents that would accuse him or confirm the veracity of the charges. Hunot came to the conclusion that the notary's documents used by Ibn Daoud to acquit himself were false. Following this investigation, Drummond Hay insisted on the application of the second article of the Convention of Peace and Friendship, concluded between Morocco and Britain in 1856, to punish Ibn Daoud and pay all the fees, which covered Hunot's trips from Safi to Marrakech and his stay in the city while the investigation took place.[14] At the same time, Drummond Hay sent a private letter to the new Moroccan minister, Idriss Belyamani, warning him against covering up and protecting Ibn Daoud. He also alluded that he was sure that the chamberlain Ahmed Ben Moussa was protecting the Marrakech governor.[15]

One of the proofs sent by Drummond Hay to Bargach included evidence that the Marrakech governor forged El-Ghanjaoui's signature on notarized documents and fabricated others through threats and intimidation to discharge him from any accusation. The British traders accused Qa'id Guerraoui of helping Ibn Daoud fabricate notarized documents by exerting pressure on some Muslims and Jews from Marrakech, either through threats or bribes. The *semsar* (brokers) of the British traders in Marrakech lodged a complaint against the governor claiming that he threatened their lives. Drummond Hay accused the makhzen and held it responsible for any losses that might affect the British traders' interests in Marrakech, where Ibn Daoud and his aides were dominant.[16]

Following the escalation of the quarrel, the sultan ordered his *khalifa* Sidi Hassan in Marrakech to look into the matter and inform him about the results of the investigation. His report concluded that El-Ghanjaoui's accusations against Ibn Daoud were groundless. The *khalifa* assured his father (the sultan) that the document that El-Ghanjaoui claimed to be false was in fact written by a scribe working for El-Ghanjaoui, and that "El-Ghanjaoui had scribes who made up documents for him, which he himself sometimes signed or authorized. It was shown that this was a trick that would enable him to deny whatever need be."[17]

Even if Consul White, the deputy of Drummond Hay, who was then abroad, approved such contradictory proofs and claims made by El-Ghanjaoui, he refused to consider them to be final. He was convinced that the truth would be difficult to determine in a place where Ibn Daoud and his aides controlled everything. Therefore, White suggested that to put an end to the matter, further investigation should take place in Tangier in the presence of the conflicting parties or their delegates.[18]

The Protection of El-Ghanjaoui by the Sultan's *Khalifa*

The events that followed prevented bringing the case to justice in Tangier. El-Ghanjaoui came to Tangier and informed White that Ibn Daoud had jailed some of his assistants who managed the business of Perry Company. He added that he had fled from Marrakech at night because Ibn Daoud attempted to have him murdered. White reacted quickly and strongly and warned the sultan's *naib* Bargach to prevent any losses that would affect the British traders' interests while El-Ghanjaoui, their agent, was away from Marrakech. To stop things from worsening and tension between the two parties becoming more bitter, White stressed that Bargach should ensure that El-Ghanjaoui receive a document from the sultan, which would include an explicit order allowing him to be directly protected by the sultan's *khalifa* in Marrakech.

It seems that after following the case from the beginning, the sultan preferred White's suggestion in order to avoid any escalation in the tension between the British traders' agents and his governor Ibn Daoud. To avoid any material losses—be they real or made up—he would find himself obliged to pay compensation from the treasury. Thanks to the sultan's decision, the *semsar* Boubeker El-Ghanjaoui was able to carry on his duties as an agent working for the British traders, supervising their interests in Marrakech, under the protection of the sultan's *khalifa*. In that way, he was safe from any unexpected attacks from the powerful Qa'id Ibn Daoud and his aides.[19]

Given the circumstances, the makhzen had to change its views about Boubeker El-Ghanjaoui. Formerly, the *naib* Bargach described him as "not chivalrous, but rabble."[20] The sultan himself insulted El-Ghanjaoui when he declaimed, "Look what the ill-mannered man said about the governor of Marrakech, because he was just backed up by some British traders."[21]

The sultan's agreement that El-Ghanjaoui should, despite his vile qualities, be protected by his *khalifa* Sidi Hassan demonstrates the importance of British influence in Morocco during the mid-nineteenth century. The strengthening of the *semsar*'s position in Marrakech meant that the makhzen backed up British trade interests and also strengthened them in other Moroccan inland areas, which were miles away from Marrakech. It opened the way for a little known and illiterate man to foster his relations not only with the sultan, but with many important dignitaries of the court as well as powerful Muslim and Jewish traders. In this way, while enriching himself, he served and expanded British interests.

Drummond Hay returned from his annual home leave to Tangier after being promoted by the Foreign Office for what he did to foster British influence and its reputation in Morocco to the post of plenipotentiary minister. He therefore had to pay an official visit to the Court to hand his new credentials to the sultan and let him know about his promotion.[22]

Meanwhile, Governor Ibn Daoud died in mysterious circumstances and was replaced by Ibn Daoud's son Mohamed before Drummond Hay set foot in Marrakech on April 5, 1873. The new governor received the British plenipotentiary minister and his accompanying delegation upon their arrival in the town. In such circumstances, Drummond Hay stated in a secret memorandum sent to the Foreign Office that he did not exclude the hypothesis that Ibn Daoud was a victim of poisoning for the harshness with which he treated Marrakech citizens.[23]

El-Ghanjaoui's Secret Mediation between the Sultan and the British Legation

In the wake of Ibn Daoud's frequent clashes with El-Ghanjaoui as the supervisor of British trade interests in Marrakech, the death of the former a few days before Drummond Hay's arrival in that town raised questions about El-Ghanjaoui's destiny. Drummond Hay and the sultan discussed the intensified clash between Ibn Daoud and the British *semsar*. Hay drew the sultan's attention to the difficulties he had faced whenever he wanted to get in urgent touch with His Majesty, especially in important cases. After considering the best ways to overcome this problem, the two parties agreed, in the presence of the sultan's chamberlain Ahmed Ben Moussa, on April 13, 1873, that El-Ghanjaoui should be protected by the British (by becoming a British protégé), and become a secret liaison with the head of the British Legation in Tangier. His task would be to act as an undercover go-between in charge of secret mail exchanged between the sultan and the British Legation.[24] In the presence of the sultan and his chamberlain, the British plenipotentiary minister ordered El-Ghanjaoui to be at their disposal to do everything that would serve British interests in Morocco.[25]

Following the British Mission's visit to the court, the sultan sent a letter to Queen Victoria, in which he praised John Drummond Hay and said that "he was warmly welcomed and generously rewarded."[26] Such expressions were not said out of courtesy or out of common diplomatic dealings, but they reflected reality. In fact, the Sultan Mohamed Ben Abderrahman gratified Drummond Hay in a special and unprecedented way, which no foreign country's representative in Morocco had ever received at that time. He gave him the exceptional opportunity to get in touch directly and quickly with top key figures in the makhzen without the official mediation of the sultan's *naib* residing at Dar Niyaba (the defacto ministry of foreign affairs) in Tangier. Thus, Drummond Hay had made it possible for his legation to obtain an exclusive privilege that enabled him to serve his country's interests with great efficiency while continuing to carry out his classical role as the "beloved adviser"[27] to makhzen authorities. The sultan and his ministers relied on him for help in instituting reforms and for carrying out its foreign policy.[28]

The quick promotion of El-Ghanjaoui was very special in the history of the Moroccan protégé system.[29] After being accused by the makhzen of forgery and ill behavior toward Moroccan authorities in Marrakech,[30] things seemed topsy-turvy since April 13, 1873, when El-Ghanjaoui was secretly charged by the sultan and John Drummond Hay to carry out an important mission, to faithfully foster the relations between Morocco and Britain.

From *Semsar* and Trader to Nobility and Wealth

El-Ghanjaoui devoted his life to achieve two goals: first, to serve British interests faithfully and do his best to foster these interests inside Morocco; second, to benefit from his unique legal position to strengthen his personal interests and hoard colossal sums of money. What makes the case of El-Ghanjaoui interesting is that after April 13, 1873, the man was officially put under British government protection, while officially and secretly supported by the sultan and his chamberlain Ahmed Ben Moussa. The two parties agreed that he should be assigned the secret, permanent, and direct link between the head of the British Legation in Tangier and the sultan whenever required. The official document, which stands as an official protecting document for El-Ghanjaoui, openly stressed one main point, that "all the sultan's governors shall respectfully deal with El-Ghanjaoui, given his position."[31]

This quotation demonstrates that Boubeker El-Ghanjaoui now had strong immunity usually granted, in old Morocco, to the *shurafa* (descendants of the Prophet), heads of *zawaya* (religious brotherhoods), or religious groups who influenced or were related to the ruling family. He did not receive this immunity because he belonged to the ranks of these distinguished people. Rather, he received these honors despite his unknown origins and his near illiteracy. He could neither write nor read until he was thirty, as shown through samples of his handwriting.

Following this, El-Ghanjaoui sent three private letters to John Drummond Hay in Tangier via the British vice consulates of El Jadida, Safi, and Essaouira. All letters were in poor, difficult to read, colloquial Arabic.[32] However, he owed much of his success to holding a new and distinguished position and as a result of his cleverness and his strong relations with the British traders in Marrakech and Safi, as well as with other Moroccan and Jewish traders. Despite his poor education, El-Ghanjaoui succeeded thanks to his numerous visits to his mentor John Drummond Hay in Tangier, who taught him to become a cunning person and a great expert on makhzen politics and international affairs.[33]

Documents demonstrate that in his last visit to the Sultan Mohamed Ben Abderrahman in his Marrakech palace in 1873, John Drummond Hay agreed with the former to concretize a reform plan to set up a telegraph line between Morocco and Europe, to build a dock in Tangier, and to build a dyke to protect the Casablanca harbor from sea waves.[34] They also agreed to think over the way to settle the accumulated British traders' debts due to some governors and tribal chiefs.[35] El-Ghanjaoui was about to inform the British Legation in Tangier about the makhzen's points of view on such issues, when the sultan suddenly died in September 1873.[36]

Following this, El-Ghanjaoui sent three private letters to John Drummond Hay in Tangier via the British vice consulate of El Jadida,

Safi, and Essaouira. All of the three letters dealt with the circumstances of the sultan's death and the nomination of his son Moulay Al-Hassan.[37] The new sultan had a special and close relationship with El-Ghanjaoui since the time when the latter used to be a modest trader trying hard to earn his living. In one of the letters, sent to Drummond Hay, El-Ghanjaoui expressed his happiness and optimism when Moulay Al-Hassan took power. It was said that El-Ghanjaoui was one of the first to have declared his allegiance to the new sultan when he said:

> Everything will be ok with this wonderful sultan. He is a man to rely on, with good manners, well educated and a clever person. Since he was *khalifa* and up to now we have had close relations with him. . . . We are by the side of the *Faqih* (learned man) [Ahmed Ben Moussa] and playing up to him as you told us to do so as to serve our purpose and help him enthrone the sultan. We were the first to do so as did our friends.[38]

Upon the arrival of the new sultan in Marrakech, El-Ghanjaoui handed him a letter sent by John Drummond Hay to present his condolences for his late father's death and congratulate him on being enthroned unanimously by all Moroccans.[39] El-Ghanjaoui remained with the sultan in Marrakech until the latter left for Fez because of the famous tanners' rebellion.[40] Then, El-Ghanjaoui travelled to Tangier where he met John Drummond Hay, who gave him some letters dealing with various bilateral issues to be handed to the sultan. El-Ghanjaoui sailed from Tangier to Casablanca, and then went by road to the Chaouia region where he met Moulay Al-Hassan camping near Sidi Hajjaj. The two men met four times and talked over the issues raised in Drummond Hay's letters. El-Ghanjaoui remained in the sultan's camp until they both went to the Rabat palace, where he got the sultan's answers to all the aforementioned issues.[41]

It seems that Moulay Al-Hassan was very satisfied, until that date, with El-Ghanjaoui's intermediary role. The latter carried mail to and from the sultan in a better and faster way, including some issues of high importance to the makhzen. Meanwhile, the sultan ordered El-Ghanjaoui to come back to Marrakech and stay there for two months, just to have some time to keep an eye on his business. Then the sultan invited El-Ghanjaoui to visit him in his Fez palace, but this time accompanied by his family. Later, the sultan issued some *dahir*s (sultan's decree) in which he granted exclusive immunity, tax breaks, and respect for the man and the services he did for him.[42] Here is a sample in which Moulay Al-Hassan ordered that such respect should not be confined to Boubeker El-Ghanjaoui but include his son as well:

> Our very distinguished *dahir* entitles his bearer al-Haj al-Bachir El-Ghanjaoui to be respected, be waited on and be exempt from makhzen duties and taxes paid by common people. By virtue of the same *dahir* his son shall enjoy the same privileges for his loyalty and valuable advice. We order our servants and *amils* to be bound to the contents of the *dahir* to the letter.[43]

The aim behind the *dahir*'s extension to cover El-Ghanjaoui's son was to protect him so that he could represent his father, be it in Marrakech or elsewhere, and look after his business while his father was away from Marrakech. As time went by, successive *dahirs* made El-Ghanjaoui stronger inside and outside of makhzen circles. This also made him a double protégé, first by the country's highest authority and second by the head of the British Legation in Tangier. It was a special and unique status to which no other Moroccan protégé had been entitled, even the famous sharif of Ouezzane, El Haj Abdessalam, who lost such privileges in 1884 when he become a French protégé.[44] British protection granted to El-Ghanjaoui in 1873 sufficed to give him immunity and exemption from various taxes, makhzen duties, and other levies on common people. The good personal relations established between El-Ghanjaoui and Moulay Al-Hassan up to the 1880s made the sultan issue such *dahirs* to compensate El-Ghanjaoui for his services.

All throughout the year, El-Ghanjaoui visited the sultan's courts in Fez, Marrakech, Meknes, and Rabat. Despite the difficulties such tiresome and dangerous journeys required, El-Ghanjaoui benefited from them and established close ties with key figures in the makhzen such as the chamberlain Ahmed Ben Moussa, other ministers, and army officers. A number of these well-positioned personalities and dignitaries within the makhzen would not hesitate to get close to El-Ghanjaoui to borrow significant sums of cash from him. Some ministers were among his constant creditors, which enabled him, sometimes, to use their power to settle some claims to the benefit of British subjects.[45] El-Ghanjaoui was by the side of the sultan whenever the latter was with his army and great tribal leaders throughout Morocco. If he was unable to be there in person, he would charge one of his aids or acquaintances to represent him and collect information for him.

Whenever El-Ghanjaoui was away from the sultan, he joined John Drummond Hay in Tangier or his successors, Kirby Green or Charles Euan-Smith. There, he would disclose makhzen secrets. He would inform them about the sultan and his health, the problems that occupied him, his opinions and attitudes about current affairs—be they related to the army, finances, the country's economy, and so on. He also informed them about the ministers' behavior. He would praise a given minister, relating details about his impartiality, or denounce another, backed up by evidence about his greed and corruptibility, or his taking people's money, running after women, or his addiction to wine, and so on. In a word, he used to inform the British about everything related to the sultan's ministers, be it good or bad. Besides acting as a mediator to carry out verbal and written messages between the sultan and the British Legation in Tangier during the last sixteen years' service of John Drummond Hay's career, El-Ghanjaoui was assigned a very sensitive task that reflects the trust both the Moroccan and English parties had in this man.

Yet the position held by El-Ghanjaoui made many Moroccan and British people angry. Some British subjects in Morocco spared no effort to denounce how the British Legation relied on his services. They described him in very negative terms and demanded that he be fired. When John Drummond Hay's term came to an end in 1886, he was replaced by Kirby Green, who immediately told El-Ghanjaoui that the British Legation, based on a recommendation made by the retired British plenipotentiary minister, was still in need of his services.[46]

Gradual Tension in El-Ghanjaoui's Relations with the Makhzen: The Repercussion of Plundering El-Ghanjaoui's Properties in Marrakech

Despite the many missions El-Ghanjaoui undertook for the British Legation and the many trips he made to the sultan's courts in every part of Morocco, he still kept an eye on his business and widened its scope every year. The protégé status granted him and his close family members by Britain and the sultan's *dahir*s, allowed him to expand his trade, sometimes using illegal methods, and invest his profits in urban and rural real estate.[47] In this way, he became the wealthiest man in Marrakech,[48] perhaps one of the wealthiest Moroccans of his time after the sultan and his chamberlain Ahmed Ben Moussa.[49]

Since he was exempt from all taxes and charges, his name did not appear in taxation registers in Marrakech, or other towns where El-Ghanjaoui or one of his agents did business. Due to lack of comprehensive documents, which listed all the properties owned by El-Ghanjaoui, it was difficult to know the extent of his wealth. Some hints found here and there in Moroccan and foreign documents gave an approximate idea.

When El-Ghanjaoui and the Marrakech governor clashed, some aspects related to El-Ghanjaoui's activities became clear. In the spring of 1889, the British Legation asked El-Ghanjaoui to visit the sultan's court at Fez frequently and speed up claims related to British subjects in Morocco.[50] On one occasion, the Marrakech *muhtassib* complained to the sultan that El-Ghanjaoui had usurped the public domain and built a wall on one of his properties, which prevented people from getting to nearby districts. He even destroyed a house near where he lived in Dar Saboun in Marrakech and built instead eight shops and small rooms and a wall to protect these shops. He also confiscated four feet from the road used by people to move to Bab Doukkala and other places in the town.[51]

By order of a *qadi* (judge), the governor sent auxiliary forces and two *udul*s to stop the building process and close the new shops. The governor seems to have loosely interpreted the sultan's orders and confiscated El-Ghanjaoui's properties in Marrakech, including houses and shops. The common people of Marrakech wrongly believed that El-Ghanjaoui was no longer on good terms with the sultan, signalling that they could plunder everything in sight belonging to the British protégé since he was a known agent working for a Christian state.

A demonstration against him spread all over the town and lasted for hours, threatening the lives of Muslim and Jewish notables. Such vandalism would have spilled over into the *Mellah* (the Jewish district) if the *khalifa* (viceroy) Moulay Othman had not intervened and brought things under control. El-Ghanjaoui heard about what had happened while he was in Tangier to hand official mail to Kirby Green. The latter comforted El-Ghanjaoui and encouraged him to go to Marrakech to see what had happened to his properties and shops, evaluate damages, and be ready to file a claim for full compensation.[52]

When El-Ghanjaoui reached El Jadida on his way to Marrakech, he found out that news about his catastrophe had already spread. He then wrote to K. Green asking him to back him up and help him get back his lost rights. He explained that the aim behind such aggression was not himself, but Green and Great Britain. In his letter, he also stated, following the Marrakech events, that he did not exclude the idea that the great British state and its legation in Tangier would be a fertile subject for people to talk about inside and outside of Morocco. He further said that what happened in Marrakech would lead all consular corps, without exception, to ask their countries to appoint vice consuls in interior towns. El-Ghanjaoui stated that he would act to prevent others from being victims of such acts.[53]

Upon his arrival in Marrakech, El-Ghanjaoui saw what had become of his plundered properties and heard about threats to his family and how frightened they had felt. He then reported to K. Green:

> We reached Marrakech and found our family members very angry and in disarray about what the Marrakech governor had done to us. . . . all the consuls in all seaports, foreign traders, their protégé and *semsars*, all people from different social classes, males and females, governors, judges who were present in the city to celebrate the 'Aid with the *khalifa* and the neighbouring tribes, have witnessed the events that took place at our doorstep. . . . On that day, the entire town went topsy-turvy. Plunderers were very happy and wanted to enter our house as has happened with Bennis' house in Fez. Traders and rich people were afraid for their properties in the event the Marrakech governor would do the same to them as he did to us. Even the Jewish traders did not open their houses in the *Mellah* for three consecutive days out of fear of being plundered like us. They (the Jews) informed all seaports, and said that since there were no consuls or ambassadors in such towns, such things could happen.
>
> After the event, the judge sent knowledgeable people to the aforementioned place and found no evidence. Then the judge blamed the governor for what had happened. The latter gathered witnesses who claimed that the governor's aids made a mistake for they were not told to do what they did. As for the sultan, may God help him, he did what was right. I am on my way aboard a ship after leaving my family, still suffering from the impact of what had happened. Even my eldest son, who was looking after my commerce in our *fundouk* (caravansary), became crazy because of the large sums which were stolen and fled out of fear of being killed. Women were the only ones to stay at home and were afraid that the doors to our houses would be broken down. Tomorrow is Thursday, and we leave for El Jadida.[54]

In the light of such written details and other data which El-Ghanjaoui himself verbally transmitted to K. Green upon reaching Tangier, the latter wrote, in the name of the legation, to the sultan's minister Ghar-

nit asking him to compensate El-Ghanjaoui for all his losses, to officially apologize to the British Legation for the losses and harm caused
to its mediator and his family, especially since he was on official duty at
the court to discuss important issues for the sultan and the makhzen.[55]
In his answer, Gharnit explained that the first investigations showed
that "Boubeker's properties were not closed up by order of the Governor, but as a result of a mistake made by an assistant of the governor and
not by the governor himself . . . and that mistakes and forgetfulness are
forgiven in all codes of conduct."[56]

In his answer, Gharnit went on to defend the Marrakech governor
and blamed El-Ghanjaoui for exaggerating and overstating the event,
claiming that:

> You were taken in by an event which does not fall within the scope of
> the governor's jurisdiction. It was not reported to the Sultan, but was
> dealt with by an intermediary by the name of Bouafiya, as you know. So,
> how could it be possible that he could execute orders without permis-
> sion from the makhzen to do so; especially since the *qadi* was a party to
> the case?
>
> It is worthy to mention that El-Ghanjaoui was protected through
> only one document issued by you and many *dahir*s issued by the
> makhzen which entitle him to be respected and not be harmed. So, how
> could he be hurt by someone without the makhzen's consent? If he had
> shown love and respect for the two states, he would not have troubled
> you. Instead he would have filed a case as he did on many occasions re-
> lated to his loans and affairs . . .
>
> He should have brought the matter before the makhzen. If the latter
> did nothing, then he could have reported it to you. He was not only pro-
> tected by the British, but he was also part of the makhzen. . . .
>
> Our Sultan, Glory be to him, approved the idea of not reporting the
> event to your beloved country, but directly to Him. It was an expression
> of the love that you show for the two countries.[57]

In fact, K. Green wrote nothing to inform the British foreign minister, Salisbury, about the event. However, one of the House of Commons
representatives raised a question, on August 8, 1889, inquiring about the
veracity of what was written in the newspapers about the outrage committed by the Marrakech governor against the property of the native
agent of the British Legation and the truth about El-Ghanjaoui's acts.
Those newspapers accused him of being a notorious slave dealer in Mo-

rocco and the owner of certain houses of ill repute—in Marrakech—which the governor had closed by order of the sultan. To answer such questions, the British government stated that the Foreign Office did not receive information from Tangier relevant to the subject.[58] Consequently, Salisbury asked K. Green to provide him with a detailed report on the events as soon as possible.[59]

To execute such instructions, Green explained what happened in the clash between El-Ghanjaoui and the Marrakech governor. He also referred to the efforts made by the makhzen to compensate for the losses. In the many letters exchanged between Gharnit and K. Green, it became clear that the latter succeeded in convincing El-Ghanjaoui of the importance of reaching a compromise after direct negotiations with the sultan in order to avoid aggravation of his relations with His Royal Highness and his ministers.

In this context, El-Ghanjaoui joined the sultan on one of his *harka* (military maneuvers) in the Zemmour region, carrying a letter from K. Green. After being received by Moulay Al-Hassan, El-Ghanjaoui related his misfortune. The sultan told him about the information he collected concerning the event and informed him about his intention to issue orders to his son and *khalifa* Moulay Othman to punish Mohamed Ibn Daoud. When asked about the total sum lost in the event, El-Ghanjaoui said that he lost 87,000 *riyal* but confessed that his son had given him back 43,000 *riyal*, which he had hidden from the plunderers, besides other objects returned to him. El-Ghanjaoui asked for 56,500 *riyal* in compensation from the makhzen. The sultan agreed that he would issue urgent orders to his son to arrest the persons in Marrakech who took part in the plundering of El-Ghanjaoui's properties. He would also use whatever means necessary to get back what they had stolen.[60]

The Accusation of El-Ghanjaoui's Participation in the Slave Trade and His Ownership of Houses of Ill Repute

What about the charges leveled against El-Ghanjaoui concerning his slave trading and owning houses of ill repute in Marrakech? Regarding slavery, we need to recall the efforts made by Great Britain to put an end to the slave trade in Morocco during the last years of the nineteenth century, a move that was part of Britain's worldwide antislavery campaign.[61]

The question raised by one of the representatives of the British

House of Commons on August 8, 1889, was provoked by Budgett Meakin, the owner of the *Times of Morocco*, published in Tangier. The latter was then in Britain and had several meetings with key figures to raise the question about El-Ghanjaoui in the House of Commons.[62]

The reasons for Meakin's initiative go back to the times when John Drummond Hay represented his country in Morocco. During the last years of his long service, he was criticized by some British subjects living in Morocco and Gibraltar who accused him of not doing enough to defend their trade interests in Morocco.[63] Meakin, a critic, used his newspaper to sensationalize the issue. Meakin also succeeded in establishing close relations with the sultan's *naib* (representative) Mohamed Torres in Tangier. He found in him a valuable source of information for his newspaper regarding current issues preoccupying the makhzen.

The representative of the British and foreign antislavery society, Mr. Crawford, paid a visit to Tangier and took a tour along the Moroccan coastal towns to collect information on slavery and the slave trading in Morocco. In a meeting he held in Tangier on November 30, 1886, Crawford raised the question of ownership of slaves and that of slave trading by British subjects and protégés in Morocco. The name of Boubeker El-Ghanjaoui had been mentioned during the meeting. He was described as one of the great Moroccan British protégés involved in the slave trade in Morocco. This contradicted what John Drummond Hay had confirmed in one of his reports to the Foreign Office, that it was strictly forbidden for British subjects living in Morocco and for any Moroccan British protégé to own slaves or to exploit them commercially. Crawford reacted to this by stressing that he inquired at the British Legation in Tangier concerning El-Ghanjaoui, and he was told that Boubeker was neither vice consul nor even a British protégé, and that the legation had no information to confirm or to deny his involvement in the slave trade. People present at the meeting expressed their astonishment regarding what had transpired. Consequently, Crawford promised to write to Salisbury to get official clarification about the issue. Meakin was quick to declare in his newspaper that he had information confirming El-Ghanjaoui's possession of more than seventy female slaves, as well as males. He also mentioned that some of them had been mistreated and some killed.[64]

Obviously, El-Ghanjaoui knew what the foreign press in Tangier published regarding his involvement in the slave trade, but he always protested his innocence, denying any involvement in this heinous traffic. El-Ghanjaoui claimed in the spring of 1886 that he had already emancipated the fifteen female and three male slaves who lived for a long time in his home; he also confirmed that he had already sent the documents attesting to their freedom to J. D. Hay, and that acquiring them had cost him 5,000 *riyal*s. He added that once emancipated, his former slaves preferred to stay in his household as members of his family.[65]

Despite all the arguments advanced by El-Ghanjaoui to deny the accusations against to him, Meakin remained firm in his positions and insisted on the harassment of his opponent by boosting the level of defamation against him, either by using the columns of his newspaper in Tangier or by referring to his case during any lecture given on Morocco in British academic circles and learned societies. Meakin devoted an editorial in which he spoke of El-Ghanjaoui's obscure and humble beginnings as a broker (*semsar*) in the service of a British trader. Then, he described the circumstances in which his relations were forged gradually with J. D. Hay to the point of his becoming an indispensable intermediary with the makhzen authorities. Meakin asked what reasons prompted J. D. Hay to make this choice even though El-Ghanjaoui did not possess the requirements for a vice consul to carry out his tasks and lacked knowledge of foreign languages and the basic principles of European culture. Meakin returned to the attack declaring that El-Ghanjaoui remained a slaveholder, despite Britain's declared war against slavery around the world. Meakin considered the confiscation of his properties in Marrakech as a golden opportunity to attack him again, and believed that it should be exploited to its maximum to push British public opinion to press the Foreign Office to dismiss El-Ghanjaoui and put an end to his mission.[66]

Although this press campaign attracted the attention of the Foreign Office, in his response to Salisbury, Green succeeded in minimizing the serious charges against the wealthy trader of Marrakech. He pointed out that the leader of this smear campaign had for many years written hostile articles about the British Legation. Simultaneously he denied any involvement of El-Ghanjaoui in the slave trade. Green avowed that he had raised the matter in Tangier with the British agent, who had confirmed that he never considered the slave trade in Morocco as a profitable business.[67]

As for charges relating to the exploitation of houses of ill repute, El-Ghanjaoui told Green that he considered himself an upright and honorable man and would not respond to these baseless charges. Yet, he explained to Green that since he was one of the greatest real estate owners in Marrakech, he had to use the services of three assistants who collected rents on his properties. So it was possible that "he did not know all of his tenants in many of his properties, whom he never saw himself."[68]

At El-Ghanjaoui's request, Green attached extracts from two articles published in the *Times of Morocco* containing the charges against him, and announced that the accused man wanted to bring to justice the newspaper and its editor, but he declined to do so after consultations with the British Consul. Green considered the above-mentioned editorials as defamatory, and as the expression of a virulent and fierce desire on the part of Meakin to undermine the memory of his predecessor John Drummond Hay. Consequently, Salisbury instructed Green to convince El-Ghanjaoui to renounce his desire to pursue Meakin and his newspaper in court, and to advise him not to pay any attention to what he published about him.[69]

Meakin continued his campaign by complaining about the British government's silence regarding the acts of his opponent. Moreover, he accused British officials residing in Morocco of sharing in El-Ghanjaoui's profits. He also asserted that the British Legation pressed the sultan to indemnify El-Ghanjaoui for his losses, and that the latter met the sultan in Tetuan to finalize the procedures for his indemnification. Meakin further revealed cooperation between the makhzen and Kirby Green to instruct the governor of Marrakech to jail everyone suspected of having participated in the looting. According to Meakin, the number of suspects concerned was twenty-six individuals including the most respected men of Marrakech. Meakin also revealed that El-Ghanjaoui received 26,000 *riyal* as compensation for his financial loses.[70]

Green denied all these allegations and stated that he had only requested the makhzen authorities in Marrakech to correct their illegal actions by providing apologies to the man concerned. He confirmed that he encouraged El-Ghanjaoui to reach a friendly settlement with the sultan in person regarding his indemnification. Thereafter, Green continued to defend his protégé by saying that his huge fortune allowed him to refrain from the practice of such despicable and dishonorable activities as the slave trade or prostitution.[71]

Makhzen Complicity with Meakin to Bring Down El-Ghanjaoui

It seems that the makhzen felt embarrassed about El-Ghanjaoui's conduct after the plunder of his properties in Marrakech, and it decided to join forces with the British journalist Meakin in coordination with the sultan's *naib* Mohammed Torres in Tangier to mount a propaganda campaign against him. They wanted to get rid of El-Ghanjaoui by putting an end to his services and mediation between the British Legation and the sultan. Makhzen correspondence reveals information on this coordination since the beginning of the aforementioned campaign. The following are extracts from a letter sent from Torres to the sultan at the end of August 1889:

> Our master glorified by God should know that when El-Ghanjaoui arrived here after what happened to his properties in Marrakech, he spread the word in connivance with his supporters among the Jewish and other dishonorable people that his case had been submitted to the British Government. This coincided with the docking of some English battleships in Tangier harbor en route to India to allow for the sailors to rest, and El-Ghanjaoui and his allies had pretended that this armada arrived in his support. Some newspapers referred to his affair to such an extent that news of it reached London. An Englishman in contact with Morocco had drawn up several questions with the intention to put them before some British governmental organizations, but before doing so, he submitted them to us for confirmation or refutation.
>
> After attentive reading, we have responded that all that we read was consistent with reality. . . . Everyone knows that Boubeker is the representative of the British Government as well as His Sharifian Majesty. In addition, he possesses houses in Marrakech where suspicious activities take place, and has a business as a slave trader and as an unscrupulous loan shark.
>
> All this had been submitted to a governmental body which denied that the man in question had any relation to the service of the British State. Therefore, a request for clarification was submitted to the British Legation in Tangier. The reply was that the man concerned does not even benefit from British protection, and it is inconceivable that he could be an agent in the service of the British Government. What is true is that the man concerned knew the former chief of the British Legation, and he got to know English tourists who traveled in Marrakech or elsewhere, for whom he provided services.[72]

Meakin and Torres secretly collaborated to present the man concerned in the highest political spheres in Britain in negative terms. Meakin was indeed in Britain to bring the question referred to earlier about El-Ghanjaoui to the House of Commons. En route to Britain, he had received from Torres official proof that would confirm the truthfulness of the charges against his opponent. Moreover, Torres had added another charge, namely the practice of usury.

When the sultan visited Tangier for the first time on September 22, 1889, he received the members of the diplomatic corps and expressed his desire to further strengthen contacts between his administration and their governments. On the same occasion, the sultan met in private with Budgett Meakin, and they raised the case of El-Ghanjaoui and agreed to coordinate their propaganda against him in the newspapers of Tangier and Great Britain. We have strong evidence demonstrating that Torres openly recognized the existence of close cooperation between the makhzen and Meakin to bring down El-Ghanjaoui. In a letter sent from Torres to Minister Gharnit the former wrote:

> Your Excellency is aware that the makhzen has solicited the services of Meakin, the British journalist, to give wide coverage to the illicit dealings of al-Ghanjaoui and to spread details about his crimes and misbehavior. This reporter has worked very hard to undermine al-Ghanjaoui.[73]

Following the sudden death of K. Green in Marrakech, Charles Euan-Smith was nominated as the British plenipotentiary minister in Morocco in December 1891.[74] During this transitional period, El-Ghanjaoui was afraid of losing his position as British protégé, since Meakin had published another editorial to attract the attention of the new British minister to the importance of stopping his services for the British Legation.[75] However, John Drummond Hay met Charles Euan-Smith in Britain before his arrival in Morocco, and recommended that he rely on the "faithful" services of El-Ghanjaoui, who never committed any fault that could be detrimental to British interests in Morocco. Consequently, Charles Euan-Smith decided not only to confirm El-Ghanjaoui in his post as an intermediary with the sultan, but he also proposed to the Foreign Office to allow him to initiate legal procedures against Meakin and his newspaper.[76] As soon as El-Ghanjaoui initiated legal procedures in a Gibraltar court against the newspaper in question, Meakin immediately published the following apologies in his newspaper:

> We desire to express our sincere regret that we incautiously made statements in the *Times of Morocco* of the 19th ultimo affecting the character and reputation of Cid Boobker-el-Ganjawi [*sic*], the British Agent at

the Shereefian Court. We have now reason to believe such statements to have been wholly unfounded, and we beg to withdraw and contradict the same, and to apologize to Cid Boobker for having made them.[77]

Meanwhile, Torres forwarded a message from the sultan to Charles Euan-Smith suggesting that he should cease to employ El-Ghanjaoui as an intermediary between his legation and the makhzen.[78] A verbal message with the same suggestion was delivered to Ch. E. Smith by Qa'id Harry Maclean in Tangier on behalf of the sultan. Ch. E. Smith suspected that this action taken by the sultan was in consequence of special advice sent to him by the French Legation at Tangier. Upon careful review of the situation, he decided not to accede to the sultan's demand, because no valid reasons would justify his taking this step, especially now that El-Ghanjaoui was in the process of prosecuting Meakin for libel. Furthermore, his dismissal would probably be followed by his being taken under French, Italian, or German protection.[79] After the excuses of Meakin, El-Ghanjaoui felt himself stronger[80] and determined to maintain legal procedures against his opponent. After having enjoyed the support of Ch. E. Smith, he traveled to Fez to prepare the official visit of the new British plenipotentiary minister to the court of Moulay Al-Hassan in order to negotiate a new commercial treaty between Morocco and Britain.

The Trial in Gibraltar, the Retirement of El-Ghanjaoui, and the End of an Era

Assisted by his Jewish friends Abensur and Pariente, both merchants and bankers residing in Tangier, and by two British traders residing in Gibraltar named Carver and Hunter, El-Ghanjaoui was able to accomplish the work required to bring Meakin and his newspaper to justice. The case also concerned the company responsible for the publication of the *Times of Morocco* called "The Exchange and Publishing Company," which constituted part of a London publishing house with branch offices in Britain and abroad. Toward the end of April 1889, when El-Ghanjaoui was already in Fez, the office of the newspaper received notice that El-Ghanjaoui had launched a lawsuit against the establishment and the editor-in-chief of the newspaper, Meakin. The complainant asked the Supreme Court of Gibraltar to request the newspaper to stop publishing slanderous articles about him as had appeared in the issues of August 6, 1889, March 21, 1891, and December 19, 1891. He also claimed damages and interest amounting to one thousand pounds as reparation for losses suffered by him due to the allegations made in the newspaper. Meakin repeated the excuses he had already made to El-Ghanjaoui, and even pretended that it was Eland, the printer-in-chief, who inserted them in the journal without his permission.[81]

Thus, a new phase of confrontation opened between the two sides, including the makhzen, and led to a lengthy trial that Meakin did not expect. He was practically certain of the veracity of the facts leveled against his adversary and that the latter would never dare to take the case to court. Since the first court sittings in Gibraltar, Meakin had to request a postponement of the case in order to provide proofs necessary to confirm the charges against his opponent. Because he had none, he asked Torres and the sultan to procure him the notaries' documents evidencing the illicit activities of the man in question as a slave dealer in Morocco and as brothel owner in Marrakech.[82]

Meanwhile, Ch. E. Smith's mission to Fez failed completely because the makhzen refused to agree to all the British propositions regarding the signing of a new, more liberal treaty of commerce. Consequently, relations between the two countries deteriorated rapidly.[83] The Foreign Office removed Ch. E. Smith from Morocco and ordered Charles Eliot, the second secretary of the legation in Tangier to manage the crisis. Once again J. D. Hay recommended that he rely on El-Ghanjaoui's services, as he considered him still very capable to serve Great Britain's interests in Morocco.[84] Earlier, the Foreign Office received a long list respecting the nature of charges made against El-Ghanjaoui from 1885 until June 1889 on behalf of "The Morocco Exchange and Publishing Company," and asked for direct intervention from the new foreign secretary Rosebey to insure impartiality at the trial and to allow this new evidence to be heard at the Gibraltar Court.[85]

To remedy the situation and put the relationship with Morocco back on the right track, Queen Victoria sent one of her Royal Council members, West Ridgeway, to spend six months in Morocco before the nomination of Ernest Satow on August 28, 1893, as the new British plenipotentiary minister.[86] Meakin tried in vain to use the arrival of West Ridgeway in Tangier for additional meetings and correspondence to try to win his assistance regarding El-Ghanjaoui's case. He also failed to use the testimony of one of the former slaves of El-Ghanjaoui named Rabha during the Gibraltar trial.[87] In these circumstances, the high court announced its sentence in favor of the plaintiff. Meakin was fined one hundred pounds sterling with reimbursement of the court fees, in addition to the absolute prohibition of publishing defamations about his opponent.[88] A few days earlier, Meakin had decided to stop the publication of his newspaper after its last issue on March 2, 1893.[89]

However, Meakin did not stop his war against El-Ghanjaoui. After leaving Tangier, he succeeded again in provoking a question about him in the House of Commons on August 7, 1893.[90] Moreover, he convinced a certain E. H. Marquis to forward a letter probably dictated or at least inspired by him to the Foreign Office mentioning that: "He (El-Ghanjaoui) is known as one of the largest slave dealers, and has amassed an immense fortune, viz., 500.000 £ and some 100.000 £ in the Bank of England, by his unscrupulous transactions."[91] Consequently, the Foreign Office instructed Ernest Satow, the new British plenipotentiary minister in Morocco, "to institute a full and careful inquiry, with view of ascertaining whether Bubekir's conduct and character rendered him unfit to be employed as an agent of the British Legation."[92]

While Satow sent a letter to El-Ghanjaoui to acquaint him with his intention to hold an inquiry, and required him to deliver the document by which he was appointed agent in the year 1873, El-Ghanjaoui anticipated this action and spontaneously offered to resign his position with the British Legation.[93] Then Rosebery regretted that Satow thought it necessary to take that severe step, since the charges against El-Ghanjaoui were unsupported by any evidence and were clearly at variance with the archives of the Foreign Office, which contained strong testimony regarding the able and efficient manner in which the wealthy trader of Marrakech and secret intermediary in the service of Britain carried out his duties. As the latter resigned his post spontaneously on the grounds of ill health, Rosebery considered that it would serve no useful purpose to pursue the investigation further, and ordered Satow to send the agent a letter regretting his infirmity, thanking him for his past services, and extending him British protection as a private individual.[94] Thus, El-Ghanjaoui did not have to face an investigation which, if conducted on Moroccan soil, might have revealed embarrassing facts about his commercial dealings. He devoted the rest of his life to his business until his death in 1905.

El-Ghanjaoui had succeeded in completing the difficult tasks assigned to him by the successive chiefs of the British Legation in Tangier over more than twenty years. This occurred at crucial moments when Morocco fought against the covetousness of many European countries who wanted to undermine its economic and political independence. El-

Ghanjaoui had benefited from protection both by the British government and the sultan, who issued *dahir*s, which exonerated him from paying taxes. This enabled him to enjoy many social and economic benefits and allowed him to join the ranks of the notables and the dignitaries of his time in Morocco. This had been concretized by very complicated relationships involving clientélism and patronage based on mutual interests as well as on maneuvers worthy of modern espionage including blackmail, compromises, and secret negotiations. These included recourse to threats to expose corruption. El-Ghanjaoui's primary goal was to succeed in collecting useful information from credible sources and transmit it secretly to the interested parties.

In the absence of modern communications in Morocco during the second half of the nineteenth century and the existence of regulations imposed by *dar niyaba* (the de facto ministry of Foreign Affairs) in Tangier for any contact with the makhzen, Drummond Hay understood the importance of using the services of a clever intermediary capable not only of exchanging correspondence secretly with the sultan, but also of collecting useful information for transmission to the British Legation as quickly as possible. In order to fully accomplish this task, El-Ghanjaoui built a very efficient network of informers from different social milieus, most of whom were located in the key posts of the Moroccan administration, informing him about all important matters. Thus, he had established close relationships with the sultan's secretaries and with the most influential ministers at the court. Recourse to money in the form of bribery or debts was one way he achieved his objectives. His close relationships with the great Jewish traders in Tangier and Marrakech and in other Moroccan cities assisted him in finding out economic and social trends in Morocco. In short, El-Ghanjaoui played a very sensitive game. Accordingly, he was hated by some and feared by others who sought to get close to him to avoid becoming his victim or to wait for an appropriate moment to bring him down and ruin him.

In this atmosphere of intrigue, El-Ghanjaoui fulfilled his functions for the British crown, without interruption, under the supervision of J. D. Hay from 1873 until the end of his mission to Morocco in 1886. He continued his service under the authority of Drummond Hay's successors: Kirby Green who died in Marrakech on February 24, 1891, Charles Euan-Smith until 1893, and finally Ernest Satow. The Foreign Office finally accepted his request for retirement by the end of 1893 for reasons of old age and ill health.

The huge correspondence related to years of El-Ghanjaoui's service

to Great Britain amply demonstrates the immense difficulties he over-
came on a number of occasions, acting with lots of patience, persever-
ance, and cleverness, in spite of his lack of education, to succeed in his
mission. Throughout the year 1889, he faced serious attempts to ruin
him from local authorities in Marrakech, but he succeeded, emerging
from this crucial experience stronger than before. He had to deal with
multiple Moroccan and British adversaries, who wished to destroy him
by accusing him of getting rich as a result of trade in slaves and prostitution. His health deteriorated over the years, in part due to many trips
during all seasons by mule and ship between Marrakech and Tangier
and between this northern town and other cities or regions where the
sultan resided with his mobile makhzen.

By coming into direct contact with politicians and diplomats from
different nationalities, in Tangier or at the sultan's court, and thanks
also to his regular meetings with successive chiefs of the British Legation in Tangier, El-Ghanjaoui had acquired rich knowledge that he
would never have had access to if he had confined himself to his original
activity as a simple merchant in Marrakesh.

When El-Ghanjaoui withdrew in 1893 from the service of Britain, he
continued increasing his wealth until his death in 1905. When Cunnighame Graham visited him at one of his trade depots in Marrakech at
the end of the 1890's, he saw him piling up golden coins in a metal box.
Within his luxurious house he was offered British tea in tiny gold cups.
Then, El-Ghanjaoui allowed his guest to see a part of what he kept in
his house, such as watches and utensils of gold and silver, in addition to
other valuable items that demonstrated the immensity of his wealth. El-
Ghanjaoui also revealed to his guest his private collection of pearls and
diamonds, and a quantity of powdered gold that he kept in sacks as well
as varieties of golden European coins. At the end, he told Cunninghame
Graham that he had only shown him one-half of his fortune, for the latter part was wholly invested in the United Kingdom, bringing him huge
profits.[95]

After his death, El-Ghanjaoui left behind him three widows, five
sons, and three daughters. On the night of his death, his house was
raided without warning by Thami Glaoui, who stole all of its contents. He kidnapped his three daughters and two of El-Ghanjaoui's widows, notwithstanding their advanced age. The wealth left by the deceased was estimated at more than two million francs in gold, which
the Glaoui usurped.[96] It seems that the situation of El-Ghanjaoui's family worsened under the French Protectorate. Over time, the glory days

of El-Ghanjaoui mostly disappeared. However, the visitor to Marrakech in our days might squeeze through narrow streets in the old medina and pass in front of a dead-end street that still bears the name of El-Ghanjaoui. The house where he used to live with his family is still there as witness to the memory of a self-made man.

Notes

Many thanks to my colleagues and friends Odile Moreau and Jessica Marglin for their help by reading my text and suggesting many relevant corrections.

1. Robert Bonting Cunnighame Graham, *Moghreb El-Acksa: A Journey in Morocco* (New York: Viking, 1930), 322.

2. Since 1704, date of the seizure of Gibraltar by the British, Morocco became so important to Britain for strategic reasons, and Britain became also so important to Morocco to allow successive sultans to obtain military and political assistance. For more details, see Khalid Ben-Srhir, *Britain and Morocco during the Embassy of John Drummond Hay, 1845–1886*, trans. Malcolm Williams and Gavin Waterson (London: Routledge Cruzon, 2005).

3. Miège was the first to underline the neglect of European writers and historians of the tumultuous career of this man. Jean-Louis Miège, *Le Maroc et l'Europe, 1830–1894* (P. U. F., 1962), vol. 3, 208 n. 5 and 6; 209 n. 1 and 3.

Among the researchers in Morocco our colleague Mohammed Kenbib had dealt with the case of El-Ghanjaoui as a British protégé on the basis of the Public Record Office documents (London), drafted mostly in English. Kenbib, *Les protégés, contribution à l'histoire contemporaine du Maroc*, Publications de la Faculté des Lettres et des Sciences Humaines, Université Mohammed V, Agdal, Rabat, 79, 80, 83, 135, 154, 220, 221. In her recent study, *The Mellah of Marrakech: Jewish and Muslim Space in Morocco's Red City* (Bloomington: Indiana University Press, 2007), 81–82, Emily Gottreich dealt also with the case of El-Ghanjaoui as a wealthy man in Marrakech on the basis of Moroccan and European sources. In her PhD dissertation "In the Courts of the Nations: Jews, Muslims, and Legal Pluralism in Nineteenth-Century Morocco," Princeton University, 2013, Jessica Marglin also dealt with El-Ghanjaoui's acquisition of properties in the *mellah* of Marrakech (135–136).

4. Graham Cunnighame, *Maghreb El-Acksa*, 322.

5. Graham Cunnighame, *Maghreb El-Acksa*, 330–331.

6. J. D. Hooker and J. Ball, *Journal of a Tour in Morocco and the Great Atlas* (London: Macmillan and Co., 1878), 127.

7. For more details respecting the signature of this very important treaty between Morocco and Britain, which contributed largely to consolidating the British influence in Morocco during the second half of the nineteenth century, see Khalid Ben-Srhir, *Britain and Morocco*, 24–57.

8. FO. 174/138, Drummond Hay to Bargach, Tangier, August 16, 1871.

9. J. D. Hooker and J. Ball, *Journal of a Tour in Morocco*, 127–131.

10. J. D. Hooker and J. Ball, *Journal of a Tour in Morocco*, 136–137.

11. FO. 174/139, Bargach to Drummond Hay, Tangier, October 13, 1871.

12. The Sultan to the Viceroy Sidi Hassan, 25 Du al-Qi'dah 1288/ February 5, 1872. Nonclassified documents, Royal Library, Rabat.

13. FO. 174/139, Bargach to Drummond Hay, Tangier, October 20, 1871.

14. FO. 174/138, Drummond Hay to Bargach, Tangier, December 20, 1871; another letter from the sultan to the Viceroy Sidi Hassan, 25 Du al-Qi'dah 1288/ February 5, 1872.

15. FO. 174/139, Drummond Hay to Idriss Belyamani, December 23, 1872; FO. 174/138, Drummond Hay to Bargach, Tangier, August 16, 1871.

16. FO. 174/139, Drummond Hay to Bargach, Tangier, March 15, 1872; FO. 174/89, Bargach to Drummond Hay, Safar 13, 1289/April 22, 1872.

17. FO. 174/139, White to Bargach, Tangier, April 27, 1872; FO. 174/89, Bargach to Drummond Hay, Safar 13, 1289/April 22, 1872.

18. FO. 174/139, White to Bargach, Tangier, May 9, 1872.

19. FO. 174/89, Bargach to Drummond Hay, Safar 13, 1289/April 22, 1872, mentioned above.

20. FO. 174/89, Bargach to Drummond Hay, Safar 13, 1289/April 22, 1872.

21. Sultan to Bargach, Safar 22, 1289/ May 1, 1872, *al-Wataiq*, vol. 4, 410, al-Matbaaa al-Malakiyya, Rabat, 1977.

22. L. A. E. Brooks, *A Memoir of Sir John Drummond Hay, Sometime Minister at the Court of Morocco, based on his journals and correspondence* (London: J. Murray, 1896).

23. Brooks, *A Memoir*, 275; Abderrahman Ibn Zaydan, *Ithaf a'lam al-nass bi jamali akhbari hadirati Maknas*, vol. 2, 121, 2nd ed. (Casablanca: Matabi' Ideal, 1990); Ahmed ibn Khalid an-Nassiri, *Al-istiqsa li-akhbari al-Maghrib al-qssa*, vol. 9 (Casablanca: Dar al-Kitab, 1956), 123.

24. FO. 174/294/3, Certificate of the nomination of El-Ghanjaoui as an undercover go-between in charge of secret mail exchanged between John Drummond Hay and the makhzen, April 13, 1873.

25. FO. 174/294/3, "Secret memorandum sent by El-Ghanjaoui to de Vismes de Ponthieu," Marrakech, July 23, 1890.

26. FO. 174/89, copy of His Majesty the sultan's reply to the Queen of Great Britain and Ireland etc., Safar 26, 1290/April 25, 1873.

27. This expression was always mentioned in the introduction of all the official correspondence sent by the makhzen to John Drummond Hay as a sign of respect and as recognition of his services to promote the welfare of Morocco.

28. See the chapter devoted to the makhzen reforms attempted under British supervision in Khalid Ben-Srhir, *Britain and Morocco*, 206–263.

29. For details respecting the long evolution of consular protection in Morocco from its origins in the eighteenth century until the conference of Madrid in 1880, see Mohammed Kenbib, *Les protégés* (Rabat: Université Mohammed V, 1996), 29–92.

30. FO. 174/89, Bargach to Drummond Hay, Safar 13, 1289/April 22, 1872.

31. FO. 174/294/3, Certificate of the nomination of El-Ghanjaoui as an undercover go-between in charge of secret mail exchanged between John Drummond Hay and the makhzen, April 13, 1873.

32. See Khalid Ben-Srhir, "On Her Majety's Service: The Secret Correspondence of Boubeker El-Ghanjaoui (1873–1893)," in *Hespéris-Tamuda* 44 (2009): 85–188.

33. See Khalid Ben-Srhir, "On Her Majety's Service."

34. FO. 174/139, note respecting the Telegram sent by J. D. Hay to Bargach, Tangier, April 8, 1873; FO. 174/89, El-Ghanjaoui to J. D. Hay, Rajab 24, 1290/September 17, 1873.

35. FO. 174/139, Note respecting British claims, October 15, 1872.

36. FO. 174/89, El-Ghanjaoui to J. D. Hay, Rajab 4, 1290/September 17, 1873.

37. FO. 174/89, El-Ghanjaoui to J. D. Hay, Rajab 4, 1290/September 17, 1873.

38. FO. 174/89, El-Ghanjaoui to J. D. Hay, Rajab 4, 1290/September 17, 1873. The document number 304 published in *al-Wataiq*, vol. 3, 17, confirms that El-Ghanjaoui was really first among the influential Marrakech persons who signed the *Bay'a* (Allegiance) to the new sultan.

39. FO. 174/140, J. D. Hay to the Sultan Moulay Al-Hassan, Tangier, November 8, 1873.

40. Abdelahad Sebti, "Chroniques de la contestation citadine: Fès et la révolte des tanneurs (1873–1874)," *Hespéris-Tamuda* 29, no. 2 (1991): 283–312.

41. FO. 174/89, El-Ghanjaoui to J. D. Hay, Ramadan 29, 1290/November 20, 1873.

42. FO. 174/89, El-Ghanjaoui to J. D. Hay, Ramadan 29, 1290/November 20, 1873.

43. FO. 174/89, Copy of a *dahir* granted by the Sultan Moulay Al-Hasan to Boubker El-Ghanjaoui who received additional *dahir*s from the same sultan during his lengthy career in the service of the British.

44. Details regarding the French consular protection of Sharif Ouazzane, in Khalid Ben-Srhir, *Britain and Morocco*, 200–205.

45. FO. 99/309, Diary of Cid Abdeslam Bennani, n.d. Bennani mentioned the name of the minister Gharnit who had heavy debts to El-Ghanjaoui in 1892.

46. FO. 174/110, El-Ghanjaoui to Kirby Green, Safar 29, 1304/November 27, 1886.

47. Qa'id Mohammed Ben Daoud to the sultan, Du al-Qi'dah 14, 1300/September 16, 1883, Kounnach (Register) 117, Royal Library, Rabat, 142. The governor draws the attention of the sultan to purchases of properties carried out by El-Ghanjaoui in the city of Marrakech and its neighboring countryside and also to his massive purchase of wheat for speculation. Caid Ahmed Oumalek to the sultan, *Rab'i al-Thani* 21, 1305/January 1, 1888, Marrakech file no. 7, Direction des Archives Royales, Rabat. Oumalek informs the sultan that El-Ghanjaoui was involved in the Ketama tobacco (cannabis) trade with Marrakech Jews in the *mellah* (the Jewish quarter).

48. Khalid Ben-Srhir, *"watiqa ghayr manchoura 'an mallah Mourrakouch fi nihayat al-qarn at-tassi' achar,"* in *Hespéris-Tamuda* 35, no. 2 (1997): 25–71. From this census of Marrakech Jews, the name El-Ghanjaoui is mentioned many

times as owner of many houses in the *mellah*. See also Eugene Aubin, *Morocco of Today* (London: E. B. Dutton, 1906), 36.

49. Graham Cunninghame, *Moghreb El-Acksa*, 271, 280.

50. FO. 174/202, El-Ghanjaoui to H. White, Shawal 4, 1306/June 3, 1889.

51. *Times of Morocco*, August 17, 1889.

52. Confidential Print (5958), letter 56, K. Green to Salisbury, Tangier, August 27, 1889.

53. FO. 174/202, Note from el Jadida regarding Marrakech proceedings to K. Green (Du al-Qi'dah 1306/June 29, 1889).

54. FO. 174/202, El-Ghanjaoui to Green, Du al-qi'da 9, 1306/July 7, 1889.

55. Ibid.

56. Gharnit to Green, n.d., file 49/ document 46, Bibliothèque Générale de Tétouan.

57. Ibid.

58. Confidential Print (5958), letter 32, Question asked in the House of Commons on August 8, 1889, and its answer.

59. Confidential Print (5958), letter 40, Salisbury to Green, Foreign Office, August 13, 1889.

60. Confidential Print (5958), letter 140, Green to Salisbury, Tangier, October 7, 1889. Enclosure in letter 40, Gharnit to Green, Muharram 21, 1307/September 17, 1889.

61. Mohammed Ennaji et Khalid Ben-Srhir, "La Grande Bretagne et l'esclavage au Maroc au XIXe siècle," *Hespéris-Tamuda* 29, no. 2 (1991): 249–281.

62. Confidential Print (5958), letter 56, K. Green to Salisbury, Tangier, August 27, 1889.

63. El-Ghanjaoui to the minister Mohammed ben Larbi Jamai, Shawal 12, 1301/August 5, 1884, Direction des Archives Royales, Rabat, Britain and Morocco files.

64. *Times of Morocco*, January 16, 1886.

65. Confidential Print (5958), Annex to letter 56, extract of letter from Cid Boo Bekir to Sir John Drummond Hay (Enclosure in Sir J. Drummond Hay's no. 21, Confidential, of April 29, 1886).

66. *Times of Morocco*, August 8, 1889, 3.

67. Confidential Print (5958), letter 56 mentioned above, K. Green to Salisbury, Tangier, August 27, 1889, and its two enclosures: Extract from *Times of Morocco* of August 27 and 14, 1889.

68. Confidential Print (5958), letter 56 mentioned above, K. Green to Salisbury, Tangier, August 27, 1889.

69. Confidential Print (5958), letter 65, Salisbury to Green, Foreign Office, September 9, 1989.

70. *Times of Morocco*, November 26, 1889, 3.

71. Confidential Print (5958), letter 81, Green to Salisbury, Tangier, November 26, 1889.

72. Torres to the Sultan, Muharram 1, 1307/August 28, 1889, Direction des Archives Royales, Rabat, files Morocco and Britain.

73. Torres to Gharnit, Muharram 28, 1310/August 22, 1892, Direction des Archives Royales, Rabat, files classified chronologically.

74. *Times of Morocco*, December 5, 1891. Meakin was thanked for his services by the sultan who ordered his *oumana* in Tangier to allow him to export to Britain a purebred horse as a present from the sultan.

75. *Times of Morocco*, December 19, 1891. The editorial was entitled "Somebody for England to Be Proud Of," 3.

76. Confidential Print (6272), letter 4, secret, E. Smith to Salisbury, Tangier, December 28, 1891; Letter 15, E. Salisbury to E. Smith, Foreign Office, January 7, 1892.

77. Confidential Print (6272), letter 43, E. Smith to Salisbury, Tangier, January 11, 1892, enclosure, extracts from the *Times of Morocco* of January 9, 1892.

78. Confidential Print (6272), Enclosure in letter 104, Hadj Mohammed Torres to Ch. E. Smith (translation), Rajeb 30, 1309/February 29, 1892.

79. Confidential Print (6272), letter 104, C. E. Smith to Salisbury, Tangier, March 14, 1892; Enclosure 2 in 104, Memorandum of instructions for Kaid Maclean's guidance with regard to Cid Boobekir; Enclosure 3 in 104, C. E. Smith to Hadj Mohammed Torres, Tangier, March 7, 1892.

80. Confidential Print (6272), letter 111, Salisbury to C. E. Smith, Foreign Office, March 23, 1892.

81. *Times of Morocco*, April 16, 1892, 3–4, and April 23, 1892, 4.

82. Torres to Gharnit, Muharram 28, 1310/August 22, 1892, Direction des Archives Royales, Rabat, files classified chronologically; FO. 174/294/3, El-Ghanjaoui to de Vismes de Ponthieu, Rabi'a II 12, 1311/October 23, 1893.

83. For details concerning this crisis see Stephen Bonsale, *Morocco as It Is, with an Account of Sir Charles Euan Smith's Recent Mission to Fez* (New York: Harper & Brothers, 1893), 73–110.

84. Confidential Print (6272), letter 307, Eliot to Rosebery, Confidential, Tangier, December 12, 1892: "Three successive British Ministers . . . whose views respecting the affairs of this country were often not identical, agreed in setting a very high value on the political services of Cid Bubekir. Sir J. D. Hay informs me that his influence, though impaired by recent events at the Court, is still very great, and that it would be fatal to alienate him from this Legation, as his talents, respecting which there seems to be no doubt, would be placed at the disposal of some other power."

85. Confidential Print (6272), letter 238, The Morocco Exchange and Publishing Company to the Foreign Office, 36, Leadenhall Buildinhs, Gracechurch Street, London, Novemebr 14, 1892. Signed, W. M. Harvie, Liquidator.

86. Eliot to Torres, January 1893, file 43/document 94, Bibliothèque Générale de Tétouan.

87. Ridgeway to Torres, May 5, 1893, file 43/document 98, Bibliothèque Générale de Tétouan; Confidential Print (6384), letter 263, Ridgeway to Rosebery, Very Confidential, Tangier, May 9, 1893; Letter 269, Rosebery to Ridgeway, Confidential, Foreign Office, May 23, 1893.

88. Confidential Print (6384), letter 276, Eliot to Rosebery, Tangier, May 27, 1893.

89. *Times of Morocco*, the last issue, number 381, dated March 2, 1893, with an editorial entitled "Au Revoir."

90. Confidential Print (6448), letter 38, Question asked in the House of Commons, August 7, 1893, and his answer. Sir Gray's answer was: "that certain grave charges were brought against him and he brought an action for libel, which was decided publicly in his favour, and a fine of 100 £ was imposed on the man who originally made the statements."

91. Confidential Print (6448), letter 60*, Private, Mr. E. H. Marquis to Mr. Forwood, M. P. (communicated to the Foreign Office, September 7, 1893).

92. Confidential Print (6448), letter 62*, Rosebery to Satow, Confidential, Foreign Office, September 13, 1893.

93. Confidential Print (6448), letter 153, Satow to Rosebery, Confidential, Tangier, October 25, 1893; Enclosure in 154, de Ponthieu. Cid Bubekir Ben El Hadj El-Bachir El-Ghanjaoui to Satow, Rabi'e II 3, 1311/October 15, 1893:

> Since that time, praise be to God, through the loss of my strength, owing to the length of the time and the number of my journeys in summer and winter. On that account, I had asked the cessation of my role as an intermediary, and to be excused from serving on this ground that my friendship remaining the same as before, retaining at the same time the protection which has been granted to me by the glorious Queen, and that I should in future have no anxiety except as to what concerns my well being until God terminates my days.

Letter 154, Satow to Rosebery, Tangier, October 25, 1893.

94. Confidential Print (6448), letter 184, Rosebery to Satow, Foreign Office, November 7, 1893; letter 389, Satow to Rosebery, Tangier, December 16, 1893; Enclosure in 389, Satow to Cid Bubeker, Jumada II 3, 1311/December 12, 1893.

95. Graham Cunnighame, *Moghreb El-Acksa*, 276.

96. Gustave Babin, *Le Maroc sans masque*, "*Son excellence*" (Paris: G. Ficker, 1932), 169.

Bibliography

English and French

Aubin, Eugene. *Morocco of Today*. London: E. B. Dutton, 1906.

Babin, Gustave. *La Maroc sans masque*, "*Son excellence*." Paris: G. Ficker, 1932.

Ben-Srhir, Khalid. *Britain and Morocco during the Embassy of John Drummond Hay, 1845–1886*. Translated from Arabic by Gavin Waterson and Malcolm Williams. London: Routledge Cruzon, 2005.

———. "On Her Majety's Service: The Secret Correspondence of Boubker El-Ghanjaoui (1873–1893)." *Hespéris-Tamuda* 44 (2009): 85–188.

Bonsale, Stephen. *Morocco as It Is, with an Account of Sir Charles Euan Smith's Recent Mission to Fez*. New York: Harper & Brothers, 1893.

Brooks, L. A. E. *A Memoir of Sir John Drummond Hay, sometime minister at the court of Morocco, based on his journals and correspondence*. London: J. Murray, 1896.

Cunnighame, Graham, and Robert Bonting. *Moghreb El-Acksa: A Journey in Morocco.* New York: Viking, 1930.

Ennaji, Mohammed, and Khalid Ben-Srhir. "La Grande Bretagne et l'esclavage au Maroc au XIXe siècle." *Hespéris-Tamuda* 29, no. 2 (1991): 249–281.

Gottreich, Emily. *The Mellah of Marrakech: Jewish and Muslim Space in Morocco's Red City.* Bloomington: Indiana University Press, 2007.

Hooker, J. D., and J. Ball. *Journal of a Tour in Morocco and the Great Atlas.* London: Macmillan and Co., 1878.

Kenbib, Mohammed. *Les protégés*, contribution à l'histoire contemporaine du Maroc. Publications de la Faculté des Lettres et des Sciences Humaines, Université Mohammed V, Agdal, Rabat, 1996.

Marglin, Jessica. "In the Courts of the Nations: Jews, Muslims, and Legal Pluralism in Nineteenth-Century Morocco." PhD diss., Princeton University, 2013.

Sebti, Abdelahad. "Chroniques de la contestation citadine: Fès et la révolte des tanneurs (1873–1874)." *Hespéris-Tamuda* 29, no. 2 (1991), 283–312.

Times Of Morocco.

Trotter, P. D., *Our Mission to the Court of Morocco in 1880*, Edinburgh: KCB, 1881.

Arabic

Ben-Srhir, Khalid. "Watiqa ghayr manchoura 'an mallah Mourrakouch fi nihayat al-qarn at-tassi' achar." *Hespéris-Tamuda* 35, no. 2 (1997), 25–71.

Ibn Zaydan, Abderrahman. *Ithaf a'lam al-nass bi jamali akhbari hadirati Maknas.* Vol. 2. 2nd ed. Casablanca: Matabi' Ideal, 1990.

Al-Nassiri, Ahmed ibn Khalid. *Al-istiqsa li-akhbari al-Maghrib al-qssa.* Vol. 9. Casablanca: Dar al-Kitab, 1956.

CHAPTER 2

Aref Taher Bey: An Ottoman Military Instructor Bridging the Maghreb and the Ottoman Mediterranean

ODILE MOREAU

Aref Taher is an unknown personality, forgotten in Ottoman and Moroccan historiography. In Morocco, he was called "Ahrif Bey" and presented himself as an Ottoman officer.[1] However, he used several aliases, such as "Taher," "Aref," and "Aref Taher" in Morocco and "Zid" in Spain.

Initially this research dealt with a short period between 1909 and 1910 when Aref Taher led an unofficial Ottoman military mission to Morocco. This adventure was kept a secret, and he remained relatively discreet about it. The original nature of my research and the lack of information available led me to attempt to identify as many personalities as possible close to my subject better to understand why this Ottoman military mission went to Morocco. I began the difficult work of identifying these personalities to fill in the gaps in my knowledge about this man's mission. The most important officer was the head of the military mission, Aref himself. In addition, very few documents exist dealing with Aref's private life. I found nothing on his childhood that would allow me to set him within a family framework as he grew up.

Understanding personal itineraries helps put into perspective the times in which individuals lived. Not being able to do more, I present a number of moments of Aref Taher's life. In doing so I hope to divulge some of the social contexts in which he worked and the complexity of his life, including his relationship to others, his friendships, and his professional networks. I also weigh his influence on other lives in various countries (Egypt, Morocco, Tripolitania).

The geographical itinerary of Aref Taher is large and rich and takes us through the vast Ottoman Empire, its various provinces as well as Morocco and Europe, including Albania, Istanbul, Egypt, Tripoli of

Taher Bey (left) explains the map to Suleiman Baruni, deputy of the Djebel and to Ferhat Bey, deputy of Tripoli. In Georges Rémond, *Aux camps turco-arabes: Notes de route et de guerre en Tripolitaine et en Cyrénaïque*, Paris, Turquoise edition, collection Altérités, 2014, p. 89.

Barbary, Spain, Italy, and France. He also had at one time in his life the opportunity to migrate to the United States. The numerous trips he made through the Mediterranean world are amazing. Each journey across the sea took several days. The time to traverse it had diminished due to the availability of new and better ships. This revolution in transportation changed people's perceptions of time and space and seemed miraculous to contemporaries.

Aref Taher Bey lived through the ups and downs of the Muslim Mediterranean's wrestling with challenges coming from Europe. Of course, he did not exist in a closed world, but in a varied number of worlds, simultaneously negotiating several frontiers.

Where Did Aref Taher Bey Come From?

Born in the Ottoman territory of Albania, he held the rank of captain of the operations staff in the Ottoman army. As an educated and cultivated officer, he belonged to the inner circle of the reformed Ottoman army, representing a minority of officers. After the Young Turk Revolution of 1908, he served in different regions of the Muslim Mediterranean. I am not sure why he left Istanbul after he graduated from the Military Academy. After all, he was destined for a brilliant career, since in the early twentieth century, hardly 20 percent of the officers had any higher education. Aref Taher Bey, thus, belonged to the elite among Ottoman officers.

Exiled to Egypt, he heard about a demand for Ottoman officers willing to serve in Morocco.[2] From late 1909 to 1910, Aref Taher led an unofficial Ottoman military mission to Morocco. After being expelled from that country, due to French machinations, he returned to Egypt where he joined an Egyptian secret society, al-Itthihâd al-Maghrabî (Maghreb Unity), involved in anticolonial fighting in Morocco. He later returned to the ranks of the Ottoman army when the Ottoman–Italian War broke out in Tripoli in today's Libya from 1911–1912. However, during his stay in Tripolitania and after, he kept up his contacts with officers on the Moroccan front.

The Young Turk Revolution of July 1908 led to a constitutional regime allied to Germany and opposed to further colonial expansion by France and Britain in the Muslim world. After a few months, the Young Turk Committee of Union and Progress took internal measures to prevent counterrevolution. According to Ottoman war minister Mahmud Shevket Pasha, Aref was court martialed because of his involvement in military students' and officers' spy activities during Sultan Abdülhamid II's reign. He was then struck off of the Ottoman army's lists and lived as a fugitive outside the empire.[3]

Given the fact that more than 90 percent of the officers of the Ottoman army continued serving the young Republic of Turkey, he belonged to a minority of officers who could have advanced high in the ranks but did not. Instead he became a persona non grata in the late Ottoman Empire and afterward in the Republic of Turkey. He was at odds with the Ottoman army. Clearly, he was not a Committee of Union and Progress partisan.

Cairo-based Six Months Exile in Egypt (Spring–Fall 1909)

In Egypt, Aref Taher Bey heard about the request made by El Muqri, an emissary of the Moroccan minister of foreign affairs, to the Khedive of Egypt, 'Abbas Hilmi Pasha, asking for Turkish officers to serve in Morocco. In fact, these ex-Ottoman officers received several job propositions, because Ottoman-educated officers from the Nizâm [reformed army] were in great demand in other Muslim countries, who emulated Ottoman army reforms. For example, Afghanistan's king Habibullah Khan also attempted to recruit officers from the same pool of ex-officers.[4]

It seems that this Moroccan invitation was extended by Mohammad Pasha al-Shara'î, member of the inner circle of the khedive 'Abbas Hilmi Pasha. Al-Shara'î, a Moroccan living in Egypt, was the president of the secret pan-Islamic Jam'iyyat al-Ittihâd al-Maghrabî (Maghrib Unity Society), which aimed at uniting the North African states (Algeria, Tunisia, Morocco, and Tripoli). This implies that, at this time, Aref Taher Bey was already in contact with the Cairo-based secret society al-Ittihâd al-Maghrabî, or at least with some of its members.

Apparently, the offer and working conditions in Morocco suited Aref Taher Bey well. In his writings in later years he would reveal yet another motive of great personal importance for working in Morocco: the unity of Islam (Ittihâd-i Islam). On November 1909, a first group of ex-Ottoman officers led by Aref Taher Bey, captain of operations, sailed to Morocco.[5]

Moroccan Resistance to European Imperialism

After the signing of the Entente Cordiale in 1904, the French aimed at promoting a de facto protectorate over Morocco. Therefore, the Moroccan government made efforts to find qualified Muslim advisors to replace the Europeans in the service of the makhzan, especially French military instructors.[6] In addition, since 1905, when Kaiser Wilhelm II visited Tangier, the Moroccan population seemed to be favorable to Germany, viewed then, rightly or wrongly, as a new protector.

The Moroccan resistance to French control over Morocco increased after 1905 and turned into open revolt in 1907. In response to blatant French intervention in Casablanca (1907), a coalition of Moroccan notables brought about the deposition of Sultan 'Abd al-'Azîz and proclaimed as ruler his more militant half-brother, 'Abd al-Hafîz (r. 1908–1912), acclaiming him "sultan of the jihad." Mawlay 'Abd al-Hafîz carried out a policy of resistance against imperialism and hoped to restore the integrity of the Moroccan central authority. As part of that strategy, it seems that the sultan secretly invited Muslim military advisors in late 1909 to Morocco to circumvent the French military mission.

The Unofficial Ottoman Military Mission to Morocco (November 1909–August 1910)

The recruitment of Ottoman instructors was kept secret by the Moroccan sultan, allowing him to claim that it was not official.[7] In fact, the recruitment of the ex-Ottoman officers was mysterious, and to this day no written proof exists verifying their presence in the country. The unofficial Ottoman military mission included about eighteen members. A first group arrived in Morocco on October 1909; the second, on February 1910.

The ex-Ottoman officers did not receive any credentials, and when they arrived in Tangier no Moroccan official welcomed them. They all had to walk the long distance from Tangier to Fez, except Aref Taher Bey, the head of the group, who traveled by horse. The only letter of recommendation he had in hand was one written by Mohammad Pasha al-Shara'î from Egypt.[8] The British Legation in Morocco considered these men as ex-Ottoman officers engaged by the Moroccan sultan as military instructors. In December 1909, Aref Taher Bey was received by the Moroccan sultan, provoking tensions between the Ottoman instructors and the French military mission.[9] In fact, from the very beginning, the French opposed the arrival of these ex-Ottoman officers in Morocco, since the Ottoman instructors considered themselves as military officers on a mission. Aref Taher Bey presented himself as "A. Tahir, comt. État-major, chef de la mission turque, Tanger" on his calling card.[10]

From the beginning of December 1909, they began to participate in the *mahalla* (the sultan's military maneuvers). Twelve Ottomans, all former officers, equipped with beautiful horses, went with Si Mahboub.[11] In fact, the French military mission refused to accompany the *mahalla* to Hiayna. However, two English instructors joined the *mahalla*. It seems that Aref Taher was the only one of the Turks who wore a military uniform, the others being dressed like natives.

The French authorities in Morocco contacted the Ottoman government demanding these mens' recall. The French did not succeed, because the Moroccans did not apparently use an official channel with the

Ottoman Porte. French authorities insisted on a full recognition of the French military mission at Fez and the dismissal of the ex-Ottoman officers whom the Moroccan sultan had taken into his service. In February 1910, a French ultimatum of forty-eight hours was given to the makhzen. It demanded the dismissal of the Ottoman instructors.[12] Although most left, some of the Turks remained with the *mahalla* until the end of May.

At this time, the British Legation to Morocco used its good offices to protect Ottoman interests in Morocco. The Ottomans were not "protégés" but enjoyed limited protection. For example, the British Legation could not insist on the Turks leaving so long as the Ottoman instructors behaved themselves. Aref Taher Bey intended to challenge an editor of a local pro-French newspaper, and then abandoned the idea.[13] The British Legation described him positively as a well-behaved man, and it played a role of intermediary between the Ottoman instructors and the French military mission to prevent the former from being expelled. Finally, the Ottoman instructors were dismissed by the Moroccan sultan, under pressure from the French, in June 1910. But some of them refused to leave the country after the French ultimatum.

In some Ottoman newspapers in Istanbul, a press campaign was led against France regarding the dismissal of the Turkish instructors in Morocco. The Turkish press praised these officers who the Ottoman government appeared to have disowned. In fact, the Ottoman war minister published on September 11, 1910, an article in *Yeni Gazete*. This article responded to a previous one published by Aref Taher under the title "Is Mawlay Hafidh a Tyrant or Not?" in which he supported the Moroccan sultan's action.[14] The Ottoman war minister assumed that this captain was an ancient informer who sent a number of his colleagues to prison or into exile. Immediately after the mutiny in April 1909, he was struck off the army rolls. Aref Taher Bey probably went back to Egypt, but first, according to Ahmed Bedevi Kuran, he moved from Morocco to Paris, while his other comrades returned directly to Cairo.[15]

Networking and Connections

After being expelled from Morocco, Aref Taher Bey worked as a journalist for one of Egypt's leading newspapers, *al-Muayyad*, where he published articles against France's presence in North Africa. In those days little information dealing with Morocco appeared in the Ottoman and

Egyptian press. Most of the time, he signed his articles by an anony-mous "A. T." The editor of *al-Muayyad*, Shaykh ʾAlî Yûsuf (1863–1913), belonged to the khedive Abbas Hilmi Pasha's entourage and was also a member of the secret society Ittihâd al-Maghrabî.

Aref Taher Bey was also involved in a project for the same secret so-ciety, which planned to open a German-Arabic language newspaper in Morroco with an anti-French editorial line. The principal actors in-volved in this project were Mohammad Pasha al-Sharaʾî, Aref Taher Bey, and Shaykh ʾAlî Yûsuf. In 1910, they began negotiations with Ger-man intermediaries in Morocco, including the Mannesmann brothers.[16] Aref Taher Bey had several meetings with the German ambassador in Egypt and Mister Singer, the director of the Deutsche Orient Bank,[17] which was a very active center spreading anti-French propaganda and the ideas of Ittihad-i Islam. He had also a very good relationship with the German diplomatic agency in Cairo.[18] Unlike the other great pow-ers, Germany had no colony in the Muslim world and did not rule over any Muslims in the Middle East. Therefore, Germany, in keeping with its growing competition with Great Britain and France, viewed anti-imperialist tendencies with sympathy. Most of the German politicians were interested in keeping the Ottoman Empire intact. The German interests were openly in competition with those of France in Morocco until France and Germany reached an agreement after the Agadir Crisis in July 1911. Until then, the Franco–German rivalry was virulent and used the press as a tool for propaganda. The German intervention in Morocco slowed French attempts at taking over the country, but could not stop it. Nevertheless, the German action in Morocco against the French authorities restarted at the beginning of World War I.

In spite of long discussions between al-Ittihâd al-Maghribî and Ger-man officials, this newspaper was never published. In June 1911, when Aref Taher Bey went to Tangier to create the newspaper, *Nahdat al-Maghreb* (Maghreb's revival), he was arrested by the French authori-ties and expelled. He then took refuge in Spain.[19] In May 1911, some members of al-Ittihad al-Maghribî made contacts with Mawlay Zayn al-ʾAbidin, a pretender to the Moroccan throne. They intended to give him military advice and monetary backing, financed by their organization. However, they never accomplished their goals, being arrested in Tan-gier by the French in June 1911.[20] Protests against the expulsion of Arif Taher were published in the Spanish Press in the newspaper *A.B.C.*[21]

When Aref Taher Bey and Muhammad Hilmi returned to Morocco in the summer 1912 and got involved in another attempt to support the resistance forces against the French, both of them were again deported. A general insurrection of the Moroccan population against the French sponsored by the secret society al-Ittihâd al-Maghrabî was supposed to break out in mid-September at the end of Ramadan. The society's agents in Tangier communicated with resistance fighters in central Morocco, and arms and money were to be smuggled to the Berber tribes. An attempt was also made to send another military mission to Morocco composed of Egyptian and Turkish officers, Aref Taher and Hilmi among them, to advise the resistance forces. However, the ever-vigilant French authorities arrested them before they reached their destination.[22]

The project of al-Ittihâd al-Maghrabî to unite the North African states was condemned to failure after the French and Germans signed a treaty on September 4, 1911. Despite this agreement, the network of al-Ittihâd al-Maghrabî continued its various activities, even after the promulgation of the French Protectorate in Morocco in 1912.

The Ottoman–Italian War (October 1911–October 1912)

Aref Taher Bey, the ex-chief of the Ottoman military mission to Morocco, was in Paris in the autumn of 1911. There he contacted a group of Turks.[23] The group included Ali Fethi Bey (Okyar), the Ottoman military attaché in Paris, and they planned to organize and join the Patriotic Officers Group at the Tripolitanian front under the command of Enver Bey. Ahmed Bedevi (Kuran), who should have joined them, had to resign for medical reasons and stayed in Paris.[24] Enver Bey divided the group of volunteers into two sections, which would reach the battlefield secretly via Egypt and Tunisia. The first section headed by Enver Bey and Mustafa Kemal Bey (who later assumed the name Atatürk) went to Cyrenaica by the way of Egypt. The second section, commanded by Ali Fethi went from Istanbul to Tunis, where Tunisian nationalists helped them join the Ottoman camp facing Tripoli. Except for personal weapons, they carried no luggage. Each member received one hundred gold liras for expenses, given to them by the Ottoman Ministry of War.[25] All of these volunteers wore civilian clothes and had false passports, travelling in disguise.

In this way Aref Taher Bey returned to the Ottoman army to participate in the struggle against Italy. He was among the first Ottoman officers to arrive in Tripolitania and distinguished himself during the fighting at the palm grove of Tripoli. He then was nominated to join the forces in Tripolitania, probably as part of the Special Services. He remained in Tripolitania with some members of the Patriotic Officers Group, even after the signature of the cease-fire Treaty of Ouchy (October 15, 1912).[26] At that point, Nazım Pasha, who replaced Mahmud Shevket Pasha, attempted to end the resistance movement in Tripolitania and Cyrenaica, since the Ottomans now had to concentrate their war efforts on the more important Balkan front.

Georges Rémond, a war correspondent of the French journal *L'Illustration*, who covered the Italian–Turkish War, met Aref Taher Bey in early 1912 in Aziziye in Tripolitania at the Ottoman headquarters. Rémond related their discussion about Ottoman international politics, and it is amazing to discover that Aref Taher Bey was advocating that there was no real pan-Islamism. According to him, pan-Islamism was no more than pipe dreams and a false argument used by the Europeans to legitimate their wars by imaginary fears. He explained to him that there was no religious unity in the Muslim world, due to the different races, skin colors, costumes, geographical distances, and diversity of languages creating problems of comprehension. He explained that the French believed that the Sanusiyya in the Sahara and the Muslims in Algeria represented a huge danger for them. On the contrary, he argued hypocritically that the Ottomans had been conciliatory. He pointed out that the French feared the Italians who settled in Tripoli, close to France's Tunisian Protectorate.[27] It seems that Aref Taher used the journalist to deflect attention from the pan-Islamic movement and tried to reassure European public opinion.

Aref Taher would continue his frequent journeys to Morocco and later traveled to Egypt and Tunisia. He was one of the leaders of the al-Ittihâd al-Maghrabî conspiracy in 1912 in Morocco, which planned a general revolt there during the spring 1912. They initiated an anti-French campaign in the Arabic newspaper *al-Haqq*, which called for an insurrection. It was planned to coincide with the abdication of Abd al-Hafidh and the arrival of al-Hiba to Marrakech.[28]

According to a French report of April 1912, Aref Taher returned to Cairo via Cyprus a few weeks before this report. That meant he continued his networking activities with Morocco during the Ottoman–Italian War. Again, Aref Taher had meetings with German personalities such as the Mannesmann brothers about the creation of a newspaper to be published in Fez in French, German, and Arabic.[29] On April 13, Aref Taher met Baron Max von Oppenheim, an archeologist and German diplomat who had been in the Middle East for twenty years. He was a top figure, one of the theorists of pan-Islam. Max von Oppenheim advised him to postpone travelling to Fez and go only to Gibraltar where the correspondent of the German newspaper *Gazette de Cologne* was based to prepare the opening of a future newspaper.[30] The activities of the secret society al-Ittihâd al-Maghrabî increased after the mutiny of Fez in April 1912.

After 1913, the network evolved into a much more formal structure organized by the Ottoman State.[31] The Tripolitanian and Balkan wars considerably affected the Committee for Union and Progress. Initially defending Ottomanism, once the Balkans were lost by 1912, the Committee stressed the unity of Islam and Turkism. The Ottoman Empire began to provide aid in fighting against all European imperialism and especially the occupation of Muslim territories.

World War I

The aims of the Special Services (Teşkilat-ı Mahsusa) were to address the twin threats to the Ottoman State: Arab separatism within the empire and Western imperialism. The Teşkilat-ı Mahsusa grew out of an informal organization established by Enver Pasha before he became Minister of War and deputy commander in chief of the Ottoman army. This informal organization took over the preexisting informal solidarities network, being at that time disconnected from the Ottoman State. Enver Pasha was convinced that a secret semimilitary organization could enhance the policies he thought would maintain the unity and territorial integrity of the Ottoman State. In fact, most of the Ottoman government's activities after 1913 against Arab separatist groups were channelled through the Special Services.[32] The primary goal of the Teşkilat-ı Mahsusa was military. Its role was to engage in military and paramilitary operations against the enemy—internal or external—and to stir up troubles in the Entente colonies where Muslims were numerous. In fact, the Teşkilat-ı Mahsusa became a tool to assist the regular Ottoman army.

When the Ottoman Empire entered World War I, the nature of the Teşkilat-ı Mahsusa changed. It was reorganized from a small covert group personally attached to Enver Pasha. It thereafter received a semiovert official status within the Ministry of War. As such, it remained under Enver Pasha's direct control and functioned as a secret intelligence service, separate from the intelligence branch of the general staff and from the Minister of Interior's secret police. This new status led to increases in personnel and a more important budgetary allocation in order to realize its new missions. During World War I, most of the Teşkilat-ı Mahsusa's activities were directed to the Ittihad-i Islam propaganda campaign. In fact, the reorganization of the Teşkilat-ı Mahsusa took place immediately after the signing of the Ottoman–German alliance in August 1914. These activities continued until the end of World War I at two levels: a military one, by recruiting volunteers, and at an ideological one, by fomenting uprisings in enemy Muslim territories.

The Teşkilat-ı Mahsusa's agents were often specialists—doctors, engineers, journalists, and guerrilla warfare specialists. But, the larger group was made up of regular army officers and enlisted men who joined the Teşkilat-ı Mahsusa for special duty. These activists, actually adventurers, came from various backgrounds but were chosen for their loyalty to the Ottoman State. Cadres of trained and experienced agents formed the nucleus of cells to be set up in British and French colonies and in regions of the Ottoman Empire, where an enemy invasion was expected.[33] At the height of its fame in 1916, the Teşkilat-ı Mahsusa consisted of about thirty thousand men.[34] After Teşkilat-ı Mahsusa's first leader Suleyman Askeri's death in April 1915, he was replaced by Ali Bey Başhamba of Tunisian origin, who held the post until the Armistice of Moudros.[35]

According to the German archives, Aref Taher moved to Spain in October 1914.[36] Then, the Ottoman Embassy in Madrid asked to send to Morocco experienced Ottoman emissaries fluent in Arabic.[37] Actually, after long negotiations, the Committee of Union and Progress agreed to dispatch a small group of experienced agents, who travelled under Bulgarian passports and arrived in Spain in November 1915. The leader of the Ottoman contingent was Prince Aziz Hasan, a liberal constitutionalist opponent of the CUP. Commandant Aref Taher Bey had considerable earlier experience in Morocco. This group, consisting of six or seven men, was attached to the staff of the Ottoman Embassy in Madrid. Aref Taher Bey was back working for the Ottoman State, at the periphery and not in its center. In fact, Aref Taher Bey was involved as an Ottoman advisor in a joint German–Ottoman program, called by the Germans "Morokko Aktion," organizing clandestine operations in the Moroccan field under the banner of pan-Islam. In contrast to the unofficial Turkish military mission to Morocco in 1909–1910, the mission of 1915 was official and organized in cooperation with the German Embassy in Madrid. An organism in charge of German–Muslim action in North Africa and the larger Mediterranean was established under the guidance of Prince von Ratibor, the German Ambassador in Madrid, and the Spanish zone in northern Morocco was utilized to foment hostilities against the French forces further south. From the beginning of the war until June 1916, they tried to spread propaganda and prepare a general insurrection, smuggling arms to Moroccan resistance fighters. From June 1916, the agenda aiming at a general insurrection was abandoned only to provide aid to the various local Moroccan resistance fighters. Major Albert Kalle, the German military attaché, was in charge of Moroccan affairs. He worked with Turkish officers and German Arabic scholars. Aref Taher Bey—who also used aliases—was called Taher, his own name, by the Germans. There were many differences between Prince von Ratibor, the German military attaché—who had overall authority for the secret operation in Morocco—and the Ottoman officers concerning the modalities of the German–Ottoman action in Morocco.[38]

All the salaries and expenses of the Ottoman military mission were paid by the German Embassy in Madrid, even though they were apparently attached to the staff of the Ottoman embassy. However, the money was actually disbursed by the Ottoman war minister. Internal disputes and financial problems were recurrent. Aref Taher Bey appears to have led these complaints. On September 1915, the German Embassy in Madrid proposed that all those who wished to go would be sent to America.[39] Apparently, for unknown reasons, no one went. By December 1915, Taher was removed from his functions and asked to return to the Ottoman Empire. Then the control over the Moroccan operations would be entirely assumed by the German Embassy.[40]

By the end of 1915, the German Embassy in Madrid proposed to pay the group of Ottoman officers five hundred pounds sterling and book them passage to the United States. According to the French Archives, Aref Taher threatened to reveal all he knew to the French, thus blackmailing the German authorities. In addition, the situation deteriorated in 1916, when news reached Spain of the outbreak of the Arab revolt and the Turkish repression of Arab dissenters in Beirut.[41] The other members of the Ottoman military mission also began to approach the French and the British to prepare their postwar situation.

All the Ottoman officers were in a very difficult financial situation. Many reports from the Ottoman Embassy in Madrid advocated the necessity to pay their salaries.[42] They also experienced troubles in receiving money sent trough the Ottoman Bank to cover the expenses of travelling to the United States.[43] Aref Taher Bey was very upset with the German Embassy, which he suspected as the cause of his dismissal. However, he refused to move from Madrid and to give back Teşkilat-ı Mahsusa's correspondance's secret key, provoking tensions with the Ottoman Embassy.[44] After very tumultuous events, in June 1918, the Ottoman officers' and Aref Taher Bey's mission was actually suspended.[45]

Back to the Center of the Ottoman Empire

During the summer of 1918, Aref Taher Bey returned to Istanbul and became aide-de-camp to the new sultan, Mehmed VI Vahidettin.[46] He was back in the center of the Ottoman Empire, holding a very important position. Mehmed VI (1861–1926), the last Ottoman sultan-caliph (r. 1918–1922), served until his overthrow by Mustafa Kemal. Only one month after ascending to power, the Ottoman Empire capitulated to the Entente forces.

Sultan Mehmed VI, to ensure the survival of the Ottoman dynasty, cooperated with the Allied forces in suppressing all nationalist groups after the empire's unconditional surrender and the signing of the Armistice of Moudros on October 30, 1918. Many leaders of the Young Turk administration sought exile in Germany after the Ottoman Empire's military defeat. An Allied military administration was created in Istanbul in December 1918, and the Ottoman Parliament was dissolved. After negotiations, the nationalists secured the sultan's agreement to organize elections in late 1919, which brought a majority of nationalists back to power in the new parliament. The Allies, frightened by the nationalists' successes, extended the Allied Military zone to Istanbul, arrested a number of nationalist leaders, and exiled some of them to Malta. On April 11, 1920, Sultan Mehmed VI again dissolved the parliament, provoking the nationalists to establish a provisional government in Ankara (in the form of a Grand National Assembly).

On August 10, 1920, Sultan Mehmed VI's representatives signed the Treaty of Sevres, with extremely harsh peace terms including the recognition of the Middle East mandates, the removal of Ottoman control over Anatolia and Izmir, and the recognition of the Hejaz as an independent state. With the Ottoman Empire's territory reduced significantly by the Treaty of Sèvres, the nationalists led by Mustafa Kemal intensified their revolt.

Civil War in the Ottoman Empire

According to Ahmed Bedevi Kuran, Aref Taher Bey was a staff commandant[47] of the Forces of Order,[48] which was founded on April 18, 1920, by the Ottoman government in Istanbul. It was a semiofficial military organization. Two days after having formed the government, Prime Minister Damat Ferit Pasha met the English High Commissioner, Admiral John de Robbeck, on April 7, 1920, in order to take measures against the nationalists. On April 11, 1920, the Seykh-ül-Islam (Arabic: Shaykh al-Islam), the highest religious authority in the land beneath the Caliph Dürrizade es-Seyyid Abdullah Efendi, proclaimed a fatwa, or religious ruling, declaring a double excommunication, civil and religious, of the nationalist rebels. He called them bandits and ordered them killed. The defection of the caliph and the Seykh-ül-Islam to the side of the foreign occupiers represented an important setback and paved the way to the development of profound divisions in the population.[49] It was the beginning of a civil war between the caliph's army and the nationalist rebels. The former contained four thousand men. The signature of the Treaty of Sevres at that point was perceived by the Ottoman public as a traitorous act. The Independence War directed by Mustafa Kemal from Ankara turned against the Ottoman sultan, who lost his legitimacy. The Grand National Assembly located in Ankara and led by Mustafa Kemal opened on April 23, 1920. The new body denounced Sultan Mehmed VI's government and drafted a new temporary constitution. Mustafa Kemal as commander of the resistance defeated the Greek invading forces in September 1922, thereby gaining control over Anatolia. The Grand National Assembly abolished the sultanate on November 1, 1922, established the new republic of Turkey, and separated the sultanate from the caliphate. Sultan Mehmet VI fled to Malta on a British warship on November 17 of the same year. This event marked the official end of the Ottoman Empire. After his flight, he was deposed as caliph and his cousin Abdülmecit II was elected in his place by the Grand National Assembly. The ex-sultan Mehmed VI tried to re-establish himself as caliph in the Hejaz without success. Afterward, in March 1924, the Assembly abolished the caliphate and sent all the members of the former Ottoman ruling family and their retainers into exile.

European Exile: Persona Non Grata

Aref Taher Bey, being part of the former Ottoman Sultan Vahidettin's retinue, had to leave the Ottoman Empire territory for exile with him. He departed with the ex-sultan and accompanied him as he moved abroad. First, it seems that he sailed to Malta with him.

Former Sultan Mehmed VI spent the rest of his life in exile under difficult economic conditions. After Malta, he left for Mecca on the invitation of King Husayn of the Hejaz in Arabia, where he was treated with respect. Later they returned to Europe by boat through Egypt and the Suez Canal to Genoa in Italy[50] to settle in San Remo on the Italian Riviera. Taher Bey was one of the fugitive's close collaborators and also served him as a translator for the Italian language[51]. The deposed sultan died there on May 16, 1926, at the age of sixty-five and was buried at the Mosque of Selim I in Damascus, because the new Turkish government did not allow him to be enterred in Turkey. Aref Taher Bey was one of the organizers of funeral arrangements and accompanied his body to Syria. At that time, he had the title of staff colonel.

After the Turkish War of Independence (1919–1923), the new Republic of Turkey presented a list of six hundred names—never made public—at the Conference of Lausanne, which were declared personae non gratae. Afterward, this list was reduced to one hundred and fifty. The National Assembly ratified the list on April 23, 1924, and included these names in the Treaty of Lausanne. The list of the Yüzelliler, the hundred and fiftyers, which was a kind of who's who of the Ottoman Empire, aimed at eliminating the Ottoman ruling elite.

Aref Taher's name was on the list. Therefore, he was not allowed to return to Turkey. These hundred and fifty personae non gratae had been either against the War of Independence in Turkey and/or had supported the Allied powers. As exiles living abroad, the National Assembly on May 28, 1927, denied them Turkish citizenship. This law had important consequences for the property rights of the hundred and fiftyers. The state confiscated their property and took away their inheritance rights in Turkey. Aref Taher's name was at the top of the list, sixth of the seven personalities in former Sultan Mehmed VI's "House of Osman."

On June 28, 1938, a few months before the death of Atatürk, the law restricting their entry into Turkey was lifted, and an amnesty law was issued.[52] However, the concerned individuals were not allowed to occupy public positions and, if necessary, their Turkish nationality could be canceled. After this amnesty, only a few survivors on the hundred and fifty persons' list returned to Turkey. Twenty-nine of them stayed abroad. However, Aref Taher Bey's name was not on the amnesty list, nor on the list of foreign residents. Was he still alive at that time? Being born circa 1885, he would have been in his fifties in 1938. The latest information we have about his life in Europe concerned his settlement in Albania. According to Ahmed Bedevi Kuran,[53] Aref Taher Bey went to Albania on the occasion of the marriage between a sister of Albania's King Ahmed Zog and a young son of Sultan Abdülhamid II. There, he was invited to join the Albanian army with the rank and salary of a general. Sixteen years after his flight from the disintegrating Ottoman Empire, he still maintained good connections with the Ottoman family in exile, being a prominent member of this imperial community in exile. We suppose that he spent the rest of his life in Albania, his home country. However, in the young Republic of Turkey, he was still considered a traitor.

Conclusion

Aref Taher Bey was a hyperactive individual, moving from one locality to another—a very mobile agent. Sometimes, I doubted colonial police reports, thinking police informants or spies confused individuals or got the wrong person. As a result, it was difficult to follow this Ottoman military officer on his numerous journeys. I tried using multiple approaches to understand facets of his personality and activities. At the very beginning, I knew he was an Ottoman instructor who came to Morocco in order to reorganize the Moroccan army, hoping to prevent the advent of the French Protectorate. He turned out to be much more than that: a tireless figure, working in the shadows, with multiple personas and networks.

The movements of Aref Taher Bey, though purposeful, appeared chaotic in a tumultuous period. He clearly had excellent qualifications due to his formation at military academies and was a qualified representative of the new Ottoman army. Many foreign rulers wanted to hire his services as a mercenary.

He experienced different kinds of exiles. He went abroad on exile during two different periods of his life. First, after the counterrevolution of March 1909 he was struck off the army rolls and spent six months in exile in Egypt. After that he worked in Morocco (November 1909–August 1910) and then became active in other parts of North Africa, including Egypt. In the fall of 1911, he returned to the Ottoman army to fight against the Italians during the Italian–Ottoman War in Tripolitania. During his second exile he fled to Europe with the deposed sultan and could never return to the Republic of Turkey. He was marginalized hypothetically because of his attachment to unpopular Ottoman rulers.

Aref Taher was a member of solidarity networks crossing the Muslim Mediterranean. He worked underground as an unofficial actor. Then, this informal network evolved into a formal structure, organized by the Ottoman State within which he had an official position. Marginality came from his secret activities with secret networks such as al-Ittihâd al-Maghrabî. He worked on different levels using journalism and press propaganda, demonstrating his multiple talents, thus making him ever more useful for those who employed him. The events he chronicled in the Arab or Ottoman newspapers dealing with Morocco were very important and were followed in the Muslim world and in European chancelleries. He excelled as an instructor in the regular army and also as a guerilla warfare leader on the battlefield in Tripolitania. He took part in all sorts of wars of his time, be they international, civil, or guerilla. He conducted subversive activities and was a member of Ottoman Special Services (Teşkilat-ı Mahsusa), being very far away from the Ottoman Empire's center. For unclear reasons he fell out with the CUP leaders. He was an actor, a participant in many experiments, a leading operator, but at a local level. At the end of the war, in 1918, he would be for four years at the center of the Ottoman Empire, very close to the sultan. Defending the Ottoman dynasty in the Caliphate army he would soon again be condemned to exile, this time without being able to return to the new Turkey.

Notes

1. Willfrid Rollman, *The "New Order" in a Pre-colonial Muslim Society: Military Reform in Morocco, 1844–1904* (Ann Arbor: University of Michigan Press, 1983), 3 vols.; Simou Bahija, *Les réformes militaires au Maroc de 1844 à 1912* (Rabat: Publications de la Faculté des Lettres et des Sciences Sociales, série thèses et mémoires, no. 28, 1995), 389.

2. Ahmed Bedevi Kuran, *Harbiye Mektebi'nde Hürriyet Mücadelesi* (Istanbul: Türkiye İş Bankası, Kültür Yayınları, 2009), 158.

3. *Yeni Gazete*, Istanbul, September 11, 1910. In these troubled times of counterrevolution, the military schools of Istanbul became the scene of numerous expulsions. The increasingly politicized students were urged to either submit to school regulations or leave. It seems that Aref Taher Bey left under obscure circumstances after the counterrevolution of April 1909, being at odds with the Committee for Union and Progress.

4. Ahmed Bedevi Kuran, *Mektebi'nde Hürriyet Mücadelesi*, 158.

5. A. E. (Affaires Etrangères, French Foreign minister's archives), n.s. 277, Maroc, Défense Nationale, 6, A. E., Tangiers, Letter No. 21, November 9, 1909, 35.

6. Edmund Burke III, "Pan-Islam and Moroccan Resistance to French Colonial Penetration, 1900–1912," *Journal of African History* 13, no. 1 (1972): 105.

7. Odile Moreau, "Une 'mision militaire' ottomane au Maroc au début du 20e siècle," *The Maghreb Review* (London) 30, no. 2–4 (2005): 213.

8. A. E. (Affaires Etrangères, French Foreign minister's archives), n.s. 277, Maroc, Défense Nationale, 6, Report, December 2, 1909, 96.

9. C. A. D. N. (Centre des Archives Diplomatiques de Nantes, French Consular Archives), Série A, 262, Fonds Tanger, French military mission to Morocco, Commandant Mangin, to War Minister, Fez, January 1, 1910, monthly report no. 1.

10. B. O. A. (Başbakanlık Osmanlı Arşivi), HR. SYS. (Hariciye Siyasi), Annex to 404/37, from the Ottoman Legation in Madrid to Rashid Pasha, Ottoman Minister of Foreign Affairs; P. R. O. (Public Record Office, London), 413/53, confidential, Sir White to Sir Edward Grey, Tangier, July 20, 1910.

11. Si Mahboub was the chief of the *mahalla* of Hiayna and was nominated by the sultan chief of the *mahalla* of Fez in December 1909, see C. A. D. N., Série A, 262, Fonds Tanger, French military mission to Morocco, Commandant Mangin, to War Minister, Fez, January 1, 1910, monthly report no. 1.

12. A. E. (Affaires Étrangères, French Foreign minister's archives), n.s. (Nouvelle Série) 278, Maroc, Défense Nationale, vol. 7, French Military Mission, Fez, March 2, 1910, Monthly Report, February, no. 13, commandant Mangin, head of the French military mission in Morocco to French Minister of War, 34–35.

13. P. R. O. (Public Record Office, London), 413/53 confidential print no. 193, Sir White to Sir Edward Grey, Tangier, July 10, 1910, 216.

14. This article was published in no. 732 of *Yeni Gazete*, Istanbul, August 25, 1326/September 7, 1910/2 Ramazan 1328.

15. Ahmed Bedevi Kuran, *Harbiye Mektebi'nde Hürriyet Mücadelesi* (Istanbul: Türkiye İş Bankası, Kültür Yayınları, 2009), 158–159.

16. The Mannesmann brothers, Max (1857–1915) and Reinhard (1856–1922), were German engineers and entrepreneurs, inventors of a method of producing seamless pipe. In 1890, they organized the Mannesmannröhren-Werke AG in southern Morocco, where they founded the Morokko Mannesmann Cie.

17. C. A. D. N., D. A. I. 220, vol. 1, Cairo, M. Defrance, chargé of the Agence and the General Consulate of France to French Minister of Foreign Affairs, M. Cruppi, April 12, 1912, 103–104.

18. C. A. D. N., D. A. I. 220, vol. 1, 102, Letter of Mr. Defrance, chargé of the Agence and the General Consulate of France in Cairo to Mr. Pichon, Minister of Foreign Affairs, February 6, 1911.

19. Aref Taher Bey was arrested on June 11, 1911. Cf. C. A. D. N., D. A. I. 220, vol. 2, 104.

20. Edmund Burke III, *Prelude to Protectorate in Morocco: Precolonial Protest and Resistance, 1860–1912* (Chicago: University of Chicago Press, 1976), 161.

21. B. O. A., HR. SYS., 404/36, annex to the report Nr. 6.894/295, Ottoman Legation in Madrid to Rifaat Pasha, Ottoman Minister of Foreign Affairs, Madrid, June 12, 1911.

22. Edmund Burke III, *Prelude to Protectorate in Morocco*, 161; See P.R.O. 413/54: Dispatch No. 159 from White to Grey, June 14, 1911; See P.R.O. 413/57: Kennard to Hunter, August 13, 1912, 205. Edmund Burke III, "Pan-Islam and Moroccan Resistance to French Colonial Penetration, 1900–1912," *Journal of African History* 13, no. 1 (1972): 97–118.

23. Ahmed Bedevi Kuran, *Osmanlı İmparatorluğunda İnkilâp Hareketleri ve Millî Mûcadele*, 1st ed. (Istanbul: Çeltüt Matabaası, 1959); 2nd ed. (Istanbul: Türkiye İş Bankası, Kültür Yayınları, 2012), 530.

24. Ahmed Bedevi Kuran, *İnkilap Tarihimiz ve Jön Türkler* (Istanbul: Tan Matbaası, 1945), 279–280.

25. Philip Hendrick Stoddard, "The Ottoman Government and the Arabs, 1911 to 1918: A Preliminary Study of the Teşkilat-ı Mahsusa," PhD diss., Princeton University, 1963 (Michigan University Microfilms International Dissertation Information Service, 1987), 80–81.

26. The treaty of Ouchy recognized the annexion of Tripolitania and Cyrenaïca by Italy. However, the Ottoman sultan-caliph's religious prerogatives on the Muslim population remained.

27. Georges Rémond, *Aux camps Turco-Arabes: Notes de route et de guerre en Cyrénaïque et en Tripolitaine* (Paris: Hachette, 1913), 77; rev. ed. Georges Rémond, *Aux camps turco-arabes: Notes de route et de guerre en Tripolitaine et en Cyrénaïque* (Paris: Turquoise édition, collection Altérités, 2014), 97. Letter by Georges Rémond to Maurice Normand, director of the French newspaper *L'Illustration*, February 2, 1912.

28. Edmund Burke III, "Moroccan Resistance, Pan-Islam and German War Strategy, 1914–1918," *Francia* (Munich) 3 (1976): 437.

29. C. A. D. N., D. A. I. 220, vol. 1, Mr. de France ministre plénipotentiaire de France to Mr. Cruppi, French Minister of Foreign Affairs, Cairo, April 12, 1912, 103.

30. C. A. D. N., D. A. I. 220, vol. 1, Mr. de France ministre plénipotentiaire de France to Mr. Cruppi, French Minister of Foreign Affairs, Cairo, April 12, 1912, Post Scriptum, 103.

31. Odile Moreau, "De l'informel au formel: l'institutionnalisation ottomane de réseaux de solidarité translocaux avant la Première Guerre mondiale," *Eurasian Studies* (Rome) 8, no. 1–2 (2010): 167–180.

32. Philip Hendrick Stoddard, *The Ottoman Government and the Arabs*, 49–50.

33. Philip Hendrick Stoddard, *The Ottoman Government and the Arabs*, 56.

34. Philip Hendrick Stoddard, *The Ottoman Government and the Arabs*, 58.

35. Ali Bey Başhamba (1876–1918) was an active leader of the Young Tunisians. In 1912, he led the tramway strike in Tunis and was later exiled. In 1913, he moved to the Ottoman Empire, where he was well connected with the Young Turks and held important positions.

36. A. A.–P. A. (Auswärtiges Amt, Politisches Archiv, archives of the German Foreign Office), WK No. 11, 1. In den Afrikanischen Besitzungen Frankreichs, vol. 2, Thérapia, telegram, October 16, 1914.

37. B. O. A., HR. SYS., 2393/4, doc. 1, Vassik Bey to the Grand Saïd Halim Pasha, Madrid, December 29, 1914.

38. C. A. D. N., D. A. I. 220, L'action allemande au Maroc, vol. 2, 10–11.

39. Edmund Burke III, "Moroccan Resistance, Pan-Islam," *Francia* 3, 1976, 460.

40. B. O. A., HR. SYS., 2393/1, doc. 93, December 8, 1915, Berlin, Hakki Pasha to Halil Bey.

41. Edmund Burke III, "Moroccan Resistance, Pan-Islam," *Francia* 3 (1976): 459.

42. B. O. A., HR. SYS., 2392/2, doc. 27, Hakkı Pasha to the Grand Vizier Saïd Halim Pasha, Ottoman Minister of Foreign Affairs, Berlin, August 25, 1916.

43. B. O. A., HR. SYS., 2392/2, doc. 29, Halil Bey to Ibrahim Ziya Bey, via Berlin, telegram, November 14, 1916.

44. B. O. A., HR. SYS., 2393/3, doc. 14, Ibrahim Zia Bey to Ahmed Nessimi Bey, March 22, 1918.

45. Ibid., 265.

46. Sultan Mehmed VI Vahidettin's investiture took place in Istanbul on July 3, 1918.

47. Ahmed Bedevi Kuran, *Osmanlı İmparatorluğunda*, 2nd ed., 527.

48. In Ottoman Turkish, these forces were called Kuvvayi Inzibatiye (Kuvâ-i Inzibâtiyye), literally Forces of Order, and in the Turkish language, Hilâfet Ordusu (the Caliphate army).

49. Odile Moreau, "La dimension religieuse de la guerre d'indépendance," in Marcel Bazin, Salgur Kançal, Roland Perez, and Jacques Thobie, ed., *La Turquie entre trois mondes* (Paris-Istanbul: L'Harmattan-IFEA [Institut Français d'Études Anatoliennes], collection Varia Turcica 32, 1998), 386–387.

50. Tarik Mümtaz Göztepe, *Osmanoğulları'nın Son Padişahı Vahideddin Gurbet Cehenneminde*, 1st ed. (Istanbul: Sebil Yayınevi, 1968); 3rd ed. (1991), 103.

51. Yılmaz Çetiner, *Son Padişah Vahidettin*, 8th ed. (Istanbul: Milliyet Yayınları, 1997), 316.

52. Cahide Sınmaz-Sönmez, "Cumhuriyetin Onuncu Yıldönümü Kutlamaları ve 26 Ekim 1933 Tarihli Genel Af Yasası" (Ankara: *Ankara Üniversitesi Türk İnkilâp Tarih Enstitüsü Atatürk Yolu Dergisi*), no. 33–34 (May–November 2004): 98. The amnesty law of the hundred and fifty persons had previously been proposed on the Tenth Anniversary of the Republic in the framework of the amnesty of October 26, 1933. However, the proposal was rejected by high ranking

Turkish officials and Atatürk himself. See Ilhami Soysal, *150 likler* (Istanbul: Gür Yayınları, 1985), 106.

53. Ahmed Bedevi Kuran, *Osmanlı İmparatorluğunda*, 2nd ed., 527.

Bibliography

Bingöl, Sedat. "150'likler Meselesi." *Bir ihanetin anatomisi.* Istanbul: Bengi Yayınları, 2010.

Burke, Edmund III. "Pan-Islam and Moroccan Resistance to French Colonial Penetration, 1900–1912," *Journal of African History* 13, no. 1 (1972), 97–118.

———. "Moroccan Resistance, Pan-Islam and German War Strategy, 1914–1918," *Francia* (Munich) 3 (1976): 434–464.

———. *Prelude to Protectorate in Morocco: Precolonial Protest and Resistance, 1860–1912.* Chicago: University of Chicago Press, 1976.

Çetiner, Yılmaz. *Son Padişah Vahidettin.* 8th ed. Istanbul: Milliyet Yayınları, 1997.

Deny, Jean. "Instructeurs militaires turcs au Maroc sous Mawlay Hafidh," in *Mémorial Henri Basset. Nouvelles études nord-africaines et orientales.* Paris: Institut des Hautes Etudes Marocaines, Paul Geuthner, 1928, 219–227.

Göztepe, Tarik Mümtaz. *Osmanoğulları'nın Son Padişahı Vahideddin Gurbet Cehenneminde.* Istanbul: Sebil Yayınevi, 1968; 3rd ed. 1991.

Kuran, Ahmed Bedevi. *Harbiye mektebi'nde hürriyet mücadelesi.* Istanbul: Türkiye İş Bankası, Kültür Yayınları, 2009.

———. *Osmanlı İmparatorluğunda İnkılâp Hareketleri ve Millî Mûcadele.* 1st ed. Istanbul: Çeltüt Matabaası, 1959; 2nd ed. Istanbul: Türkiye İş Bankası, Kültür Yayınları, 2012.

Moreau, Odile. *L'Empire ottoman à l'âge des réformes. Les hommes et les idées du "Nouvel Ordre" militaire, 1826–1914.* Paris-Istanbul: Maisonneuve et Larose-IFEA, collection "Passé ottoman, présent turc," 2007.

———. "Une 'mission militaire' ottomane au Maroc au début du 20e siècle," *The Maghreb Review* (London), 30, 2–4 (2006).

———. "La dimension religieuse de la guerre d'indépendance." In Marcel Bazin, Salgur Kançal, Roland Perez, Jacques Thobie, eds., *La Turquie entre trois mondes.* Paris-Istanbul: L'Harmattan-IFEA (Institut Français d'Etudes Anatoliennes), collection Varia Turcica 32 (1998), 386–387.

Rémond, Georges. *Aux camps Turco-Arabes. Notes de route et de guerre en Cyrénaïque et en Tripolitaine.* Paris: Hachette, 1913; rev. ed. Georges Rémond. *Aux camps turco-arabes. Notes de route et de guerre en Tripolitaine et en Cyrénaïque.* Paris: Turquoise édition, collection Altérités, 2014.

Rollman, Willfrid. *The "New Order" in a Pre-colonial Muslim Society: Military Reform in Morocco, 1844–1904.* 3 vols. Ann Arbor: University of Michigan Press, 1983.

Simou, Bahija. *Les réformes militaires au Maroc de 1844 à 1912.* Rabat: Publications de la Faculté des Lettres et des Sciences Sociales, série thèses et mémoires no. 28, 1995.

Stoddard, Philip Hendrick. "The Ottoman Government and the Arabs, 1911 to 1918: A Preliminary Study of the Teşkilat-ı Mahsusa." PhD diss., Princeton University, 1963 (Michigan University Microfilms International Dissertation Information Service, 1987).
Soysal, Ilhami. *150 likler.* Istanbul: Gür Yayınları, 1985.

CHAPTER 3

Nazli Hanem, Kmar Bayya, and Khiriya Bin Ayyad: Three Women Living between Istanbul, Cairo, and Tunis in the Late Nineteenth and the Early Twentieth Centuries

LEÏLA BLILI

The history of social change in the Arab provinces of the Ottoman Empire since the end of the nineteenth century is tied to individual experiences of men and women who, by their thoughts and actions, influenced events. While doing so, they posed the question of what would become of their countries. Such personalities mobilized a variety of means to express themselves: giving public lectures and writing pamphlets, articles, and books dealing with the backwardness of the Arab world and the Ottoman Empire while denouncing the malfunctioning of its political and military institutions.

The vast literature dealing with these subjects rarely mentions women. Why are they absent from the political landscape in a world then dominated by men? Wasn't there a feminine elite who had access to education and participated in the political processes of those countries? There were women pioneers of reform in the Arab–Ottoman world. However, for a long time they have been victims of a conspiracy of silence that makes it difficult to reconstruct their lives. How can we begin to do so when these women did not follow the same trajectories as men, who belonged to political parties or edited newspapers and magazines? Having written little, didn't these women risk being forgotten?[1] The historiography of the reform movement, having been largely analyzed from a male perspective, would benefit greatly if we could introduce female participation. Taking into account gender would inform us about the place of women in the movement, their relations with men, and where and how they expressed their views.

Nazli Hanem and Kmar Bayya.

Three Prominant Women

This chapter deals with three aristocratic women who fostered significant changes. It begins with their biographies set within the provincial
life of the Ottoman Empire. Each was a pioneer. Nazli Hanem (1853–
1913) opened the first literary and political salon in Cairo and then later
in Tunis. Khiryia bin Ayyad, while living in exile in Vienna, gave the
first public lecture on the degraded status of women in the Ottoman
sultan's harem. Kmar bint Abdullah contributed to the modernization
of the Tunisian court and pushed her husband, Nasir, the Bey of Tunis, to get involved in nationalist politics. By following their comings
and goings, whether forced or voluntary, between Istanbul, Cairo, and
Tunis, their lives illustrate aspects of the political and social history of
the Ottoman Empire at a moment when serious menace threatened the
state.

All three lived rich and opulent lives, but also faced numerous problems, such as exile, loss of power, and an assortment of prohibitions. Their biographies raise important questions such as how did their individual experiences lead them to get involved in political events and social movements? What views did they have about what would happen to their nations? Did they, by their actions and examples, reflect, over the short or long term, some sort of social evolution?

Nazli-Zeinab Hanem

Nazli-Zeinab Hanem was born in Cairo within the family founded by the ruler of Egypt, Mehemet 'Ali (r. 1805–1848).[2] Her father, Mustapha Fadhil Pasha, was the second son of Ibrahim Pasha, who inherited the Egyptian throne. Mustapha's half-brother, Ismail, was older than Mustapha by forty days. The two brothers did not get along, and their mothers intensified their antagonisms. The two men also had vastly different educational backgrounds. Mustapha was the most cultured prince of the royal family. Was that the reason why the rules were changed leading to his elimination from the succession to the throne? The change in the rules, decided by the Ottoman sultan, would have significant consequence: it eliminated from the Egyptian throne a wise prince open to modern ideas. His brother Ismail conspired with the officials of Sultan 'Abd al-'Aziz's court in Istanbul to promulgate the decree of 1866 in favor of enthroning Ismail's own son Mohamed Tewfiq, who was designated the successor to his father. The decree destroyed Mustafa Fadhil's life, as he saw himself denied the throne unjustly. He could no longer stay in Egypt under those circumstances, so he sold most of his possessions and moved into exile in Istanbul, accompanied by his family.

Fadhil, like all the oriental princes, had founded a large family. His harem included three wives and nine legal concubines who bore him ten boys and six girls, the oldest of whom was Princess Nazli. For a long time it was believed that her mother was of Russian origin, but the register of the ruling family states that she was Anatolian, whose name was Dal Azād Hanem (1837–1885), and Nazli was her only girl. The latter was thirteen years old when her father left Cairo, so she spent her adolescence in Istanbul. Like so many aristocratic girls, she probably received her education at home from tutors. The Cairo palace had probably faded in her memory quickly as her father while living in Istanbul was named minister of finance. But soon his relations with Sultan 'Abd al-ʿAziz deteriorated, and he left the Ottoman capital to live in Paris. There he wrote a pamphlet "From a Prince to a Sultan," aimed at ʿAbd al-ʿAziz. In it he denounced despotism, explaining that it was not only the Christian minorities who were oppressed but also the Muslims left to the whims of their prince. Openly announcing his rupture with the Ottoman Porte, he gathered around himself a number of dissidents who founded the Young Turk movement. However, he felt persecuted and saw no possibility for changing Ottoman politics. More and more his mental condition deteriorated until he ended up mad. Meanwhile, as an indirect victim of despotism, Nazli's political thought entered a warlike mode and she became, during this first stage of her life, an adamant adversary of the sultan's absolutism.

In 1872 she married one of her father's cousins, Khalil Pasha (1832–1879), who also belonged to the ruling family.[3] After attending military school, he became an imperial administrator and was named Ottoman ambassador in several European capitals. He lived in Paris between 1860 and 1865, married a French woman, Julie de Niverly, and socialized with important political personalities and great cultural figures. He became friends with the artist Gustave Courbet (1819–1877), from whom he ordered a painting, "The Origins of the World," which for a long time remained hidden because of its obscenity.[4] Khalil Bey matured in this tumultuous environment, accumulating debts from gambling, going from one literary salon to another where he was constantly invited. Some archival sources, mainly diplomatic correspondence not yet fully analyzed, present him as a tortured man, someone on the verge of madness.[5]

Abandoned by his first wife, Nazli married him in October 1872 and moved to Cairo with him in 1875, the same year that her father died. Khalil became the Porte's ambassador to France, so she left Cairo once more and shared with her husband his voyages and displacements to several European capitals. Her political and social formation benefitted from this diplomatic experience. Khalil Pasha died in Istanbul on January 12, 1879, leaving Nazli a widow at the age of twenty-six. Returning to Cairo, accompanied by her stepdaughter, Leila, a product of Khalil's first marriage, Nazli became an autonomous woman.

Nazli in Tunis, 1896–1913

The voyages of Nazli led her to Tunis for the first time in 1896 and a second time beginning in 1899. Apparently these were private visits:

her sister Roukaya, involved with family matters regarding her husband Tahar bin Ayyad (the oldest son of Mahmoud Bin Ayyad whom she had married in 1872), came with her to help her take care of her affairs.[6] Before embarking on this, her first trip to Tunis, Nazli contacted a Tunisian reformer living in Cairo, Mohamed Bayram V,[7] who recommended that she look up some important families such as the Baccouche and the Sellami as well as the Prince Nasir Bey.

The French authorities thought that she invented a family business as an excuse to travel and believed that the princess was "a spy in Egypt for his Imperial Majesty [the Ottoman sultan]."[8] The comings and goings of the princess were minutely followed by the French police: the French General Resident in Tunis was informed in a telegram sent from the Foreign Ministry dated May 16, 1899, that "the princess was expected to arrive in Marseilles, intending to travel through Tunisia, Algeria, and Morocco to contact leading Muslim personalities there. Her voyage will be paid for by the Caliph and she should be expected to echo his views." So Nazli was thought of by the police as another Mata Hari working for Abdülhamid II (1876–1909).

During her stays in Tunisia she went on promenades, on family and official visits, including one to the French General Resident in his palace in La Marsa. She also contacted Tunisian reformist intellectuals and participated in several of their activities. In 1896 she attended a Young Turk Congress in Paris, which provoked a severe reaction from Sultan Abdülhamid II. Immediately after, she wrote him a letter justifying her attendance at the Congress, evoking in her missive her hope to see a democratization of Ottoman political life.[9]

After receiving her letter, the sultan, despite his being furious with her, invited her to Istanbul to bring about a reconciliation. How can we explain this reconciliation with someone that she considered a despot and a deeply corrupt ruler? In 1896 she also translated her father's pamphlet written in 1866 from Turkish into Arabic, in which he denounced the ills of the empire, and sent the translation to Sultan Abdülhamid II who was enraged about that as well. She went to Istanbul despite qualms about her travelling expressed by some of her friends who feared for her life. But she took the precaution of staying at the residence of the British Ambassador and not in the royal palace, where she could have been made to disappear without a trace. And when she visited the sultan in his palace, she took with her an official of the British Embassy, who attended the audience that she had with the ruler. The sultan put on a show of receiving her with much pomp and offered her some expensive gifts, while actually holding her in great contempt to the point that palace officials did not dare to pronounce her name in the ruler's presence. This apparent contradiction led some observers to label her an Ottoman spy, while others thought that she had sold out her principles in exchange for a chest of jewels. After one of her friends sought to understand her change of heart when she began to compliment the ruler, Nazli smiled broadly and showed her precious stones and gold that Abdülhamid II had bestowed upon her.[10]

Did she really reconcile with the sultan, and did she become his secret agent? The responses to this question are mired in controversy. However, if she really did reconcile with him, it probably was not because she received a chest of jewels. Such a transaction probably hid from view her championing of the Ottoman cause against colonial expansionism while also ending her denigration of the sultan-caliph. Instead of fighting her, he made her into a collaborator.

A Political Marriage?

During her second Tunisian voyage in 1899 she met a young civil servant, Khalil Bouhajeb, a man twenty years her junior who had studied in Paris. She decided to marry him. Since becoming a widow in 1878, Nazli had refused several marriage proposals, one coming from a governmental minister, the other from a prince. Instead of accepting the constraints of marriage, she preferred the liberty that her widowhood gave her. Why did she change her mind at a relatively advanced age of fifty, when she married for a second time? Why did she choose Khalil Bouhajeb, a young civil servant without a fortune? Was this a political marriage, allowing her to remain in Tunis and momentarily leave Cairo? That is the way that the French authorities saw it, presenting the princess as "an old ruined woman, with a detestable reputation, running around the world, an adventuress who sold her services to foreign chancelleries." She represented British interests, they thought. What reasons did she really have to set up her base in Tunis? Whatever the reasons for this marriage, the betrothal was celebrated with much attention on April 22, 1900, and registered at the French consulate of Cairo. After asking the French authorities for permission, she and her husband moved to Tunis.

After her marriage, she asked one of her Cairo friends what people thought of her now.

What does Cairo society think of my marriage to the young Tunisian after I had refused to marry a minister and a prince?

They say that you are

Crazy, yes, everyone is crazy, my father was mad! She responded, followed by great laughter.[11]

Nazli lived in La Marsa in a house that she named Villa Ramses. The abode became a cultural center that attracted the Tunisian intelligentsia. The house also became the pivot of relations between Tunis and Cairo. It was there that famous Egyptian personalities, such as the reformer Mohamed 'Abduh, met the Tunisian elite. He, in turn, invited the Tunisian Bashir Sfar to accompany him when he returned to Egypt. Through her, important Egyptians established contacts with the Young Tunisians.

On October 13, 1913, Princess Nazli fell while walking. The consequences of that fall were fatal, for after being transported to Cairo, she died on December 28, 1913. After her death, Princess Kmar proclaimed several days of mourning in the Bardo palace. A police report in the Tunisian archives speaks of "less foreign political agitation regarding the Orient on the part of Kmar. They attribute this calm to the disappearance of Princess Nazli, an intimate friend of Kmar's."[12]

Nazli's husband was only informed of her death two days after it happened. A stepbrother and sister of Nazli, Prince Kamil and Princess Fatma, had in the interim emptied her villa, removing her jewels, furniture, and works of art. Khalil Bouhajeb informed the French consulate of the transgression by telegram, leading to the consul's visit to the abode where he locked the premises and opened an inquiry. The culprits were protected by their cousin, the Egyptian khedive, and therefore had nothing to fear from the inquiry. Prince Kamel even counterattacked: at the moment the case went before the Muslim court to establish the list of Nazli's heirs, he demanded the annulment of his stepsister's marriage to Khalil under the pretext that it was contracted without his consent. To facilitate his claims and remove any legal documents in support of the marriage he stole the wedding contract from Khalil's office in Cairo and tore it in two, removing from the bottom of the document proof of the payment of a dowry, thereby hoping to win the case. Khalil Bouhajeb organized his defense, recalling that only the ruler of Egypt authorized princely marriages, which he had duly done, and demanded the restitution of his property. Behind the sordid details of a struggle over inheritance, this episode demonstrates, after the fact, the refusal of Nazli's family to accept this marriage, probably viewed by them as a misalliance. At the same time, it highlights the force of character of this woman who upset all etiquette in her milieu. Khalil Bouhajeb continued his political ascendancy after Nazli's death. As we shall see, he remained in the proximity of the palace, protected by Kmar Bayya.

If Nazli was known by a handful of scholars, she was not given the recognition that she really deserved among a larger audience. Several years ago this began to change. In 2002 a small book appeared in Tunis written by a historian, Abou al-Kaçim Mohamed Kerrou (1924–2015), who called her a pioneer of the reform movement in Egypt and Tunisia. The word pioneer usually referred to the men who engaged in the reform movment, but Kerrou states that the great Egyptian reformists, such as Saad Zaghloul, Kaçim Amin, Mohamed 'Abduh, and others, were formed in the salon that the princess organized in Cairo in the second half of the nineteenth century, and that it was the first salon in the Arab world established by a woman. More than that, Kerrou argued that these men, and other reformers, were her protégés, and that they owed their existence as reformers to her alone. She played a similar role in Tunis where she lived during thirteen years. During that time, she founded another literary salon and helped form several enlightened intellectuals. The work of Kerrou renders justice and homage to her, as so many unsavory things have wrongly been written about her. No previous book demonstrated the significant role that she played in Egyptian and Tunisian modern history. The author claims that without crediting her as a catalyst of new ideas in Egypt and to a lesser extent in Tunisia, we cannot understand how several progressive intellectuals, journalists, lawyers, and politicians were formed.

Kmar Bayya, 1866–1942

Far from Cairo and its palace intrigues, in the Caucasus mountains, the woman who would be called Kmar, or "Moon," was born. Her real name remains unknown. She declared in a notarized statement her birth date as 1866 and revealed nothing of her infancy or childhood, of which she would have had only vague recollections.[13] She was merely identified as "the daughter of Abdullah," meaning the slave of God, but we know nothing about her family background. At a young age, she was purchased on the Istanbul slave market and offered to the Bey of Tunis. In about 1878 she entered the harem of the ruler, Sadak Bey (1814–

1888), in the Bardo palace, and nothing distinguished her from the other women there at the time. We also cannot affirm with any certainty that she married that bey. However, when Sadak died, she married his brother and successor, 'Ali Bey (1818–1902).[14]

This old bey, not very intelligent, was weak willed and took his marching orders from the French colonial authorities. At his death Kmar lost her status as the principal wife of the ruling bey, and lived a less luxurious life in a pavilion of the palace. But she established cordial relations with the nephew of the defunct bey, Nasir, who ascended to the throne in 1906. They immediately got married.[15] The princess was thus propelled once again to the envied high status of First Woman of the Realm. However, despite the love that her husband felt for her, and which he announced publicly, palace intrigues led the bey to repudiate her. But not being able to live without her, he married her anew. The matrimonial life of Kmar Bayya is exceptional for her successive marriages, three if we count the less certain one to Sadak, to the point that some chroniclers designated her as "the widow of the Husaynids."[16]

If the marriage of white slaves purchased on the slave markets of the Orient to the Tunisian princes took place regularly until the end of the nineteenth century, the trajectory of Kmar remains unique in the beylical court. Her status of "inherited" wife from one prince to another can be explained neither by her beauty or fertility, since she did not have any children of her own. She probably possessed other qualities that are difficult to determine. In effect, the laudatory chronicles of the era and diplomatic reports, which speak of innumerable royal intrigues and palace plots, make it difficult to discern the real person behind the hidden screens of the palace, although we know that she played a major role in Tunisian political life after World War I.

Kmar and Nazli met during the period when the former was married to Ali Bey. Kmar visited Nazli's Villa Ramses, situated about one hundred meters from the beylical palace, and learned to play chess there with Salem Bouhajeb, the father of Nazli's husband Khalil.[17] Nazli had considerable influence on Kmar. Thanks to her contacts with Nazli, Kmar evolved differently than the other women at the beylical court in that she participated in political and cultural discussions in palace literary and political salons. The young timid woman who had married 'Ali Bey quickly transformed herself into a self-possessed person who spoke about politics with her husband, listened and joined discussions behind a curtain in the councils held by the prince, and also discussed poetry and religion with courtiers. Her costumes changed as she evolved. Instead of wearing heavily brocaded robes, she adopted more the modern dress of Turkish women. We don't know much about these activities, and we have to be satisfied with innuendos found in the archives or furtive glances into the life of the palace found in laudatory biographies of the beys. However, thanks to indirect sources, such as royal palace expense records, we can gather some information about daily life in the harem, such as expenditures for the purchase of paper and crayons indicating her interest in educating the girls living in the palace. She herself knew how to read Arabic and Ottoman Turkish. Kmar Bayya was therefore an atypical princess, different from the other princely wives, several of whom, like her, came from the Caucasus mountains. She stood out for the interest she had in public affairs. The relative liberty she had in participating behind a curtain in political discussions stopped when her husband Ali Bey died in 1902. Since she was no longer the First Woman of the palace, her status deteriorated. Widows of defunct beys could not remarry, except another reigning bey. Kmar suffered ostracism within the palace from 1902 to 1906. Only then did she regain power once again by marrying Nasir Bey.

Discretely, she took part in nationalist politics and pushed her husband to take positions against the colonial regime: in 1922 she succeeded in convincing him not to receive the French President Alexandre Millerand (1859–1943), on an official visit to Tunisia. Her hostility to France expressed itself in her actions, especially in her attempts to place people whom she chose in important positions. During the crisis of 1922, we see Kmar maneuvering to change the prime minister, Taib Jallouli, considered too Francophile by the bayya's friend, Khalil Bouhajeb, the widower of Princess Nazli, who belonged to a pro-Ottoman movement close to the palace.[18]

The French General Resident reacted violently, and under threats of military action forced the bey to fulfill his diplomatic duties. This action attracted a great deal of attention in the press, because this was the first time in the history of the country that the palace took a position against the French Protectorate. The bey, with Kmar's prodding, had provoked a constitutional crisis.

When Nasir Bey died in 1922, the year of this crisis, Kmar Bayya once again lost her position as First Woman in the palace. She had taken the precaution, however, of approaching the new bey, Mohamed El Habib (r. 1922–1929) and his wife, so as to conserve some power. She succeeded in having her protégé Khalil Bouhajeb, the former husband of Nazli (who had died in 1913), named as prime minister in 1926. Her role declined once more beginning in 1929, when Ahmed Bey, her stepson by her first marriage, who hated her, ascended the throne. At that moment, roles were reversed and Khalil protected her until he himself lost power in 1932.

Kmar Bayya put her own strategy in place to protect herself from any reversals of fortune. In 1936 she turned over her property to the Muslim *Waqf* institution, which protected her possessions from state confiscation and guaranteed her and her heirs after her death an income. In the process she did something new: the *Waqf* contract was not drawn up by a Muslim notary, as was usually the case, but in the French Consulate: the last recourse of a princess to escape beylical despotism.[19]

If it was no longer possible for Kmar to take part in the world of politics, she had the satisfaction of seeing another one of her stepsons, Moncef Bey, become ruler on June 19, 1942, during World War II. She organized all the festivities surrounding his accession to the throne and watched with pleasure as he adopted nationalist positions and increasingly became estranged from the French Residency. Kmar passed away on December 30, 1942, at the moment that the Germans bombarded Tunis. She would not live to see her stepson arrested by the allied forces in May 1943 and exiled under the pretext that he had collaborated with the Axis powers. While the French considered him as an enemy collaborator, the Tunisians organized a personality cult around him and called him after his death in exile, "the people's bey." Certainly, he must have owed Kmar a great deal in helping to transform him into a Tunisian nationalist hero.

Kmar Bayya had to submit more than the two other women discussed in this chapter to social conventions within the palace. As the wife of reigning rulers she had to follow strict protocol. Nevertheless, behind closed doors she oriented the politics of the palace toward nationalist agendas. She freed herself after becoming a widow for the second time, and at a ripe old age travelled to Vichy in France, thus becoming the first Tunisian princess to go abroad.

Khiriya Bin Ayyad (1873–?)

Our third aristocrat was born in Istanbul while her father, the Tunisian Mahmoud Bin Ayyad, served during twenty years as a tax farmer and supplier of goods for the Tunisian state during the era of Ahmed Bey from 1837 to 1855. After gathering a large fortune, in 1852 bin Ayyad fled to Paris, carrying with him a colossal amount of money stolen from the Tunisian treasury. There he purchased properties and ac-

quired French citizenship. When the Tunisian state initiated legal action against him to restitute the stolen money, his immense wealth won
him the support of important French politicians, and even Napoleon III
himself intervened on his behalf, declaring himself the arbitrator of the
entire affair.[20]

After a long stay in Paris, in 1857 Mahmoud Bin Ayyad moved to Istanbul, where he began a new life. He succeeded in entering the imperial palace and establishing an influential network among the courtiers. In the process he became an important figure, calling himself bey,
playing on the ambiguity of the term, which denoted a dignitary in the
Orient, while in Tunis it was the title of the ruler. In his new residence,
he lived in the Turkish style according to the testimony of his daughter, multiplying his wives and legal concubines and producing numerous children, including Khiriya.[21] Mahmoud Bin Ayyad, although a
thief, was nevertheless an enlightened man, open to modernity. He gave
his children a good education, sending his boys to pursue their studies in Europe. Khiriya married the writer and politician 'Ali Nouri Bey,
who became Ottoman consul in the Caucasus (the main source of white
slaves for the Ottoman harems) prior to the deterioration of his relations with the sultan because 'Ali Nour favored greater liberty within
the Ottoman Empire. Because of this he had to flee to Western Europe where he settled in Rotterdam. His wife and children were blocked
from leaving Turkey until they clandestinely evaded the police and left
on a French ship to join 'Ali Nouri in Europe.[22]

This experience of political persecution and exile gave Khiriya an occasion to engage in opposition politics. She delivered several lectures in
European capitals in which she denounced both the Ottoman sultan's
despotism, the difficult status of Turkish women, and the internal dy-
namics of the royal harem, of which she had been a first-hand observer.
One of her lectures given in Vienna and translated into German in 1904
was published under the title *The Turkish Woman: Her Social Life and the
Harem.*[23] Its preface was written by a pioneer of Austrian feminism, Go-
swina von Berlepsch. In this way Khiriya became one of the first Muslim women to have published a text.[24]

The Networks Converge

Nazli's father, Mustapha Fadhil Pasha, and Mahmoud bin Ayyad, Khiriya's father, met in Istanbul, but their paths diverged because one of

them became a notorious opponent of the sultan early on, while the other joined the inner circle of Ottoman power. Mohamed bin Ayyad after a couple of years in Istanbul became part of the inner circle of Ottoman power during the reigns of ʿAbd al-Aziz and Abdülhamid II, with whom he had excellent relations. He was a dignitary of the court and specialized in commerce in white slaves, offering some beautiful women from this trade to the sultans.[25] Khiriya denounced this slave trade that her father engaged in vociferously in the same published lecture mentioned above. After this Vienna lecture we loose track of Khiriya, only to find her a few years later with her husband in Tunis to contest in court a case wherein one of her brothers attempted to deprive her of an inheritance.[26]

The meeting of Nazli and Khiriya was therefore favored by the proximity both families had at one time or another with the central power. Marriages often resulted from the closeness of such strategically located families: thus one of bin Ayyad's daughters married the sultan's doctor, while Khiriya tied the knot with a high Ottoman official, ʾAli Nouri. As for Mahmoud Bin Ayyad's oldest son Tahar Bey, born in Tunis in 1851, he married Roukaya, the stepsister of Nazli, in 1872. In this way the Egyptian princess met and befriended Khiriya. Thanks in part to this network, Nazli travelled to Tunis in 1899 and met her future husband Khalil Bouhajeb. By setting up her household in the Tunis suburbs near the royal palace, she came in contact with Kmar Bayya. These examples of marriage and friendships, in addition to others that we know little about, demand more research since they constitute the transnational social networks around the palace that formed a powerful vector for the circulation of new political ideas flowing in from abroad. Most likely during her stay in Tunis, Khiriya befriended Princess Nazli, who some years earlier had supported her stepsister in a conflict with her husband, the stepbrother of Khiriya, for debts he did not pay to his wife.

Conclusion: Precariousness of Power

Our three women owed their positions to their proximity to power, which could shift suddenly. Life for the three of them changed constantly as their fathers or husbands became estranged from power. None of them had titles to great land holdings, which might have added to their security. Nazli was the granddaughter of M'hamed ʾAli, a poor Albanian who became a janissary and then pasha of Egypt. Khiriya was the daughter of a tax farmer who absconded with a fortune belonging to the beylical state of Tunis. Kmar was a white slave born in the poor hinterlands of the Caucasus. They could lose everything they had as suddenly as they received it. This precariousness in part explains why the court milieus were always filled with intrigue and plots. Our three women, therefore, understood the fragility of their family situations. Their social status was also precarious since they received it by the will of the wielder of power, and at any moment they could be disowned or lose their fortunes and end up destitute. A slave woman could lose her status through widowhood or repudiation. It was probably this precariousness that gave them the capacity to deal with social problems such as white slavery, polygamy, and ignorance, and to comprehend firsthand the nature of despotism. They knew these evils since they lived their lives within the imperial harems. The lives of such princesses often worsened suddenly after the death of a husband or son.

Harems were therefore places where power politics produced great violence, and Ottoman history has abundant examples of this.[27] No doubt our three princesses were interested in power, but a different power than what they found surrounding them, power based on the respect of individual rights, liberty, and equality between men and women. If we are astonished that they were so engaged, it is because our understanding of harems is based on Western representations of the princely institution as being highly sensual and sexually charged.[28] In fact, in Muslim countries princesses not only had privileges, they also had social obligations. The woman with power participated in the life of the community. She got engaged in important functions, especially the creation of a *Waqf* endowing Quranic schools or other religious institutions: the proceeds of a *Waqf* nourished the poor and students and allowed *zawiyas* (brotherhoods) to play their role as charitable institutions. If we can stop viewing the harems as mindless sensual places, we can better understand their women's engagement in politics.[29] What seems important are the changes in the modalities of participation: charitable activities such as the constitution of *Waqf*s are no longer sufficient in the context of the nineteenth century. The problem was no longer merely helping the poor cope, but rather the new challenge became how to transform the entire society by wiping out the paternalism that forced people into submissive relations. More and more these notions were challenged by enlightened spirits.

At the moment European imperialism intensified its pressure on independent states and before the final scramble for Africa in the 1880s and 1890s, women became important as couriers of information between the Ottoman capital and outlying districts to the point that European chancelleries began to spy on their activities. Informal networks such as private circles of notables and even harems flourished outside the purview of European spy networks monitoring activities within the Ottoman Empire.[30] Family ties, notably the nexus of relatives and family alliances, should be highlighted for us to understand how such informal networks acted as transmitters of communications across borders. Colonial powers understood that these networks were developing, and so they intensified their espionage networks to cover these social phenomena. The products of this intensified spying have allowed historians to revisit this period and permitted us to reconstruct biographies and understand subversive activities. The three women that we have examined provide basic clues as to how their affinities allowed them to spread new ideas and bridge the varied worlds within the Ottoman Empire in the late nineteenth century.

Notes

1. Michelle Perrot, *Mon histoire des femmes* (Paris: Seuil, 2006), 16–17.

2. Mehemet 'Ali (1769–1849), an Albanian, as the leader of a contingent of janissaries from his Ottoman province, was sent to Egypt with his troops to fight the French army. Named governor of Egypt by the Ottoman sultan in 1805, he exterminated the last remnants of the Mamluke military elite in March 1811 and significantly increased his territory, even menacing the Ottoman Empire. After losing a war in 1838 against the sultan's forces that were backed by the British, he had to accept being a vassal of the empire in exchange for the creation of a hereditary monarchy, which he founded. He resigned his position due to illness in 1848 and died on April 2, 1849, leaving his son Ibrahim on the throne.

3. On this personality see Michèle Haddad, *Khalil Bey, un homme, une collection* (Paris: Amateur édition, 2000).

4. Thierry Savantier, *L'origine du monde, histoire d'un tableau de Gustave Courbet* (Paris: Bartillat, 2006).

5. French Minister of Foreign Affairs, letters of Khalid Chérif Pasha, Vol. 163–166, series "Extraordinary Acquisitions," 2001.

6. Telegram addressed to Tahar bin Ayyad installed in Paris, April 26, 1896, sent by one of his relatives, Dossier Nazli, Archives nationales tunisiennes, Carton 1, dossier 20.

7. Bayram V left Tunis October 13, 1879, because of his differences with the Tunisian prime minister, who he thought was a French agent aiding and abetting their colonial ambitions in the country. He moved to Istanbul, but quit that city for Cairo in November 1883 because of plots organized against him

in the Ottoman capital. He had psychiatric problems and received treatment in Europe, notably by Professor Charcot. Bayram consumed morphine to treat his pain. He died December 18, 1889. See his work, *Safwat al 'itibâr*, 5 vols. (Carthage: *Édition bayt al hikma*, 2005).

8. Nazli Hafsia, *La Princesse Nazli Fadhel en Tunisie, 1896–1913, une figure moderniste* (Tunis: Sagittaire édition, 2010).

9. Letter dated October 22, 1896, cited by Abou Kaçim Kerrou, *La Princesse Nazli, une pionnière du réformisme en Egypt et en Tunisie* (Tunis: Dar al Maghreb al Arabi, 2000).

10. Kerrou, *La Princesse*, 136.

11. Fahmi Pasha, cited by Kerrou, *La Princesse*, 139.

12. Archives nationales Tunisiennes, Série F, dossier 5, Kmar Bayya.

13. Archives nationales tunisiennes, Série F, Carton 5, dossier 11.

14. Leïla Blili, "Parenté et pouvoir dans la Tunisie husaynite 1705–1956," PhD thesis, University of Tunis, 245.

15. Ismahane Ben Barka, "La Princesse Kmar," mémoire de maitrise (Tunis: Faculté des letters de la Manouba, 2003), 34.

16. Mokdad Wartatani, *Al Nafkha al nadiya* (Tunis: Publisher Unknown, 1936), 37. The author is the official biographer of Bey Ahmed II (r. 1929–1942).

17. Ismahane Ben Barka, "La Princesse," 21.

18. The High Institute for the History of the Tunisian National Movement, microfilmed archives of the French Ministry of Foreign Affairs, C5, D1, p. 178.

19. National Archives of Tunisia, series F, dossier 5, Kmar Bayya, Notarized Act, dated September 12, 1936.

20. Mohamed Salah Mzali and Jean Pignon, "Khereddine homme d'Etat" (Tunis: Société tunisienne d'édition, 1971), 21.

21. Dignitairies in Tunis were rarely polygamous. This can be explained by the fact that most of the ministers of the government were of Mamluk, or slave, origin who married princesses belonging to the royal family who did not tolerate polygamy. See on this subject the state thesis of Leïla Blili, "Parenté et Pouvoir dans la Tunisie husaynite."

22. Younis Wsifi, "Khiriya bin Ayyad, l'une des pionnières de l'émancipation de la femme à la fin du 19ième siècle," in *Revue d'histoire maghrébine*, no. 119 (2005): 116–119.

23. Khiriya bin Ayyad, *La femme et la question de l'émancipation sociale dans le monde musulman au début du XXè siécle*, edited and translated from the German by Mounir Fendri (Tunis: Demeter édition, 2009). In Arabic.

24. Younis Wsifi, "Khiriya bin Ayyad," 116.

25. Khiriya Bin Ayyad gave some details of her father's successful slave trade in her published Vienna lecture cited in note 23 above, 86–87.

26. Younis Wsifi, "Khirya bin Ayyad," 22.

27. Leslie Pierce, *The Imperial Harem* (New York: Oxford University Press, 1993).

28. Jocelyne Dakhlia, *l'Empire des Passions* (Paris: Éditions Aubier, 2005).

29. Leïla Blili, "Habous et stratégie de pouvoir dans la Tunisie husaynite 18è-20è siècles," in Randi Deguilhem and Abdelhamid Hénia, *Les Foundations*

pieuses, waqf, en Méditerranée: enjeux de société, enjeux de pouvoir (Kuwait: Public Foundation of Waqfs [pl., *Awfaq*], 2004), 157–172; Mustafa ʾAli Hind, "Princess Fatima Ismael, *Waqf* as a Reformatory Project," in *Awqaf*, no. 13 (November 2007): 93–107 (in Arabic).

30. Michelle Perrot, *Mon histoire des femmes* (Paris: Seuil, 2006), 16–17.

Qaʾid Najem with Merebih Rebbo and the notables of the Ait Ba Amran on a visit to Spain (August–September 1937), in El Mukhtar Soussi, "Le Qaʾid Najem." Presentation, tradition et annotations by Rachid Agrour and Mbark Wanaim. Rabat: IRCAM (Institut Royal de la Culture Amazighe), 2013, Fonds iconographic Mbark Aït Mzgou, p. 246.

CHAPTER 4

Servant, Officer, and Resistance Fighter: The Autobiography of Qaʾid al-Raha al-Najim al-Akhsassi (1867/68–1964)

WILFRID ROLLMAN

Sometimes, fame and renown are to be found in their proper places and do conform to the actual merit of the person who enjoys them.
IBN KHALDUN[1]

Al-Najim bin Mubarak bin Masʿud was born in 1284AH (Anno Hijri)/ 1867–68 of parents who were second generation freed slaves in the clan of Ida Jalul of the Ait Bu Yasin of the tribe of al-Akhsas (located about twenty miles southeast of Tiznit) in Morocco. His father, Mubarak ibn Masʿud (d. 1878), seems to have made the transition from client to respected independent leader in the area by the time of al-Najim's birth, and his family was at the time at least modestly comfortable economically.[2] He went to *kuttab* (Quʾran school) in a nearby village, but because of his poor skills in Arabic and because he was a black descendant of slaves, he was treated so harshly by the master of this school that he fled and never returned. Nonetheless, he seems to have later acquired some level of literacy in Arabic and says he wrote letters regarding supplies and other military matters during his years as a senior military officer leading troops in the field.[3]

The young al-Najim's life would change even more drastically when famine carried off both of his parents in 1878. To escape starvation, he moved with some of his relatives to the house of Qaʾid Dahman ibn Bayruk (Tekna), one of the most powerful households in the Wad Nun region, where he remained for a number of years as a servant of the *qaʾid*'s wife and his slave concubine.[4] While there, he narrowly escaped the first of several attempts by people around him, who sought to capitalize on his color and marginal social status as an orphan child of freed slaves, to kidnap him in order to sell him into slavery, or for the purpose of presenting him as a gift to the sultan.[5] In relating these experiences, al-Najim makes very clear his great fear and resistance to the idea of being enslaved, a return to a past that he, like his father, was quite proud and pleased to have left behind. At the same time, he shows a keen awareness of how his color made him a prime target for slave traders.[6]

In 1300AH/1882–1883, al-Najim returned to his birthplace and joined the domestic service of Sultan Mawlay al-Hassan's (r. 1873–1894) recently appointed *qa'id*, Bu Hiya al-Buyasini al-Akhsasi who was at that moment preparing for the arduous journey to Marrakech to pay homage to the sultan. The *qa'id* invited al-Najim to go along, because he knew *darija* (colloquial Arabic), which the *qa'id* and the other elders of the tribe did not. The *qa'id* thought that al-Najim would be quite useful to the delegation during their visit to Marrakech, which he was.[7]

Despite having to escape yet another attempt to enslave him, al-Najim was greatly impressed with the city and the makhzan's hospitality. His visit also resulted in his making contact with the *jaysh qa'id* Muhammad ibn Tahir al-Dlimi, who gave him sanctuary from his most recent would-be captors. Qa'id al-Dlimi then included him in his entourage when the *qa'id* led the makhzan's campaign to block the efforts of an English businessman to establish a trading station on the Sus coast. After this al-Najim returned to Marrakech as a domestic servant in the housefuld of *qa'id* Muhammad ibn Tahir al-Dlimi (in Marrakech) and accompanied him on royal expeditions (sing. *mahalla*) led by the Sultan Mawlay al-Hassan from that city. In 1885–1886, al-Najim was part of the Dlimi contingent in Mawlay al-Hassan's second expedition to the Sus and remained there when his patron, Qa'id Muhammad ibn Tahir was ordered to garrison the makhzen's *qasbah* in the Ait Ba'Amran. A short time later (after 1308AH/1890–1891), Qa'id Muhammad ibn Tahar died, leaving al-Najim in the hands of his brother Yahya, who had succeeded the deceased as commander of the Ait Ba'Amran garrison. Al-Najim soon after left the service of this *qa'id*, saying, "He needed a change in life." He became an itinerant merchant in the Sus, seeking to better his fortune by working in the new Saharan-North African-Atlantic trade networks that had been developing in the Wad Nun region, and were strongly contested by the Moroccan government and the local tribal and religious power centers during the second half of the nineteenth century. His former protector, the Qa'id Dahman bin Bayrouk was part of this struggle to control the transregional trade. It is quite possible, therefore, that al-Najim was not at all unfamiliar with the mechanisms of this economy from an early age and so could access it with some degree of confidence in a beneficial outcome. In addition to the opportunity to improve his economic situation, engagement in the itinerant trade no doubt facilitated the broadening of his social and political contacts in the region as well.[8]

With the death of Mawlay al-Hassan (June 1894) and the subsequent unrest in the Haouz region around Marrakech, al-Najim, thanks to his long-term relationship with the Dlimi Shararda, joined the Dlimi garrison at Ait BaʿAmran when it was called up to help defend Marrakech against the Rahamna factions which had rebelled against the makhzen and its supporters among neighboring tribes.[9] Al-Najim's capable military and political performance in lifting the siege of Marrakech and suppressing the Rahamna uprising brought him to the attention of makhzen officials and led to his appointment to the ʿaskar nizami and his rapid promotion to the rank of qaʾid raha of a tabor (battalion consisting of five hundred plus officers and men), all volunteers, raised at his initiative, primarily from his native Sus and the Haouz. He would hold this rank for the rest of his career in the army, save for several years of the nineteenth century when he was demoted and reassigned after a confrontation with the Vizier Ahmad ibn Musa. His tabor, like the Harraba, the demonstration battalion organized, equipped, and trained by Sir Harry Maclean, the most prominent of the makhzen's European advisors, but without the trappings of a British colonial unit, would become one of the largest and most reliable units in the ʿaskar nizami and would continue in service until the reorganization of the army under the reforms of Commandant Mangin in 1910.[10] In addition to military operations in the field, he worked in the office of the minister of war, Saʿid ibn Musa, where he met and developed a close friendship with al-Mahdi ibn al-ʿArabi al-Manibhi (d. 1939), a young qaʾid miʾa (commander of one hundred men) in the ʿaskar nizami and a fellow southerner. Al-Manibhi would later become minister of war with close ties to Sultan Mawlay ʿAbd al-ʿAziz and Qaʾid Maclean.

After the death of Ahmad ibn Musa in 1900, al-Najim requested and received a new field command and reappointment to the rank of qaʾid raha, with authorization to raise an infantry tabor of up to 1,700 men.[11] From then on, al-Najim participated in all of the makhzen's campaigns against rebellious tribes, especially the movement of Bu Himara in the area north and east of Fez from 1902 to 1909. He gained great fame and the favor of the new sultan, Mawlay ʿAbd al-Hafidh (r. 1908–1912) when he and his tabor surrounded and captured Bu Himara, putting an end to one of the most serious rebellions against the makhzen's authority dur-

ing the preprotectorate period. It was an action that he saw as "a won-
derful duty, an action by which I rendered service to my government
and to my country because this man has caused the ruination of Morocco."[12] Others were not so certain about the merits of al-Najim's military success, suggesting that he may have captured the wrong person,
that the real traitor to Morocco was the incumbent sultan.[13]

Thus began a time of great anguish for al-Najim. He had joined the
'askar nizami to defend the sultan and his Islamic realm against Christian attack only to find that neither Mawlay 'Abd al-'Aziz nor Mawlay
'Abd al-Hafidh seemed really committed to, or capable of, such resistance. Faced with a choice between the two brothers during their civil
war in 1907–1908, he chose not to choose and sought the protection of
Spain at Melilla rather than become involved in an armed confrontation
with his sovereign.[14] On his return and reconciliation with Mawlay 'Abd
al-Hafidh, he took up again his long struggle to capture Bu Himara and
to put an end to his rebellion. However, having succeeded in doing so
he saw himself criticized by government officials such as al-Madani al
Glawi and ridiculed by elements of the populace as a "Christian qa'id."[15]

The very appearance of the 'askar nizami officers and troops on
the scene, both in an operational and sartorial sense, increasingly became seen as a provocation and flash point for opposition to broader
makhzen policies and practices, rather than as providers of order and security. This was due also to the new army's wretched state of well being and lack of discipline in the last years before the protectorate.[16] But
the problem was broader and deeper than this. The makhzen itself was
well aware of this and made every effort to mitigate the "European-
izing" impact of its reforms on its new troops. From the beginning, it
had associated its reform initiatives with similar programs put in place
by Muslim governments elsewhere in the Middle East and North Africa at the time. Ottoman, Egyptian, and Tunisian veterans of the 'askar
nizami in those places were hired as instructors, and instructional materials produced there were brought to Morocco to help with the establishment of the new military system. Much attention was paid to issues
like uniforms, nomenclature, and orders of battle to assure that the imported system was made to look and operate within the context of local Islamic culture. This desire to "Islamisize" the New Order remained
strong throughout the nineteenth and early twentieth centuries. If anything it grew stronger as Europe, especially France, became more determined to establish greater control over Moroccan affairs and the
country itself. As late as 1909, long after the makhzen had lost effec-

tive control over the military reform process, Sultan Mawlay ʿAbd al-Hafidh sought to employ Turkish renegade military advisors, provided by the Egyptian khedive in Cairo, in response to intensifying popular and even makhzen opposition to any increase in the role of French military advisors or further "Europeanization" of the new army. This last effort to attenuate the European character of the new military forces, like all the others, failed. France compelled the sultan to dismiss his Turkish advisors (see chapter 3), and French control of the form and substance of the *ʿaksar nizami* program intensified to the point where the makhzen's regular army disintegrated in a maelstrom of foreign invasion and internal unrest.[17]

As a senior military officer (*qaʾid al-raha*) in the *ʿaskar nizami* from the 1890s to 1912, Qaʾid al-Najim was at the center of the struggle by state and society to confront, and creatively accommodate, the formidable array of interventions imposed on them by European powers intent upon incorporating Morocco into their imperial systems and modern culture, while preserving Islamic and Moroccan values and identity. A professional in the same organization as his—Hajj Salim al-ʿAbdi, a senior officer in Maclean's *Harraba* (training demonstration) battalion and proud wearer of the British-style uniforms distributed to this unit—took a decidedly different view than his on what a modern Moroccan army should look like and how, and to what end, it should function.[18]

Al-Najim, nonetheless, continued his service, even accepting the comprehensive reform of the army proposed and initiated by Commandant Mangin (Joseph Emile Mangin, Chief of the French Military Mission in Morocco, January 1909–March 1912) in 1910. He did so, even though these reforms meant a significant reduction in his authority and economic well-being, as well as a substantial increase in "Europeanization" of the *ʿaskeri nizami*'s appearance and organization as French officers began to play a dominant role in the sultanate's military affairs. He seems to have done so with deep misgivings, but accepted this new regimen because he was ordered to do so, and because he accepted the sultan's explanation that he was reorganizing his army because it was no longer functioning effectively as protector of the *umma*. As an experienced military officer he may have agreed, but committing to a French sponsored and managed program must have been difficult, even though the sultan expressed his conviction that this was the best course of action.[19] In this matter the sultan was most explicit and public, saying that the awful condition of the *ʿaskar nizami* required that he "have recourse to experienced people and to follow, step by step, their method which is moreover, the only one practiced in the civilized world, at the head of which is France."[20] Furthermore, he assured his officers that he was "assured that this method contains nothing contrary to Qu'ranic prescriptions" as proven by the fact that "Turkey, an Islamic nation *par excellence*, who has adopted it [a European military system]."[21] As commander of a new battalion, al-Najim participated in makhzen efforts to quell revolts among military and nonmilitary tribes in the region of Fez and elsewhere, which did nothing to encourage his enthusiasm for the new forces or his confidence in Mawlay 'Abd al-Hafidh as the "sultan of the jihad."[22]

Moreover, the new army and hundreds of veterans who had been discharged by Commandant Mangin as unfit to serve were becoming increasingly restless. Strict rules of military discipline mandated in the Mangin reforms were rigorously enforced. Rumors and signs of rebellion abounded, reaching a point where, ironically, significant elements of both the new and old military establishments, which had been more and more vilified by popular voices as servants of the Christian *Harraba*, were tending toward an alliance with popular urban and rural resistance to the makhzen's apparent acceptance of French control.[23]

These tensions would explode soon after Mawlay 'Abd al-Hafidh was forced to sign a Protectorate treaty with France (Treaty of Fez, March 30, 1912) in the famous Army mutiny of Fez (April 17–18, 1912), which resulted in the deaths of a number of French military advisors at the hands of their troops and several days of destructive looting and fighting in the city and immediate environs before French and Moroccan forces suppressed the rebellion and imposed martial law.[24]

From 1910 to 1912, he remained committed to Mawlay 'Abd al-Hafidh and to the idea of jihad, but with increasing difficulty. Always reluctant to oppose his sultan, he sought a way to absent himself from the politics and practice of the army under the Mangin regime and in Fez. He described his state of mind in those days many years later to al-Susi in the following words:

> The observer now sees what happened to us in those bad times of al-Madani al-Glawi (1907–1911). We lost our military and personal honor. I struggled with myself and I did not find any way that I might get out of the situation I was in. So I gritted my teeth and grumbled always in the presence of the sultan about army service. I said to him that I had been wounded more than once and my power is weakening. I am not able to stand up to the maneuvers of the new army as is required of anyone who accepts my position.[25]

The sultan would hear none of it and stated his need for people like al-Najim to continue in his service, even if not fully active in the new military system because "you bring *baraka* to this army."[26]

However, in 1911, he did reassign al-Najim away from the turmoil of Fez to Marrakech, where he and a small force of new troops supported Dris Mannu, the newly appointed governor of that city. He served as Dris Mannu's *qaʾid* of the Haouz tribes and then as *qaʾid* of Demnat. They worked together to hold these areas for Mawlay ʿAbd al-Hafidh against furious resistance from the Glawis and popular outrage at the sultan's signature of the Treaty of Fez. The imposition of the French Protectorate meant the abdication of Mawlay ʿAbd al-Hafiz and restoration of the Glawis to power in Marrakech and much of the south.[27] The pasha Dris Mannu was dismissed and exiled to Meknes by Protectorate authorities for four years, after which he was permitted to retire to Marrakech, where he lived until his death in 1940.[28]

Qaʾid al-Najim chose, even at his already considerable age, to continue pursuit of his priority objective of using his military skills to resist foreign influence and intervention in Morocco. After al-Hiba's death, he continued to participate in tribal resistance to French expansion into Morocco's southern and Saharan area until it was finally overwhelmed in 1934. Al-Najim then took refuge with the Ait BaʿAmran where he joined local opposition to Spanish rule. He spent 1947–1956 under house arrest there. When Morocco achieved its independence, Qaʾid al-Najim was part of the Ait BaʿAmran delegation that traveled to Rabat to pay homage to King Muhammad V. He was subsequently assigned a house in Marrakech where he lived in very modest circumstances until his death in 1964.[29]

For Morocco, like other Middle Eastern and North African states, the creation of a modern army based on European models was a central focus in their responses to the challenges of European power and policies in the nineteenth and early twentieth centuries. Its attempt to create a new military order (*nizam al-jadid*) was justified in terms of the state's religious obligation to defend Muslims from foreign attack. This it never succeeded in doing, but its efforts to do so created an important arena of contact between European values, technology, and models of organization. It meant growing numbers of Moroccans from very diverse backgrounds became engaged, whether voluntarily or not, in the process of redefining themselves and their relationships to the state under which they lived and to the territory over which it claimed to have authority. Finding some balance between what European models proposed as ideal and what were considered essential elements of local belief and practice, some understanding of what to embrace and what to resist in a rapidly changing world for the security of the self and the community became an abiding quest especially for those participating in the new army. Just by being part of the state's most ambitious project to create something like what existed in Europe, but still remaining Moroccan, meant that they were at the heart of a process of reconstruction and re-invention that went well beyond the sphere of military practice. Qa'id al-Najim eagerly sought to be part of this process for reasons personal, religious, economic, and possibly political. He clearly believed that responding to the sultan's call for men to defend his state and territory was his obligation. He furthermore believed that he could fulfill this obligation by participating in a new army, which in significant ways was an import from Europe, without subordinating his own values and identity to that of the providers of this innovation. His commitment to resistance was consistent all his life on the level of practice and on the symbolic level as well. On the question of uniforms, for example, the only image we have of him shows his rejection of this aspect of the new army. He never says so, but becoming part of a unit such as the *Harraba* was never considered a serious or necessary option for him. Al-Najim was a pious Muslim, but he seemed to conceive his notion of the obligation to resist foreign intervention in somewhat broader terms than just the community of believers. His participation in the new army was to preserve the sultanate and to defend territory, as well as to protect the community of believers. His desire to join the new army and to achieve a leadership role in it also had several personal components. Service in the new army, as an officer and professional soldier, provided al-Najim with the means to secure his own personal freedom. As a son of freed slaves at a time when slavery was still practiced, al-Najim was painfully aware of discrimination against him in a range of matters, such as his struggle to become literate in Arabic and gain a better education.[30] The new army offered new possibilities for him to become a respected professional person with responsibilities and the opportunity to advance economically beyond the limited horizons of a slave or domestic servant. He was adamant throughout his life story that he was not interested in being a *wasif*, a servant in some official's entourage. That role, for him, was but a stepping stone to greater freedom, professional expertise, and wealth. He served such an "apprenticeship" in the entourage of the qa'id Muhammad ibn Tahir al-Dlimi, where he gained invaluable military experience and made useful contacts that he later used to gain an appointment as *qa'id raha* with his own *tabor* of volunteer soldiers in the new system. In this position he became a prominent individual in the new army and in the country, a position that he abandoned only when it was certain that in a French system he would again be subjected to a new form of servitude. There is no question too that al-Najim saw participation in the new army as an economic opportunity. A *qa'id raha* had access to considerable revenues (licit and illicit) and opportunities for anyone with an entrepreneurial flair such as al-Najim seemed to have. Had not politics intervened, he might well have ended his career a wealthy man. Although there is no evidence that he lived anything but a modest lifestyle, he mentions in several places in his life account ownership, or claims to ownership, of several urban properties in Marrakech and Fez.[31] He died poor, but he was a free man. He was for many a hero of the national resistance and for himself a proud veteran of many campaigns that brought him success and prestige because of his professional expertise. His place in the modern nation was small, but his claim to be there was, he felt, authentic and perhaps made with a sense that he had found a balance between the imported modernity of the institution he served and the Moroccan identity he lived.

> I do not know how the sociologists will account for such a character, who grew up a poor illiterate orphan, a mere shepherd, but who later made a name for himself among the most heroic figures of the army.[32]

Thus opens Muhammad al-Mukhtar al-Susi's redaction of the oral autobiography told to him in Moroccan colloquial Arabic (*darija*) by Qa'id al-Raha al-Najim al-Akhsassi, the soldier and officer in the *'askar nizami* (1894–1912), and a respected leader and combatant in the anticolonial resistance (1912–1956). Al-Najim had resettled in Marrakech after independence. He was ninety-two years old when he related his life story to al-Susi, a renowned historian who was in the process of creating an encyclopedic biographical dictionary of persons originating from the Sous region of southwestern Morocco.[33] Al-Susi was a man of letters in the Arab-Muslim tradition, an intellectual, a nationalist, who actively resisted the French Protectorate, a religious reformer (Salafi) and a Sufi. He was a Tashelhit speaker, born in Iligh in the Sous, very proud of his origins, and solicitous "to demonstrate the excellence of the intellectual quality of the periphery even within the framework of Arabo-Muslim culture."[34] He went to Marrakech and Fez for his advanced education and to partake of the greater economic and professional opportunities available to him there and not at all in the impoverished, rural milieu of his youth. In Fez and Marrakech, al-Susi had not only to face the challenges of reconstructing his Moroccan identity in such a way as to fit in with, and be respected by, the educated elites of these capital cities. He, at the same time, had to find ways to negotiate and accommodate the new cultural and political realities of European influence and occupation, which had reached a new level of intensity just as he began his studies at the madrassa Ibn Yusuf in autumn 1919.[35]

Both Qa'id al-Najim and Muhammad al-Mukhtar al-Susi had, therefore, very much in common in terms of their origins, their life trajectories—albeit in quite different registers—their concerns, and their struggles. Both were in many ways transitional figures, individuals that bridged cultures, historical eras, and personal struggles for professional respect and success. Their stories provide a very rich, and in many respects quite rare, source for the historian interested in reconstructing these passages from a Moroccan perspective.[36] Their narratives intersect and overlap, although there is no evidence that they actually met until quite late in their lives and well after both had achieved national distinction in their respective careers. Although they shared regional origins, they came from different social backgrounds: al-Susi was born into a family of Sufis, a free man with access to literacy and education that would allow him to pursue a life in scholarship and teaching. Al-Najim was a black freed slave, denied access to education and constrained to a life of service and subservience until his extraordinary fighting and leadership skills opened the way for him to become an officer in the *'askar nizami*.[37]

Al-Najim's autobiography, as presented in al-Susi's *al-Ma'sul*, without doubt offers a wealth of detailed information. It amply contributes to al-Susi's "archive" for the Sous, his well-laid table of savory dishes ready for the tasting of anyone interested in the history and culture of this area.[38] However, al-Susi, in his introduction, alerts his readers to the fact that in the autobiography of al-Najim, like all of the other biographical and autobiographical material included in his twenty-volume work, his interpretive choices have all along shaped the menu. His focus is explicitly on the elites, religious and nonreligious, of his region. He gives ample space to religious men from a broad spectrum of Islamic practice: he, himself, insisting that he was a follower of both the mystical (Sufi) and Salafi (modern reformist) paths to a true Muslim life. He acknowledges his, and the region's, *Amazigh/Tashilhit* (Berber) identity and celebrates those who, like himself and Qa'id al-Najim, successfully navigated between this and broader Islamo-Arabic cultural fields. He was clearly enthusiastic about people like al-Najim, who made connections: intellectual, political, social, and geographical, between the Sous and the wider world, especially with the emergent Moroccan nation.[39] Hence, along with the methodological issues commonly involved in the use of these materials—problems of oral testimony, memory, biographical focus, imposed narratives, and so forth—the biographies and autobiographies in *al-Ma'sul* must be used with these specific interpretive issues in mind.[40] They must also be used with an appreciation of the ways in which al-Najim's inclusion in *al-Ma'sul* ably serves both his and al-Susi's project of self-definition, validation, and commemoration. Within the context of a Sous participating in the construction of a unified Islamic *umma* and a Moroccan national community, resistance to foreign domination and insistence on national independence and cultural liberation became significant factors for maintaining the institution of the makhzen, which later would form the core of an independent state and modern Moroccan kingship.

This critique is not intended to suggest that al-Najim's long (170 pp.) autobiographical entry in *al-Ma'sul* is essentially the creation of al-Susi, or a tale confected by al-Najim to secure a place for himself in the renowned chronicler's publication. Even while accepting that oral autobiographies of the kind recounted to al-Susi by al-Najim are fraught with possibilities for historical "creativity," external sources document unambiguously at least the military accomplishments of Qa'id al-Najim, both as an officer in the Moroccan army[41] and as a participant in the anticolonial resistance in the Sahara and southern Morocco.[42]

Moreover, recent scholarship on slavery and service in precolonial and colonial Morocco by scholars such as Mohammed Ennaji has verified, in part by documenting how exceptional al-Najim was, much of his narrative regarding his experiences as a black freed slave. This provided historians with a critical sociological dimension to this man's strenuous efforts to move beyond the constraints of region, culture, and social status. He accomplished this through the skillful mobilization of social and political networks among powerful patrons. These included the vizier Ahmad bin Musa (Ba Ahmad, d. 1900) and the minister of war al-Mahdi al-Manabhi (1900–1904), and officers of the French military mission in Morocco during the decade before the imposition of the Franco-Spanish Protectorate in 1912.[43]

It is a challenge to give an analysis of all the stages in the unfolding of Qa'id al-Najim's very long life (c. 96 years) and the development of his military career. He was active in both the precolonial period before

1912, the colonial periods of Moroccan history (1912–1956), and he lived through much of the first decade of the country's independence after 1956. The focus of attention in these remarks is on the precolonial period of his trajectory, from the time of his military service with the makhzen until his decision in 1912, to join the popular resistance. The resistance was led at the time by Ahmad Haybat Allah ibn Ma al-ʿAynayn (known as al-Hiba, d. 1919) against the installation of the Franco-Spanish Protectorates. Even with this narrow focus, the account of al-Najim's life, as presented through al-Susi's biographical dictionary, offers useful material on a variety of themes crucial to the discussion of Moroccan society's transformation in the nineteenth and twentieth centuries. Al-Susi raises important questions and provides potentially useful information on the challenges to "traditional" social categories and boundaries. Al-Najim's struggle to decide his course of action regarding foreign invasion and influence brought into conflict his sense of loyalty to his sultan and his sense of obligation to live by prescriptions of the Islamic shariʿa (law) as he understood them. His account of this process sheds light on the meaning and purpose of jihad for Moroccan Muslims at the time. His choice to seek a career in the ʿaksar nizami brought the need to acquire new skills and to think about military service in a different and more European-influenced manner, but also the opportunity to challenge traditional patterns of military service, which he found onerous. His accounts of makhzen politics provide a precious insider's view, rarely available to the contemporary scholar. His story also reveals some sense of the man, his emotional side, his hopes and disappointments, his drive to achieve, as his father had urged for him, "a future that was something better than the life usually left to slaves and freedmen in nineteenth century Morocco."[44]

His experience and his account of it, hence, mixes analytical and literary genres. He does not fit easily into any one. He seems to be a subaltern who serves the state, a "southerner" who seeks out a national scope for his actions, and a man from a largely oral tradition in Tashalhit and colloquial Arabic seeking to inscribe his life story in a classical Arabic literary form, the biographical dictionary. His story embodies multiple narratives that he, with the help of Muhammad al-Mukhtar al-Susi, seeks to organize into one. That he, and his "biographer," only partially succeed in doing so, and that they have left a record of their efforts, provides contemporary scholars an invaluable point of departure for the further study and understanding of the Moroccan society these two men lived in and sought to reshape. Their versions of themselves, as expressed in al-Susi's *al-Maʿsul*, often hint at or betray aspirations, projections, and historical reinterpretations along with historical information. Much more study of these sources is needed to appreciate fully the relationship between al-Najim's oral autobiographical account and al-Susi's recollection, transcription, and edition of it. This essay is a first, and hence, a necessarily tentative effort to reconstruct from these materials a plausible account of al-Najim's life and his motivations for and responses to service in *nizami* during the first phases of his life and career. Hopefully time and resources will permit further and deeper investigations which could provide us with a more nuanced and better documented analysis of his whole life and the times in which he lived.

Notes

1. ʿAbd al-Rahman ibn Khaldun, *The Muqaddimah: An Introduction to History*, trans. Franz Rosenthal, 3 vols., 2nd ed. (Princeton: Princeton University Press, 1967); Bollingen Series, 43, vol. 2, 88.

2. *Al-Maʿsul* 20, 6. On the region of al-Akhsas, see *Maʿalima al-Maghrib* (Sale: Matabiʿ Sla, 23 vols., 1984–2005), vol. I (1984), 200–201.

3. *Al-Maʿsul* 20, 7, and 51; Mohammed Ennaji, *Serving the Master: Slavery in Nineteenth Century Morocco* (New York: Palgrave Macmillan, 1999), trans. Seth Graebner, 59.

4. Ibid.; "Ibn Bayruk," *Maʿlama al-Maghrib* 6 (1992), 1, 934–939.

5. Ibid., 8; and Louis Arnaud, *Au Temps des Mehallas*, 7. Here Dr. Arnaud's informant, al-Hajj Salim al-ʿAbdi reports that the Qaʾid ʿAbd al-Malik Mtouggi gave, at one time, to sultan Mawlay al-Hassan (r. 1873–1894) as many as two hundred black slaves from the Sus and Draʿa Valley.

6. *Al-Maʿsul* 20, 10–13; U Naʿim Mubarak, "Al-Qaʾid al-Najim bin Mubarak al-Akhsasi" (Agadir: Universite de Ibn Rushd, Faculte des Lettres, 1997–1998), unpublished memoire for a degree in history (in Arabic). I am grateful to Dr. Bin Bin, Director of the Royal Palace Archives in Rabat, for bringing this valuable source to my attention.

7. *Al-Maʿsul* 20, 8.

8. Ibid., 16–17; regarding politics and transregional trade in this region, see Rahal Boubrik, *Saints et Société en Islam: la Confrérie Ouest-Saharienne Fadiliyya* (Paris: CNRS Éditions, 1999); and Gislaine Lyndon, *On Trans-Saharan Trails: Islamic Law, Trade, Networks, and Cross-Cultural Exchange in Nineteenth-Century Western Africa* (Cambridge: Cambridge University Press, 2009).

9. *Al-Maʿsul* 20, 18–19.

10. Eugene Aubin, *Le Maroc d'aujourd hui* (Paris: Colin Édition, 1913), 251–252; *Al-Maʿsul* 20, 20.

11. *Al-Maʿsul* 20, p. 3.2. On al-Manibhi, see *Maʿalima al-Maghrib* 21 (2005), 7, 275–279.

12. Mohammed Essaghir al-Khalloufi, *Bouhmara: Du Jihad a la Compromis-*

sion, Le Maroc Oriental et le Rif de 1900–1909 (Rabat: Imprimerie El-Maarif al-Jadida, 1993), 117, quoting *Al-Maʿsul* 20, 74.

13. The question was raised by, among others, Qaʾid al-Madani al-Glawi, at the time a public supporter of Mawlay ʿAbd al-Hafidh and a minister in his government.

14. U Naʿim Mubarak, "Al-Qaʾid al-Najim," 20; and *Al-Maʿsul* 20, 57.

15. Ahmad Toufiq, *Al-Mujtamaʿ al-Maghrib fi al-Qarn al-Tasiʿ ʿAshr: Inoultan (1850–1912)*, 2nd ed. (Rabat: Manshurat Kuliyat al-Adab, 1983), 166.

16. Muhammad bin al-Hassan al-Hajwi, *Intihar al-Maghrib al-Aqsa bi-yad al-thawara*, trans. and ed. Muhammad al-Saghir al-Khalufi (Rabat: Matbaʿat al-Maʿarif al-Jadida, 1994), 36–42.

17. Bahija Simou, *Les Reformes Militaires au Maroc de 1844 a 1912* (Rabat: Publications de la Faculte des Lettres et des Sciences Humaines, 1995), 441; Arnaud, *Au Temps des Mehallas*, 219, 434–436.

18. Louis Arnaud, *Au Temps des Mehallas ou le Maroc de 1860–1912* (Casablanca: Éditions Atlantides, 1952), 16ff, 58–59, 151.

19. Bahija Simou, *Les Reformes Militaires au Maroc*, 433.

20. Ibid.

21. Ibid.

22. *Al-Maʿsul* 20, 80–81.

23. Bahija Simou, *Les Reformes Militaires au Maroc*, 439–444.

24. Ibid., 455; and F. Wiesgerber, *Au Seuil du Maroc Moderne* (Rabat: Les Editions La Porte, 1947), 284–286.

25. *Al-Maʿsu* 20, 82.

26. Ibid.

27. Ibid., 85–87; and Ahmad Toufiq, *Al-Mujtamaʿ al-Maghribi*, 165–168.

28. Muhammad al-Mukhtar al-Susi, *Autour d'une Table d'Hote*, trans. Alain Roussillan, ed. Mohamed Adiouan, Revisions by Hassan Aourid (Rabat: Publications du Centre Tarik Ibn Zyad, 2003), 159–180.

29. U Naʿim Mubarak, "Al-Qaʾid al-Najim," 38; *Al-Maʿsul* 20, 169, and 10, 264.

30. Mohammed Ennaji, *Soldats, Domestiques et Concubines: L'Esclavage au Maroc au XIXe Siècle* (Paris: Balard, 1994), 100–101.

31. *Al-Maʿsul* 20, 81; and U Naʿim Mubarak, "Al-Qaʾid al-Najim," 43.

32. Muhammad al-Mukhtar al-Susi, *al-Maʿsul* (Casablanca: Matbaʿat al-Jamaʿa, 1961), vol. 20, 5. Quotation translated by Mohammed Ennaji and published in his *Serving the Master*, 60.

33. *Al-Maʿsul* (Ar. lit., the "sweetest part," i.e., the elite) was completely written, but only partially published at the time of al-Susi's death in 1963. When completely published it comprised twenty volumes.

34. Ahmad Boukous, "Mohammed Mukhtar Soussi, figure emblematique de la difference," *Naqd: Revue d'Etudes et de Critique sociale* (Algiers), no. 11 (1998): 102. For further materials on Muhammad al-Mukhtar al-Susi, see Ahmad Toufiq, "Al-Tarikh fil-zaman *al-Maʿsul* aw Muhammad al-Mukhtar al-Susi min zaman al-nahw ila zaman al-tarikh," in *Al-Mukhtar al-Susi al-Dhakirah al-Mustaʿadah* (Casablanca: Matbaʿat al-Najjah al-Jadida, 1987), 65–80; Rida Allah ʿAbd al-Wafi al-Mukhtar al-Susi, *Dalil Makhtutat wa Muʾalifat al-Marhum al-ʿAlama Muhammad al-Mukhtar al-Susi* (Rabat: Privately published, 1988).

35. 'Umar Afa, "Muhammad al-Mukhtar al-Susi bin 'Ali al-Ilighi," *Ma'lama al-Maghrib* 15 (2002): 5185; Ahmad Boukous, "Mohammed Mokhtar Soussi," *Naqd*, 104–106.

36. Mohammad Benjelloun Touimi, Abdelkebir Khatibi, and Mohammad Kably, ed. and trans., *Ecrivains Marocaines de Protectorat a 1965* (Paris: Sindbad, 1974), 40–43; Ahmad Boukous, "Mohammed Mokhtar Soussi," *Naqd*, 101–102.

37. On Qa'id al-Najim's education, see al-Susi, *al-Ma'sul* 20, 7; Mohammad Ennaji, *Serving the Master*, 58–60.

38. Al-Susi, *al-Ma'sul* 1, p. z.

39. Ibid., pp. h–z.

40. Limited space does not allow a full elaboration of these issues here, but useful discussions on the issues involved can be found in *American Historical Review*, "Round Table on Biography and History," 114, no. 3 (June 2009): 573–661; Linda Shopes, "Oral History and the Study of Communities: Problems, Paradoxes, and Possibilities," *Journal of American History* (September 2002): 588–598; Martin Elnagger, "The Language of the Self: Autobiographies and Testimonies," *Alif: Journal of Comparative Poetics*, no. 22 (2002): 169–197; Louise Marlow, ed., *The Rhetoric of Biography: Narrating Lives in Persianate Societies* (Boston: ILEX Foundation, 2011), esp. 1–10, 89–105; Thomas Spear, "Methods and Sources for African History Revisited," *Journal of African History* 47 (2006): 305–319.

41. Chateau de Vincennes, Ministere de la Defense, Etat Major de l'Armee de Terre, Service Historique, Carton 3H/90, Le Chef de Bataillon Verlet-Hanus (Marrakech) to the Resident General de France (Rabat), "Rapport sur les evenements de Marrakech (August–September 1912), Marrakech, October 1, 1912, 8; Muhammed Essaghir al-Khalloufi, *Bouhmara du Jihad a la Compromission: Le Maroc Oriental et le Rif de 1900–1909* (Rabat: Imprimerie El-Ma'arif al-Jadida, 1993), 85; Abd al-Wahhab bin Mansur, *'Allam al-Maghrib al-'Arabi* (Rabat: al-Matba'ah al-Malikiyah, 1979–) 1, 382–386.

42. Muhammad Binsa'id Ait Idir, *Safahat min malhamat Jaysh al-Tahrir al-Maghribi* (Casablanca: Matba'at al-Tayasir, 2001), 28; Mubarak u Na'im, "*Al-Qa'id al-Najim bin Mubarak al-Akhsasi*," Memoire d'Histoire (Agadir: University of Ibn Rushd, Faculty of Letters, 1997–1998), unpublished. A work based in part on oral accounts from the Sous: Mustafa Shabbi, *Al-Jaysh al-Maghribi fil-Qarn al-Tasi' 'ashr, 1830–1912*. 2 vols. (Marrakech: al-Matba'ah wal-Waraqah al-Wataniyah, 2008), 1, 325.

43. Mohammed Ennaji, *Serving the Master*, 60; Chateau Vincennes, Service Historique, Carton 3H/90, report of October 1, 1912.

44. Mohammed Ennaji, *Serving the Master*, 59–60.

Bibliography

Ennaji, Mohammed. *Serving the Master: Slavery and Society in Nineteenth-Century Morocco*. Translated by Seth Graebner. New York: St. Martin's Press, 1998.

Laroui, Abdallah. *Les Origines sociales et culturelles du nationalisme marocain (1830–1912)*. Paris: Francois Maspero, 1977.

Má alama al-Maghrib, 23 vols. Sale: Imprimerie de Sale, 1989–2005.

Al-Mukhtar al-Susi: al-Dhakirah al-Mustiʿadah. Casablanca: Matbʿat al-Jadida, 1986 ('Amaal al-nadwah allati nuzhimaha Itihhad Kitb al-Maghrib bi-taʿawan maʿ al-Majlis al-Baladi li-Madina 'Agadir, December 21–23, 1984).

Pascon, Paul, et. al. *La Maison d'Iligh et l'histoire sociale du Tazerwalt*. Rabat: Société Marocaine des Editeurs Réunis (SMER), 1984.

Pennell, C. R. *Morocco since 1830: A History*. London: Hurst & Co., 2000.

Shabbi, Mustafa. *al-Jaysh al-Maghribi fil-Qarn al-Tasiʿ ʿashr, 1830–1912*. 2 vols. Marrakech: al-Matbaʿah wal-Waraqah al-Wataniyah, 2008.

Al-Shlih, Mustafa, Ahmad al-Slimani, Bushta al-Sakkiwi. *Muhammad al-Mukhtar al-Susi*. Rabat: Matbaʿah Idiyal, 1996.

Al-Susi, Muhammad al-Mukhtar. *al-Maʿsul*. 20 vols. Casablanca: Matbaʿat al-Jamaʿa, 1961.

———. *al-Sirat al-dhatiyah lil-ʿAlamah Rida Allah Muhammad al-Mukhtar al-Susi Majriyat Atwar Hayyatihi*. Compiled by ʿAbd al-Wafi al-Mukhtar al-Susi. Rabat: Matbaʿat al-Maʿarif al-Jadidah, 2009.

CHAPTER 5

Little Known Roots of Islamism: al-Kawakibi's *Umm al-Qura*

SANAA MAKHLOUF

By the mid-twentieth century, Abd al-Rahman al-Kawakibi[1] became celebrated as part of the Middle Eastern reform movement centered around Mohamed 'Abduh and Jamal al-Din al-Afghani. He was a virulent critic of despotism (mainly through his book *Taba'i' al-istibdad* [*The Nature of Despotism*] and propagator of an Arab-centered Muslim revival commonly alluded to as Pan-Arabism in his semiautobiographical novel *Umm al-Qura: Proceedings of the First Conference on Islamic Awakening Held in Mecca in 1899.* However, he is almost always regarded as secondary to the main figures of reform of the nineteenth to early twentieth centuries,[2] and his role in shaping the concepts of Islamism (*al-islamiyya*) often goes unacknowledged.[3] A careful examination of his major works and, in particular *Umm al-Qura*, would, however, reveal the foundations of the most basic creeds, rhetoric, and strategies of what has become today's Arab-centered Islamist ideology.[4] Nevertheless, few Islamists would like to admit such a possible parentage of their most cherished ideologies since they identify al-Kawakibi with the secular reform movement that evolved around 'Abduh and al-Afghani, which reached its maturity in the Arab nationalism of the twentieth century. However, topoi developed by al-Kawakibi lay the foundation for an Islamic revival, as with situating the quest for the pure uncorrupted faith of the *salaf as-salih* (the pious forefathers) as preserved by the Najdi Arabs of the Arabian Peninsula at the heart of political Islam and constituting the ideology of *al-islamiyya* (Islamism) as distinct from the religion itself. He also identified the times as the second *jahiliya*[5] and advocated initiating a jihad against a Muslim "other." He identified the corruption of traditional sources of Islamic learning from within, with its disregard for the intellectual legacy of the (often non-Arab) ulama and *sufi shuyukh* (pl. of shaykh); as well as the widening of the doors of personal *ijtihad*[6] to include the "laic" expert. All of this reveals a common ground for many of the arguments both explicit and implicit that modern Islamists have adopted for their causes.

The question of "what went wrong with Islam?" central to the novel *Umm al-Qura*—and admitted to by al-Kawakibi in the introduction to *Taba'i' al-istibdad* as the question of a lifetime of research—has been kept alive throughout the twentieth century. It helps to construct a common and uninterrupted space where Muslim and Arab activists could re-confirm their shared worldviews, jihadi missions, goals, and common enemies.[7] It has also kept both of his works as relevant today as when he wrote them at the end of the nineteenth century. However, despite the wide propagation of his work and biography, relatively little is known for certain about the man, "a Janus figure in modern Arabic political thought."[8]

The Legend

Abd al-Rahman ibn Ahmad Baha'i ibn Masud al-Kawakibi, the staunch proponent of Arabism, born in Aleppo to a Persian father and a Kurdish mother, is paradoxically claimed by most of his biographers as an "Arab" thinker and reformer.[9] According to his grandson, Abd al-Rahman al-Kawakibi, the family originates from Ardabil in northwestern Iran, from the stock of the eponymous founder of the Safaviyya, Safi al-Din Ardabili (1252–1334). From this lineage came Shah Ismail I, the founder of the Safavid Ahi'i dynasty in Iran (1501–1722).[10] Though the direct ancestor of the Kawakibi family, Ibrahim Safavi (d. 1447), moved to Aleppo before the conversion of this area to Shi'ism, hardly any of the studies question the "Arabness" of al-Kawakibi. Neither do they allude to a problem of his "national" identity; an omission similar to that associated with the most prominent leader of the modern reform movement, Jamal al-Din al-Afghani.[11] Sources give different birth dates for him, varying from 1849 to 1854, with his family confirming that he was born on 23rd of Shawwal 1271 AH or July 9, 1855.[12] He spoke and wrote in three languages: Arabic, Turkish, and Persian and worked as a journalist, then a lawyer, and later, as an administrator in Aleppo.

During the years 1872–1876, he started his career in journalism, editing and writing for the official bilingual Turkish and Arabic Aleppo weekly *Furat*. In 1877, he co-published and edited his own journal, *al-*

Shahba', Aleppo's first and only Arabic journal. His writings reveal a growing political awareness of the global and local scene and the rivalry of Western states for power and dominance that would ensnare the weakening Ottoman Empire and the Arab region. His writings also reveal his keen sense of the power of journalism in forming public opinion. *Al-Shahba'* was censored and banned by its sixteenth issue for its overt criticism of the Ottoman administration.[13]

Undaunted, al-Kawakibi published the weekly *al-I'tidal* two years later in 1879. However, this time he had to include a Turkish section. *Al-I'tidal* had an even shorter life; its license was revoked by the tenth issue.[14] With this, al-Kawakibi's journalism career in Aleppo seemed to have come to an end.

Al-Kawakibi was appointed to successive administrative posts in the following period, where he seemed to gain local support for his endeavors to reform the running of his offices, even becoming mayor of Aleppo in 1892. However, both his challenging of Ottoman administrators and his political activities repeatedly got him into trouble with the Turkish authorities. According to his family and biographers, he was falsely accused of conspiring with foreign agents, of forming an underground secret society against the Ottoman government, and of being part of an assassination plot against the Aleppo Ottoman governor Jamil Pasha. For all of these charges he faced no less than capital punishment.[15] This period of intense political activity, coupled with the end of his journalism career, is revealed in the novel *Umm al-Qura*, which allows us to reconstruct al-Kawakibi's activism in Aleppo prior to his sudden appearance in Cairo.

Escaping to Egypt a decade later in 1899 with manuscripts of his political writings, al-Kawakibi published his novel *Umm al-Qura* under the pseudonym al-Sayyid al-Furati. Al-Kawakibi apparently managed to send two copies of the published novel to Khedive Abbas, and a copy to both Muhammad 'Abduh and Shaykh Ali Yusuf, publisher of *al-Mu'ayyid*. Pleased with the novel and probably assuming that it was based on real events, the khedive had both 'Abduh and Yusuf locate the anonymous author. They finally tracked him down.[16] Thus, the novel gained him admission into the 'Abduh reform circle. With the patronage of Khedive Abbas II, he was sent on missions networking against the Ottoman sultan and promoting Khedive Abbas as the natural leader of an "Arab" caliphate. He travelled to East and North Africa, the Arabian Peninsula, Yemen, Central Asia, and East Asia. Back in Cairo, al-Kawakibi's promising career abruptly came to an end in 1902 when he was allegedly poisoned in a downtown café frequented by reform activists such as Shaykh Ali Yusuf and Muhammad Rashid Rida. The continued posthumous publication of his works in *al-Manar* and *al-Mu'ayyad* gained him prominence as a spokesperson for Arabism and a critic of Ottoman despotism.

Protocols of Reform: al-Kawakibi's *Umm al-Qura* Revisited

O you who fall upon these notes!

Know that they are a chain of analogies for which the knowledge of the first does not dispense with the need to know its last; they are a series of meanings linked together in sequence for which the skimming through would not suffice for their attainment. So, if you are from the *umma* of guidance and find in yourself the fervor for life and religion and the quality/spirit of chivalry then do not quickly reject them until you have given them their due and have fully comprehended their opening lines and their endings. From that moment, it is entirely up to you. But if you are from the *umma* of *taqlid* (imitation) and held by the fetters of illusions; far from introspection; and do not care to know who you are and on which path you are going and disregard the rightful claims of your religion and yourself and do not care to know wherefore you are destined; and you are agitated by real life and the good advice; and feel the shame of your degradation and the heaviness of responsibilities/duties—so much so that you cannot bear to go on with reading [these lines] and employing your mind and acquired knowledge to consider the premises and conclusions—then I implore you to treat these notes with the customary neglect. Throw them aside to others who may examine their contents for themselves.

PREFACE TO *UMM AL-QURA*: PROCEEDINGS OF THE FIRST CONFERENCE ON ISLAMIC RENAISSANCE 1316 AH/1898[17]

With these words begins *Umm al-Qura*, that is to say "Mecca, mother of all cities," the short political novel that records twelve of the fictional secret meetings of the organization of *Umm al-Qura* in Mecca in 1898 during the hajj season. The story tells of the gathering of twenty-three male activists, including al-Kawakibi, representing Arab and Islamic communities from across the Western colonized world, who convene in Mecca in search of answers to al-Kawakibi's lifelong question, "What went wrong with Muslims?" It is narrated by al-Sayyid al-Furati, a pseudonym for al-Kawakibi, who is the convener of this conference. The novel traces al-Kawakibi's political trajectory in Aleppo and his escape to Cairo.

The Storyline: Flattening of History

Understand! For the religion has lost its might ['izz]
when once it was mighty without any weakness!
For then, it had its folk who gave it all its due
of guidance, teaching, and proper doctrination!
Wherefore has it come to when the [so-called] folk of knowledge
    confine themselves to the confines of their homes [in the embraces
    of their women]?
Has it not become a religious obligation [*fard*] to put an end to this
    weakness/feebleness?
Come forth together to exert our effort!
Lest by its neglect the faithful incur sinfulness!
Come forth to *Umm al-qura* and conspire/confer!
Do not despair from the wrath of an all-protecting God.
For that which swords could once accomplish
Now, needs no more than tongues!
OPENING VERSES BY AL-SAYYID AL-FURATI (276)

The story follows a very simple line. It is a day-by-day account of twelve of the secret meetings of the Society of Mecca, *Jam'iyyat Umm al-Qura*, which uses the hajj (pilgrimage) season as a cover for its clandestine activities. Al-Sayyid al-Furati, alias al-Kawakibi, leads twenty-two others[18] in discussions around the most pertinent question of the day: "What went wrong with Muslims?" (275). The characters represent activists from Aleppo (Furat), Damascus, Jerusalem, Alexandria, Cairo (Misr), Yemen, Basra, Najd, Medina, Mecca, Tunisia, Fez, Britain, Ottoman Turkey, Kurdistan, Tabriz, Russia (Tatar), Kazakhstan (Kazan), Central Asia (Turkistan), Afghanistan, India, Sindh, and China. The Arab delegates assume a higher point of authority and the other nationalities naturally defer to them the role of defining the concepts of "*islamiyya*." The Meccan elected conference president presents the participants with a list of ten questions that they should debate:

(1) Locate the illness
(2) Describe the symptoms
(3) Determine the sources of infections (the microbes)
(4) Identify the illness
(5) Find the remedies
(6) Define [the concept of] *islamiyyah*
(7) Identify the means to practice it (*taddayun biha*)
(8) Determine what is hidden (*shirk*)
(9) Determine how to fight [dangerous] innovation (*bid'a*)
(10) Formulate laws and by-laws for the establishment of an educational society[19]

Al-Sayyid al-Furati, as secretary of the conference, was assigned the function of recording the conversations and deliberations as well as the final resolutions reached by the conference participants who represented Muslim communities from all over the colonized world, including a British Muslim convert from the society of Liverpool.[20] The novel ends with a conversation that takes place about two months later between the Indian delegate and an unnamed "most noble" prince who strongly approves of the conference findings and deliberations. Though the novel does not include any details about the characters except for their nation-based coded titles, individual reform views, and contributions to the thorny ten questions, and that they all speak Arabic, yet careful reading can suggest the real-life figures who might have inspired the literary construction.

It would probably be fruitful for researchers to retrace the possible parallel trajectories between the novel and al-Kawakibi's real life in order to identify the existing networks disseminating Islamism at the end of the nineteenth century. Al-Furati—al-Kawakibi's own character—certainly reflects many of the influences of al-Kawakibi's idol, al-Sayyid Jamal al-Din al-Afghani, who might also have inspired the character of al-Muhaqqaq al-Madani, elected as president of the conference; al-'alim al-Najdi might have been based on the Wahhabi defender, Mahmud Shukri al-Alusi, the foremost proponent of Islamic reform/Wahhibism in Iraq; and the Yemeni delegate could be al-Imam al-Shawkani; while al-Adib al-Bayruti could very well be Muhammad 'Abduh, who had spent his years of exile in Beirut a decade earlier lecturing and propagating Islamic activism to the youth and where al-Kawakibi—and most probably Muhammad Rashid Rida—might have first met or heard of him prior to joining him in Egypt in 1899. The prince, as he himself seems to have identified with, could very well have been based on the youthful figure of Khedive Abbas II, who shares the same ambition of displacing the Ottoman sultanate with his Arab caliphate. The felicitous Said from England (Liverpool) could have been based on Wilfrid Scawen Blunt, who was to play an influential role in the Muhammad 'Abduh circle and from whose *The Future of Islam* (1882) purportedly— as suggested by Sylvia Haim—al-Kawakibi adapted many of his ideas, especially the call for establishing an Arab caliphate.[21] Al-Kawakibi, similar to his protagonist al-Sayyid al-Furati, was reported to have rented a house in Aleppo where he allegedly met in secret with his unidentified foreign friends—some of whom could also have been Italian activists—to discuss political affairs of the day (Al-Tahhan, 26). Following the publication of the novel, al-Kawakibi was sent on missions to northwest Africa, East Africa, the Arabian Pennisula—though ironically enough not on hajj—Yemen, India, and East Asia to spread the message of political Islam—and presumably anti-Ottomanism—among activists in the colonized Muslim world. His insistence on secrecy so detailed in the novel seems to have been justified when he was allegedly poisoned in Cairo in 1902.

Meeting for the first time, Ikhwan al-tawhid, as they are called in the novel, identify themselves to each other through their religious slogan: the minimalist *shahada*, "we worship none other than Allah" (*la na'budu illa Allah*). After professing an oath of allegiance to the forthcoming jihad and fealty to the group *"'ala 'ahd allah bi 'l-jihad wa 'l-amanah,"* the twenty-three "members of this blessed society" discuss the reasons for the decline of the Muslim world. Though the decline had started over a thousand years ago, the times are now pressing, their Meccan brother urges them, since they need to thwart the imminent danger[22] to the "heart of the Muslim world": the Arabian peninsula![23] Ironically, though initiated as an insider response to the crisis of the time, the meetings are conducted in the most thoroughly Western fashion. A chair for the conference is appointed, secretary for the minutes of the meetings elected, and prints of a secret cipher are distributed among the anonymous participants—included in the first publication of the novel. Briefs and setting of procedures and by-laws are approved by all within a modern Western paradigm.

However, at no point in the novel do the Muslim Ikhwan[24] ever doubt the religious and cultural authenticity of their enterprise, or question the appropriateness of the Western "awakening" (*nahda*) and the Protestant Reformation paradigm that they have adopted for their political cause and to which al-Kawakibi repeatedly refers. He sees the causes for the political, economic, and military decline and the subsequent remedies within the framework of religion. The convergence of the religious with the political is affirmed through the words of the protagonists.

The Ikhwan al-tawhid embark on their endeavor with a sense of history in the making. The "moment is now ripe," the Meccan Muhaqqiq claims, for changing the tide in favor of the Muslim nations. He heralds the rise of a "vanguard of free and noble men . . . each one of whom counts for a thousand and the thousand for one-thousand thousand" who will wake the *umma* from its slumber and revitalize it (283). The Ikhwan identifying themselves with such men profess their allegiance to the forthcoming jihad on the sources of the decline. They themselves strategically adopt the nonsectarian "irrefutable" Salafi creed as their religious orientation (*madhhab as-salaf aladhdhi la yuradd*), so that their findings and conclusions would be acceptable to all of the followers of the "*Qiblah*," that is, all Muslims (281). Their war cry adopted as a conference resolution, "Zealous guardianship of religion over and beyond compassion for Muslims" (*al-ghira 'ala 'l-din qabla 'sh-shafaqa 'ala 'l-muslimin*) (380) indicates the beginning of a conscious rift that will henceforth be ever widening: the rift between a loyalty for Islam—as defined by them—and a loyalty to Muslims or, more pointedly, those whom the Ikhwan al-tawhid will deem Muslim only in name.[25]

Each speaker offers in turn his analysis of what ails the *umma*, trying to locate within its traditional structures the sources of the infection. Curiously, none stops to question the validity of the diagnosis itself. The lowliness of the Muslims is all too evident. In what has become— through the writings of the reform movement—by the mid-twentieth century a standard perception, they all agree that the decline had started "more than a 1,000 years ago" when the Arab Umayyad dynasty lost its powers to "non-Arab elements" (280, expounded in 353).[26] However, after Western nations had reversed their fortunes (through their successful religious Reformation and Enlightenment) they gained the upper hand over the Muslims, and the latter's decline became more discernable. Thus, the regression that supposedly had begun long ago and had made its way largely unnoticed could now be identified precisely because of being able to be seen from the outside: the vantage point of the *nahda* activists. And the question of "what went wrong?" could be asked, and more importantly, answered by those who were willing and dared to do so. These concerned activists would leave behind their "inherited means of comprehension" and do for Islam what "Luther and Voltaire had done for the West" (373–374): to locate the sources of the illness within the *umma* and displace the corruptive forces with necessary remedies.

Al-Kawakibi already anticipates that these remedies would not necessarily be palatable to the *umma*, and accordingly he has his Ikhwan proclaim from the very start that their mission includes finding ways to administer carefully the needed (bitter) remedies to the body of the resisting *umma* so as to "overcome the flinching susceptibilities of its taste and smell faculties" (280).

The Three Corrupting Elements: Contamination by Foreign Elements

The Ikhwan's combined efforts center on one urgent finding as declared by the Meccan delegate in the opening session: What must be resisted by all means is the "imminent danger to the 'heart of the Muslim world,'" mainly the claim of the Ottomans to be the legitimate representatives of the caliphate and sovereigns over the Arabian Peninsula. In order to remove the religious legitimacy of these Muslim contenders from their position at the head of the *umma*, a formulation was needed to effectively keep them out of the fold of Islam. According to al-Kawakibi and his circle, such a formulation must be both theological and political at the same time. He has his Ikhwan find it in the reformist Wahhabi theology, which excludes Muslims who do not adhere to their particular Unitarian doctrine from the faith altogether and grants legitimacy to the fight against them. However, the term Wahhabi itself is strategically not used. Instead, the nonpartisan but positively loaded terms *salafiya*, the irrefutable true *tawhid* of *al-salaf asalih*, with its adherents, and the *muwahhiddun*, Unitarians, or Ikhwan al-tawhid—these being the self-appointed designations of the Wahhabi[27]—are appropriated to describe the religious affiliation of the participants.

Accordingly, al-Kawakibi's Ikhwan hold that it is only the Arab *muwahhiddun* from the heartland of Islam who have preserved the religion from the corrupting forces that had assailed the rest of the Muslim world and immersed it in a second state of *jahiliya* (ignorance) (310–12, 320).[28] These Arabs with their Salafi orientation, Arabic language proficiency, "pure racial stock,"[29] "tribal solidarity," "aversion to frivolous intellectualism," and rejection of exotic forms of Islam such as Sufism, or *bid'a*, or foreign accretions, represent the most authentic version of Islam, *al-Islamiyyah*.[30] "The religion has originated from among them and in their tongue," the Meccan delegate unabashedly argues, "they are its people, carriers, protectors, and its defenders. . . . We should not feel reluctant to give in to their superior understanding of their religion" and accordingly be ready to "join them in thwarting the threat to the heart" of Islamdom (281–282). The final resolutions of the conference dedicate a 26-point elaboration of the virtues of the Arabs favoring their leadership of the coming religious revival and the re-instatement of hereditary rights.

Al-Kawakibi has no compunction to condemn non-Arab Muslims for the decline of the Islamic creed. Through the spread of Islam outside of Arabia, the non-Arab converts brought into the fold the remnants of their pagan beliefs: "the religion has departed from the custody of its people and the word/unity of its *umma* has dispersed," al-Kawakibi claims. "The opinions of intruders have gained hold over the principles of religious rulings/*shar'* and have resorted to those which suit their pagan inclinations" (289). This sentiment is further emphasized in a footnote on the same page by al-Kawakibi: "Would they [the non-Arabs following the Ummayad period] had not entered the religion, thereby desecrating it, and overcoming its people and [usurping] their rightful claim [for the caliphate]! Muslims from outside of the Arabian Peninsula are a mixture of mongrel intruders and remnants of diverse peoples (riffraff/*akhlat dukhala' wa baqaya aqwam shatta*) with nothing to hold them together other than that they face [direct their prayers to] the glorious *ka'ba*" (294).

The correspondence between this newly emerging Salafism or Islamism and Arabism is no accident. The allocation of the Arabian Peninsula to the center of the Islamic world as its heart seems to serve the Ikhwan al-tawhid a double function: it overrides the geopolitical realities of Muslim civilization and its historical centers of power—mainly cosmopolitan Baghdad, Cairo, Damascus, Tlemcen, and Constantinople where the Ottoman authority was recognized—while conferring to the Arab *Umm al-Qura* area a newly conflated religio-political symbolic level.[31] Al-Kawakibi thereby reinstates the "Arab" origin of the religious giving legitimacy to the claims of the Wahhabi Arab movement as the keeper of the authentic message of Islam, *islamiyyah*.[32] Secondly, to alienate the non-Arab Muslim elements (mostly, the Turkish Ottomans), from the heart of Islam and designate them as the threatening other whose Islam merely serves as a front for political opportunism. With the identification of the other two culprits for the decline the net is drawn close on all possible non-Arab elements that might influence

the definition of Islam for the modern world and ensure Arab and therefore the newly constructed Wahhabi–Salafi hegemony over the religion.

Corrupt Ulama and *Fuqaha*: Guardians of the Outward Knowledge

"Our innermost illness is the falling of our religion into the hands of its
official ulama; in other words under the rule of the turbaned ignorant
ones" (298). Given such Arab-centered perceptions of Islamic ethnicity,
history, and geography, it is not surprising that the causes, and thereby
the targets of reform, are located in the traditional institutions and re-
positories of knowledge that have for centuries informed and helped
shape the pluralistic diversity of the Islamic self. These are the ulama
and jurists of the different *madhahib* (schools of law or jurisprudence),
keepers of the outward knowledge of the law; and the Sufis and Sufi orders, keepers of the inward knowledge of the heart. They are, after all,
the only serious contenders to the religious legitimacy of the emerging
Salafi/Wahhabism.[33]

Accordingly, the ulama are accused of cowardly and hypocritical par-
tisanship; corruption and opportunistic collaboration with the Ottoman
rulers; blind imitation of their predecessors; irrational and arrogant bigotry; pedantic scholasticism; and preaching fatalism and political res-
ignation. They had, furthermore, contributed to decline by closing the
door of *ijtihad* and accumulating worthless scholastic knowledge that
has led to deepening sectarianism, dogmatic divisions, and confusion.
Finally, their *tashdid* drove the populace to find refuge in charlatan Sufis
(324–325).[34] Al-Kawakibi's Ikhwan reach one conclusion: the turbaned
ones have gone astray becoming more harmful to the religion than the
devil (301).

Strangely, al-Kawakibi's culprits resemble more the priests and clergy
of Catholicism and the charlatans of folk religion and exonerating practices of the church than anything out of an Islamic milieu. Even the
Ikhwan's diatribe against them mimics Reformation accusations against
the Papist Church and Enlightenment scorn for folk religions (294).
The Ikhwan draw parallels between the practices of fraudulent ulama
and Sufi extremists and those pagan ones of Christianity and Judaism
(294–298). Though the inspiration for these ideas could be traced more
to Western critiques of Christianity, especially Catholicism and popular
religion,[35] than to the Islamic traditional genre of anti-Sufism, yet the
imagery and the rhetoric have had such a strong hold that it has been ac-

cepted by mainstream Muslim culture as the valid representation of the state of traditional ulama and Sufis evoking derision, ridicule, and contempt for the offenders.

The conversation recorded as an addenda to the conference between the Indian delegate and "the noble prince" further shows the contempt that al-Kawakibi's Ikhwan have for traditional scholarship and statesmanship in general, an *istighna* (richness) for any kind of learning or expertise that comes from without the fold of Wahhabism: "I don't suppose that there are among the nobles and Muslim viziers/politicians any who are more politically astute than some of the members of the society [of *Umm al-Qura*], whose views show an extensive scope and insight" (393–394).

Best Jihad: Silencing the Tradition

Such self-congratulatory pronouncements allow the reformers—solely on the basis of their convictions and claims of sincerity—to levy accusations against the scholars of Islam and ascertain that they are excluded from any serious role in informing the reform movement. Instead, they are to be publicly discredited. The Ikhwan lay their strategies by which to achieve their end: they are to wage a rhetorical war on the traditional ulama, lampooning them and depicting them as incompetent and suspect objects of scorn and derision. The Ikhwan's final resolutions even call upon the state to help suppress these dissident ulama and put them under quarantine until they submit to the will of the new Salafi teachings.

The reform/Salafi movement was so successful in its war against traditional Islam and the recruitment of the institutions of the emerging postcolonial nation states that by the end of the century Osama bin Laden could publicly proclaim: "The fatwa of any official *'alim* (religious scholar, singular of ulama) has no value for me" and few could blame him for that act of defiance.[36]

Emptying the Hearts of Muslims

The third and final culprit that had to be contained was Sufism, the premodern loci of popular faith and contender for the hearts of Muslims, and incidentally, the source of much of the anticolonial resistance movements that had emerged in the late nineteenth and early twentieth century. Al-Kawakibi's Ikhwan mainly accuse them of providing a safe haven from the *tashdid* narrowing of the doors of salvation by the formal ulama who offered lax definitions of Islam, *iman* (faith), and *kufr* (disbelief), that supported the thriving of pagan rituals and beliefs within Muslim communities.

By teaching the simple-minded commoners subversive religious innovations, cheating them with false spiritual hierarchies and religiosity, pretending supernatural powers, promising power of intercession, preaching hidden *shirk* (idolatry), and sometimes outright *shirk*, fabricating hadiths, and spreading corrupt customs and beliefs like advocating the use of music, *dhikr* (rhythmic invocation), apathy, fatalism, and the rejection of the rational and the scientific, corrupt Sufis had thus led their ignorant and gullible followers astray (319–323).

Through these attractions Sufi cults of *baraka* (blessing) gained control over the folk and helped define a religion that places spiritual self realization and moral excellence, that is, social and political apathy, above real jihad. Sufism also introduced a social order and gradation of knowledge and a hierarchy based on a spiritual dimension that could expand interpretations and allow for a nonmonolithic, nonconformist, individualized understanding of religion. As such, traditional Sufism offered a real challenge to the Ikhwan *al-tawhid* and their claims of being the custodians of the pure unadulterated Unitarian Islam of Salafism and of being the advocates of personal *ijtihad*.

Again, al-Kawakibi has his Ikhwan resort to the institutions of the state to help curb the powers of these informal centers of authority and their popular image of piety and authenticity. The conference resolutions call upon the Sufi orders to confine their activities to social and civic philanthropy and networks of charity. During the last years of his life al-Kawakibi travelled near and far mimicking the travels purportedly done by al-Sayyid al-Furati in the early pages of the novel to gather the activists for the conference and to spread the message of *Islamiyya* and its activism against the oppressive Ottomans, "decadent" local scholars, and charlatan Sufis. Fulfilling their share of the best jihad, the 'Abduh circle routinely targeted the ulama and Sufis, lampooning them, and engraving them in the popular memory as the culprits for "what had gone wrong" (373).

Inventing Salafism: A Religion for Modern Times

With these perceptions of the carriers of the Islamic learning and culture, the need for a redefinition of Islam along lines compatible with the spirit of the times becomes crucial. That al-Kawakibi finds it in the champions of unitarian Wahhabi Islam is no accident. Blunt, just a decade earlier, had identified it as the source for the revival of Islam and the mobilization of the Muslim peoples against their Ottoman rulers and their decadent scholars:

> Wahhabism, as a political regeneration of the world has failed, but the spirit of reform has remained. Indeed, the present unquiet attitude of expectation in Islam has been its indirect result. Just as the Lutheran reformation in Europe, though it failed to convert the Christian Church, caused its real reform, so Wahhabism has produced a real desire for reform if not yet reform itself in Musulmans. Islam is no longer asleep, and were another and a wiser Abd el Wahab to appear, not as a heretic, but in the body of the Orthodox sect, he might play the part of Loyola or Borromeo with success.[37]

The poem, sent to the conference members by al-Adib al-Bayruti (i.e., Muhammad 'Abduh), shows the powerful appeal of such a grand reformation project:

> O our folk! Rectify your faith in the unicity/*tawhid* of your Lord
> Do not associate with His living creatures and other riffraff
> Purify the religion from all sorts of false accretions and fabrications
> Return to the fundamental religion of your forefathers/*salaf* who have integrity
> Hold on to divine ordinations [Qur'anic verses] that are certain
> and a *sunna* that has come to you with most clear wording
> Forsake innovation in religion even if [claimed to be] good
> Do not be seduced by the [seeming eloquence of] wise interpretations.
> The beauty of the religion is in its [pure] thought and deed
> Much more worthy than the captivity, chains, and illnesses [of false beliefs]
> . . . Other than in the circle of *tawhid* you will not find a place of gathering [for] you are not related by blood. (389)

This circle of *islamiyyah* then is the distinct form of Islam, which sets apart the unitarians from the Muslims by name only. But why would *al-islamiyyah* have the power to mobilize Muslim youth and provide a viable alternative to traditional premodern Islamic institutions? Precisely because it sells itself as a new beginning that seems to break away from the past, circumventing its realities while reaching out to the uncontaminated sources, and in the process allowing one to pretend that the legacies of the past do not matter. The power of this creed is unleashed through the "opening" of the door of *ijtihad* supposedly closed by the Turkish/non-Arab ulama.

As an added appeal embedded in the reconstructed Salafi/Wahhabi creed is a rejection of any hierarchy—except naturally that of the Najdi Arabian—of any sort, including those of knowledge, social order, and age.[38] The reforms introduced by Muhammad 'Abduh to the curricula of al-Azhar University and the gradual exclusion of Sufi texts from mainstream religious schools must be revisited within this context. [39]

Playing *Ijtihad*

One of the main features of Islamists today is their attraction to *ijtihad* as a way to overcome generations of authoritative scholastic texts and legitimize their positions concerning issues like the blowing up of noncombatant civilians, killing of hostages, forbidding marriages with Christian and Jewish women, and so on. The recourse to *ijtihad* without the necessary learning that would qualify a would-be-*mujtahid* was one of the main accusations levelled against the Wahhabi theologians by their contemporaries already apparent within the context of al-Kawakibi's times.[40]

It is not too improbable to see al-Kawakibi's novel as an advocate of *ijtihad* as a way to bypass the "corrupt" and "corrupting" legacies of Islamic scholarship and mysticism and their figures of authority and displace them with newer authorities that identified with the Arab legacy of the Wahhabi reform movement. His characters are all part of a lay and literate circle that can access information for themselves and know enough to interpret the "linguistic" and "literal" meanings of the clear verses: the people of this level are guided by their own perspicacity and do not need to imitate except after examining the evidence of the one they might choose to follow (resolution no. 15 of the last meeting).

Alongside their revived concept of individual *ijtihad* appears the more seemingly modest term of *istihda'* (direct guidance by the sources, that is, without recourse to a "human" guide) (203), which alludes to the literal interpretation of the religious sources as opposed to *taqlid* or intellectual interpretations (*ta'wil*). Together with *ijtihad* they become the cornerstones of *al-islamiyyah* and the great equalizer of movements based on political Islam. Through *istihda'* (direct guidance by the sources) the self-styled *mujtahid*s predetermine what constitutes admissible evidence and reject evidence of more inclusive and tolerant definitions of *tawhid* and dismiss religious support for liberal behaviour as idolatry. Through their *ijtihad* they purify the fundamental tenants of the religion from centuries of *ta'wil* (esoteric interpretation), *tahrif* (distortion, alteration), and dogmatism, and distortions and infestations of hidden *shirk* (hidden or covert idolatry, which encompasses much more than blatant forms of idolatry or denial of Allah's Unity) and *bid'a* (innovation) (331–342).[41]

Shackling *Ijtihad*

Al-Kawakibi's Ikhwan al-tawhid propose a liberation of *ijtihad* from any meaningful requirements or restrictions. The criteria they deem necessary or sufficient for *mujtahid*s[42] to exercise *ijtihad* and be eligible for membership in the legislative body of those qualified to express the community's will on matters of public policy and law call into question the true nature of this opening. The Yemeni delegate outlines the five points of knowledge required for performing independent interpretation of the Islamic legal sources:

> 1. [He] should be knowledgeable of *quraishi* Arabic, acquired through learning and practice, enough to understand oral speech and NOT to encompass knowledge of extensive vocabulary and idiomatic usage, verbal forms and the irregular verbs, rules of grammar, figures of speech and usage, or rhetoric and its genres, the acquisition of which would require more than two thirds of one's life! . . . even though such knowledge would only be useful for one who pursues the study of literature.
> 2. [He] should be able to read the Qu'ran with a proficiency such that he can discern the meanings of its vocabulary and its sentence constructions, plus be familiar with the historical contexts of the revelation and explanations of the circumstances governing them as available from books composed on the sunna and history, and the exegeses offered by the Prophet or his companions. Besides, it is quite commonly known that the verses that deal with legislation do not exceed the one hundred and fifty! A footnote claims that information is available in the *Tafsir* of al-Ahmadi al-Hindi.[43]
> 3. [He] should be well versed in the prophetic sunna compiled during

the lifetime of the followers of the companions of the Prophet and their followers and their followers in turn without being held by the condition of knowing 100,000 or 200,000 hadiths. It suffices for him what sufficed [Imam] Malik in his *Muwatta'* and [Imam] Ahmad [Ibn Hanbal] in his *Musnad*. Besides, it is commonly known that the hadiths [*ahadith*] concerning legislation do not in any way exceed the one thousand and five hundred! A footnote explains that *Imam* al-Shawkani al-Yamani encompassed these *ahadith*.[44]

4. [He] should have extensive knowledge of the *sira* [life] of the Prophet, and those of his companions, and their states/affairs as recorded in the early *sira* books, and the history works accredited by *Ahl al-Hadith* [hadith specialist] like al-Hafiz al-Dhahabi, Ibn Kathir, and earlier ones like Ibn Jarir, and Ibn Qutaiba and earlier ones like Malik and al-Zuhari and their likes.

5. [He] should have a naturally intact intelligence unspoiled by teachings of theories of logic and argumentation—A footnote indicates that Westerners have established that there is absolutely no benefit to be derived from [the study of] logic and so they neglected it, even though they are concerned with researching means of studying foreign languages[?], Greek philosophy, Pythagorean metaphysics, theology, doctrines of the wise ones, disputes of the rationalists, deviations of the Sufis, extremism of *al-khawarij* [sect of Islam along with the Sunni and Shi'a], conclusions of later day *fuqaha'*, the interjections of the over suspicious, the rhetorical ornamentations of the hypocrites, and the forgeries of the swindlers. (336–338)

The doors of *ijtihad* now being declared open—and eligibility criteria relaxed—would yield rationally controlled pragmatic rulings that could be easily codified and taught to Muslim youth (376). Only this time around, *ijtihad* would not be left to the specialized *faqih*s and their onerous requirements, but rather handed over to the newly defined intellectuals to "reinterpret, reconstruct, and reformulate Islamic normativity, and dismantle the classical representations of Islamic law."[45]

But then, how to determine which *ijtihad* ruling to define the day? The sign of its authenticity would be measured by its position vis à vis countenancing the strategies used by the Islamists and their wars against competing movements: "The *mujtahid*s of this rank guide themselves and do not need to imitate except if they be convinced of the evidence of those whom they follow" (338). Thus, the matter becomes a closed circle where "*mujtahid*s" with such rudimentary knowledge as stated above have to make the final decision on a body of evidence that they may not necessarily have studied in terms of their own personal conviction. The exponential growth of fatwas and fatwa wars in the past decades reveal the unfortunate effect of this relaxation of the criteria for *ijtihad* as promoted by the Wahhabi informed "liberal" reform movement.

Popular Appeal of the Novel: Forging New Identities

The novel helped forge new identities and religious values. It proposed a new social order built on common ideologies and causes—mostly in resistance to the established order. The fraternity of Ikhwan al-tawhid is built on a transnational shared ideology and activist agenda that supersedes their local cultures. Here indeed are the seeds of a globalized Islam that aims to displace local and living figures of authority with standardized books, schools, societies, and social networks: "Other than in the circle of *tawhid* you will not find a place of gathering [for] you are not related by blood" (389).

Moreover, these fraternities or organizations appear to be free from social gradation, where all are equal and have equal voices and votes. Al-Kawakibi clearly sets out that these are the rules for the coming social order where all positions are by election and agreement. As such these fraternities mimic Sufi orders as a social equalizer while rejecting the spiritual dimension, which precludes a hierarchy as claimed by the master-disciple relationship.[46] Not surprisingly, the novel includes a born-again Muslim who revokes the Sufi traditions of his forefathers and converts to the new *islamiyyah* (343).

These fraternities were instrumental in the dissemination of an emerging quasi-Wahhabi Islamism that is politically centered since they provide a support system where: "each one sees that there are companions who agree with matters the way one sees them and walk the same path as he and so his heart/spirit becomes steadfast and his tongue grows stronger in voicing/speaking out the words of god, fearless of blame or criticism of ignorant ones" (330).

The novel also feeds a sense of heroism and lust for adventure, which is driving these young men, the vanguard of religious revival and the reinstatement of past glories.[47] The need for secrecy and anonymity is exciting and contagious. The characters of the novel seem to emanate from al-Kawakibi's other work *Taba'i' al-Istibdad* as representations of *Ahl al-Aza'im* (People of Determination).

The defiant says: the malady is to withstand shackles and the remedy is to stand up against humiliation

the steadfast says: the malady is the unrestrained leaders and the remedy is to bind them with heavy chains

the free one says: the malady is unjust arrogance and the remedy is to humiliate the arrogant and [finally] "the martyrs say: I love death as much as you love life." (436)

The latter call finds a resonance today in Osama bin Laden's ominous words "we love death as much as you love life, so we will win."

The romantic adventurous mood created by the novel and its actors is one of the main appeals of Islamism—an appeal that is often ignored in the studies on Islamism. That and also the comfortably safe—mentally—world it depicts of the struggle between good and evil and the triumph of the good. Their goodness is self-evident: the world has sunk into a second *jahiliya* (age of ignorance) and those who dare to oppose it are by virtue of their opposition the true Muslims. They are in no need of the teachers, elders, *shuyukh* of this treacherous world. Their sincerity and fraternity will ensure their salvation.

These young men are propelled forward through the seeming rationality of their quest. Estranged from their own tradition—"the problem is that our religion is not our ancestor's original religion" (310)—they find comfort in mirroring each other as concerned modern Muslims, looking at their tradition from the outside. The question of "what went wrong?" never disappears from their horizon. It helps them construct an echo chamber where they can hear each other and confirm themselves in their shared (and quite often ambivalent) worldviews, mission, goals, and common enemies.

For over a century traditional Islam, the culprit of all such searches, has effectively been sealed and not allowed to speak for itself. To say something about it, one has to stand outside of it. *Islamiyyah* speaks for it.

Al-Kawakibi's rhetorically powerful writings with their slogans and memorable quotes quickly became staple food for the Egyptian-influenced awakening and dissemination of Islamism in the Islamic world. And, although al-Afghani's and 'Abduh's reform circle does not find much favor with present-day Islamists, the common genealogy and rampant suspicion of traditional Islam can even be heard through their vociferous antagonism to the reformist agenda as well as their variants of "what went wrong?"

By the middle of the twentieth century, al-Kawakibi's writings had become part of the popular culture of political activism expressed through what would later emerge as a particular and recognizable type of discourse: the rhetoric of reform Islamism and political activism.[48] Arguably, more than a record of the reform consciousness of the times, this widely popular legacy helped shape the identity of Arab Muslim activists for more than a century. Moreover, the story has presented Arab youth for over a century with a facile romantic rendition of modern Islamic history with implicitly embedded culprits to blame for "what went wrong with Islam" which has effectively circumvented the need for critical thinking on the events that underlay the nation building of the modern Middle East, as well as on the given model of Reformation and Enlightenment for modern political activism.

Though written over a century ago, the views expressed by the novel's young protagonists resonate with the rhetoric and ideologies of today's contemporary Muslim activists, raising the strong claim that al-Kawakibi be justifiably considered one of the founding fathers of modern day Islamism, on a par with al-Afghani and Muhammad 'Abduh. The fact that al-Kawakibi was not really an Arab, was proud of his Shi'i lineage, never went on hajj or visited Mecca, was in the pay of the Egyptian khedive to help topple the Ottoman caliphate, and was implicitly or explicitly aiding the British to realize their control of the Arab world and re-map the region into colonies of Western influence, does not diminish the power of al-Kawakibi's *Umm al-Qura* to seduce more and more into its intrigues.

Notes

1. In the mid-twentieth century many studies focused on al-Kawakibi, extolling his works as an "Arab" reformer such as: Muhammad Ahmad Khalf Allah, *al-Kawakibi: Hayatuhu wa Ara'uhu* (Cairo, 1955); Sylvia Haim, "Alfieri and Al-Kawakibi," *Oriente Moderno* 34, no. 7 (July 1954): 321–334; and Haim, "*Blunt and al-Kawakibi*," *Oriente Moderno* 35 (1955): 132–143; Norbert Tapiero, *Les Idées Reformistes D'al-Kawakibi* (Paris, 1956); Khaldun S. al-Husri, *Three Reformers: A Study in Modern Arab Political Thought* (Beirut: Khayats, 1966), chapter 4; Elie Kedourie, "The Politics of Political Literature: Kawakibi, Azoury, and Jung," in *Arabic Political Memories and Other Studies*, ed. Elie Kedourie (London: Frank Cass, 1974); Muhammad 'Amara, *al-A'mal al-Kamila li-'Abd al-Rahman al-Kawakibi* (Beirut: n.s., 1975); 'Abbas Mahmud al-'Aqqad, *al-Rahhala (Kaf) 'Abd al-Rahman al-Kawakibi* (Cairo: *Matbu'at al-Majlis al-A'la*, 1958); Jan Daya, *Sahafat al-Kawakibi, Silsilat Fajr al-Nahda*, 2 (Beirut: *Mu'assasat Fikr*, 1984) and

al-Imam al-Kawakibi: Fasl al-din 'an al-dawla (London and Syria: *Nashr*, 1988); Eliezer Tauber, *The Emergence of the Arab Movements* (London: Frank Cass, 1993), chapter 5; Muhammad Jamal Tahhan, *al-Istibdad wa-bada 'ilahu fi fikr al-Kawakibi* (Damascus: Ittihad al-Kitab al-'Arabi, 1992); and Tahhan, *al-A'mal al-kamila lil-Kawakibi* (Beirut: Markaz Dirasat al-Wihda al-'Arabiyya, 1995); Ronen Raz, "Interpretations of al-Kawakibi's Thought, 1950–1980s," *Middle Eastern Studies* 32 (January 1996): 179–190; Joseph G. Rahme, "Abd al Rahman al-Kawakibi's Reformist Ideology, Arab Pan-Islamism, and the Internal Other," *Journal of Islamic Studies* 10, no. 2 (1999): 159–177; Ryuichi Funatsu "Al-Kawākibī's Thesis and Its Echoes in the Arab World Today," *Harvard Middle Eastern and Islamic Review* 7 (2006): 1–40.

2. Almost all studies of the modern reform movement exclusively cite al-Afghani, followed by Muhammad 'Abduh and finally Muhammad Rashid Rida as the founding fathers of modern Islamic movements, while for Islamism, in particular, they skip a generation to Sayyid Qutb and the Indian/Pakistani Muslim Abul Ala al-Maududi in the mid-twentieth century. See, for example, "The Genealogy of Islamism," 92–93, in Peter R. Demant and Asghar Ali Engineer, *Islam vs. Islamism* (Westport, CT: Greenwood, 2006). That may also be due in part because with al-Kawakibi's untimely early death; he, as a political actor, ceased to play a direct role in the propagation of the ideas presented in the novel. However, the repeated publication of his two major works on political Islam made certain that the "ideas" put forward by al-Afghani's reform movement were kept alive among a young readership well into the twentieth century.

3. I will be referring to Islamism as generally defined by the International Crisis Group Middle East/North Africa Report No. 37, "Understanding Islamism" (March 2, 2005): It is "synonymous with 'Islamic activism,' the active assertion and promotion of beliefs, prescriptions, laws, or policies that are held to be Islamic in character. There are numerous currents of Islamism in this sense: what they hold in common is that they found their activism on traditions and teachings of Islam as contained in scripture and authoritative commentaries," 1.

4. Since 1899 the novel has been reprinted in whole or in extracts in Arabic and in translations. Chapters of the book were published by Shaykh Yusuf 'Ali in *al-Mu'ayyid* in 1899, and an edited complete version was published in 1902 by Rashid Rida in his newspaper *al-Manar*. Citations to the text will be from the edition of Mahmoud effendi Taher of *Jaridat al-'Arab* journal, n.d., registered in *Dar al-Kutub*, 1923.

5. The concept of the return of the "un-Islamic" historical epoch, generally attributed to the prominent ideologist of the Muslim Brotherhood, Sayyid Qutb, half a century later.

6. A legal decision by independent interpretation of the legal sources, the Qu'ran and sunna.

7. The question has led to a genre on crisis and renaissance that included famous responses such as that of Amir Shakib Arsalan's *Our Decline: Its Causes and Remedies* (largely based on Lothrop Stoddard's introduction, "The Decline and Fall of The Old Islamic World," in his *The New World of Islam*, London 1922),

and Marmaduke Pickthall's speech in Madras, India, in 1927, entitled "Causes of the Rise and Decline of Islam." Repeated like a mantra by reformers and Islamists alike, the question was brought back to center stage by Bernard Lewis's *What Went Wrong?: The Clash between Islam and Modernity in the Middle East* (New York: Oxford University Press, 2002), and the events of September 11, 2001.

8. "Abd al-Rahman al-Kawakibi, a Janus figure in modern Arabic political thought, makes this statement as well: 'Free man is a complete master of himself and is completely owned by his qaum.'" Sylvia G. Haim, "Islam and the Theory of Arab Nationalism," *Die Welt des Islams*, n.s. 4, no. 2/3 (1955): 124–149. According to Haim, the conception of the *umma* in modern Arabic, to which al-Kawakibi has largely contributed, has become almost inseparable from the notion of nationalism, a secular notion imported from the West, 137–138.

9. Norbert Tapiero, *Les Idees Reformistes D'al-Kawakibi 1265–1320 = 1849–1902 contribution a l'étude de l'Islam moderne* (Paris: Les Éditions Arabes, 1956); and Antonino Pellitteri, "Abd al Rahman al-Kawakibi (1853/54–1902): Oriente Moderno," n.s. 15, no. 76 (1966): 1, 3–7, 9–49, 51–55, 57–69.

10. Abd al-Rahman al-Kawakibi Jr., "Introduction," in *Al-A'mal al-kamila lil-Kawakibi (The Complete Works of al-Kawakibi)*, ed. Mohamed Jamal Tahhan (Beirut, 1995), 16.

11. Nikki Keddie, *An Islamic Response to Imperialism: Political and Religious Writings of Sayyid Jamāl ad-Dīn "al-Afghān"* (Berkeley: University of California Press, 1983), 3ff.

12. Tahhan, 17.

13. *Al-Shahba'*, issues 1–11, Tahhan, 111–251. Issues twelve to sixteen are missing. On the troubled course of its publications see Tahhan, 65–71.

14. Tahhan, 43, 252–258.

15. Tahhan, 24–29.

16. Tahhan, 29–30. For a slight variation see also Martin Kramer, "Azoury: A Further Episode," *Middle Eastern Studies* 18, no. 4 (October 1982), 351–358. Quoting W. S. Blunt in his *Diaries II* (London, 1920): "Urfi Pasha . . . an informant in the Khedive's service, . . . with transparent excitement, reported to the Khedive the initial appearance and content of Kawakibi's *Umm al-Qura*, and later provided the Khedive with a copy of the rare book," 355. Apparently all were under the impression that the events of the novel had really taken place.

17. Otherwise stated, all translations of the text are mine. Since the novel is written primarily as a memoir and employs strong rhetorical strategies, I have allowed myself some poetic license.

18. Interestingly, to see how the fictional and the real interweave, the real General or World Muslim Congress held in Mecca, 1926, and convened by King 'Abd al-Aziz Ibn Saud, similarly had delegates from Palestine, the Hijaz, Egypt, the Sudan, Russia, Turkey, India, and Java.

19. Tahhan, 284.

20. What is remarkably missing is a representative of the Sudan, where the story of al-Mahdi's revolt was unfolding, and also the total omission of the historicity of the novel.

21. Al-Kawakibi, similar to his protagonist al-Sayyid al-Furati, was reported to have rented a second house in Aleppo where he allegedly met in secret

with his unidentified foreign friends—some of whom could also have been Italian activists—to discuss political affairs of the day. See Tahhan, 26.

22. These threats are never identified or articulated by the speakers. However, using the thesis of the novel that the Ottomans are the main causes of decline, one can safely conclude the probable threats: the possibility of growing power of the Ottomans in the region which would threaten Arab ambition to establish autonomous rule. High on the list was the Hijaz Railway Project running from Damascus to Medina, which would help strengthen the authority of the Ottoman Empire over Arab provinces. The railway would also protect Mecca and Arab provinces from British invasion by facilitating the movement of troops, which would in turn provide Ottoman support for al-Rashidi against their rivals, the House of Saud, leading to the defeat of the latter. The ambition of the British government, as well as Western powers, to displace Ottoman influence in the region by promoting the "Arab Caliphate" can be inferred from W. S. Blunt's, *The Future of Islam*, first published in 1882. See "The Modern Question of the Caliphate," *The Future of Islam*, ed. Riad Nourallah (London: Routledge, 2002).

23. The novel takes place during the period between the fall of the second Saudi-Wahhabi State (1824–1891) and the rise of 'Abd al-'Aziz ibn Saud in 1902 against the Ottoman-backed al-Rashid family.

24. Though this appellation now refers to the Muslim Brotherhood almost exclusively, it is a reminder of the thread between the early Wahhabi informed Salafi trends and the more formal present day Ikhwanis passing through the late nineteenth century "liberal" reformers.

25. This formula points to two main trends that are interrelated: an objectification of Islam as an actor that has its interests and character independent of its carriers—one that becomes gradually formed through the writings of the Orientalists and reformers of this period and which is later inculcated in curricula of the modern education system (as noted in the works of Dale Eicklemann) and modern religious studies; and secondly, a corresponding distinction between those who call themselves Muslim and the "true" Muslims who represent the interests of that essentialized Islam (as developed in the later works of Sayyid Qutb).

26. A footnote by al-Kawakibi unabashedly expresses through the voice of his Meccan delegate regrets that these non-Arab "intruders," who had injected the rules of shari'a with the remnants of their pagan beliefs had converted, joining the ranks of Muslims: "Would that they had not joined it thereby desecrating it and usurping the rightful claims of *Quraish [Qurayish]* to leadership!" 289.

27. "*Madhhab as-salaf as-salih* is no new viewpoint among Muslims, for it is the view of all of the people of the Arabian Pennisula except for the [racially] intermixed Hijaz population" (281). The distinction is a strategic one since the people of Hijaz's amenability to diverse cultures, intellectual movements, and Sufism is thereby attributed to a racial defect and a contamination by foreign elements, therefore confirming the natural superiority of the Wahhabi Najdis over their own brethren. The pure religion can only be sought from among the *muwahhiddun* tribes of Najd.

28. A concept utilized by Sayyid Qutb, ideologist of the Muslim Brother-

hood, half a century later in order to justify breaking away from the mainstream *umma*. It is also the underlying concept developed by later Islamists and followers of Qutb that allows jihad against professed Muslims in the name of defending the faith and which later produces the more radical modern *takfiri* (Muslims who reserve the right to accuse other Muslims of apostasy) concepts.

29. Disregarding the irony of al-Kawakib's own questionable Arab ethnicity, his claim should not be taken lightly. Al-Kawakibi repeatedly stresses the mythical "fact" that the Arabs of the peninsula have not intermarried with women of "inferior/despicable" blood unlike other urbanized Muslims: "They marry from Arab stock of reputed birth and morals and have preserved their race and customs intact; they mix with others but do not intermarry" (391). This myth finds its way through the rhetoric of so-called "transnational" Islamists and surfaces in unlikely places as in an interview with Osama bin Laden. Though he starts out with a religious based identity ("I am a Muslim born to Muslim parents"), he inadvertently boasts of the one that is based in his "pure" Arab racial stock. When asked, "Is it correct that a daughter of Mulla Omar [the Afghan Taliban leader] is your wife or your daughter is Mulla Omar's wife?" Osama Bin Laden answers laughingly, "All my wives are Arabs (and all my daughters are married to Arab *Mujahidīn*). I have a spiritual relationship with Mulla Omar. He is a great and brave Muslim of this age. He does not fear anyone but Allah. He is not under any personal relationship or obligation to me. He is only discharging his religious duty. I, too, have not chosen this life out of any personal consideration" (Hamid Mir, the last journalist to interview Osama bin Laden, at http://www.maldivesculture.com/maldives_osama_bin_laden.html). It would seem that though Mulla Omar enjoyed fine religious qualities, his blood was still not fit for procreating with an Arab woman, since it would then devalue her offspring and become an impediment to its ascension to leadership. It is as though the supremacy of the Arab Wahhabi *mujahid* becomes almost a birthright. Osama bin Laden also conveniently disregards the intermarriage of the house of Saud with many non-Arabs.

30. For a history of the term Islamism, see Martin Kramer, "Coming to Terms: Fundamentalists or Islamists?" *Middle East Quarterly* (Spring 2003): 65–77. Even though French Orientalists such as Ernest Renan, in his essay *L'Islamisme et la science*, in 1883, used this term to refer to Islam as the religion of the Muslim people, al-Kawakibi strategically adopts it because of its nuanced meanings. It suggests both an identification with Islam as a religion, as well as a distinction from what would currently be believed to be Islam. Accordingly, he includes the need to define it and to determine the means by which to adhere to *Islamiyya* among the ten questions posed to the conference participants: "What is Islamism?" and "How can one practice or adopt *Islamiyya*?"

31. One should not underestimate the appeal of this sacred geography to subsequent Islamic activists and their manipulative use of it to gain support for their actions. One has only to examine the use of rhetorical appeals used by Osama bin Laden in justifying his grievances against the United States and claiming it as a legitimate target for his jihad: the placing of "infidel" American troops around *Harmain Sharifain* (the Noble Sanctuaries: Mecca and Me-

dina). By conflating Saudi Arabia, the modern nation state, with the mosques of Mecca and Medina, the most sacred symbols of Islam, he thereby evokes affront at the supposed injury of desecration of the kingdom's sanctity. Hamid Mir, the last journalist to interview Osama bin Laden, at http://www.maldives culture.com/maldives_osama_bin_laden.html. It would be interesting in this light to re-read Blunt's words: "Indeed 'Mecca, the seat of the Caliphate' is, as far as I have had an opportunity of judging, the cry of the day with Mussulmans; nor is it one likely to lose strength in the future. Like the cry of 'Roma capitale,' it seems to exercise a strong influence on the imagination of all to whom it is suggested, and when to it is added 'a Caliphate from the Koryyesh,' the idea is to Arabs at least irresistible. How indeed should it be otherwise when we look back on history?" in his chapter "The True Metropolis—Mecca," *The Future of Islam*, 130.

32. Blunt's account of the pivotal role that Wahhabism played and continues to play in movements of Islamic revival reveals a correspondence between Orientalist rhetoric and constructions and those of the reformers: "Politically and religiously the Mussulman world was asleep, when suddenly it awoke, and like a young giant refreshed stood once more erect in Arabia. The reform preached by Abd el Wahab was radical." *The Future of Islam*, 83.

33. See Tamara Albertini, "The Seductiveness of Certainty: The Destruction of Islam's Intellectual Legacy by the Fundamentalists," *Philosophy East & West*, University of Hawaii, 53, no. 4 (October 2003): 455–470. Her thesis: "The damage they [fundamentalists] are doing to Islam's intellectual and scholarly legacy is of such a systematic nature that it is hard to believe this to be an expression of sheer ignorance of how theological and legal matters ought to be dealt with. It is my deepest conviction that this state of affairs is the result of a well-thought-out strategy designed eventually to remove any scholarly resistance to fundamentalism from within the Muslim world. Whereas much attention has been devoted to its anti-Western ideology, almost no mention has been made so far of its massive assault on the intellectual culture of Islam" is easily corroborated by the novel's deliberations and findings, which aim to discredit the ulama and their scholarship.

34. See for instance Blunt's summary dismissal of the legacy of the Ottoman ulama: "The Turkish *ulema*, ever since their first appearance in the Arabian schools in the eleventh century, finding themselves at a disadvantage through their ignorance of the sacred language, and being constitutionally adverse to intellectual effort, had maintained the proposition that mental repose was the true feature of orthodoxy, and in their fatwas had consistently relied on authority and rejected original argument. They therefore readily seconded the sultan in his views. Argument on first principles was formally forbidden in the schools; and for the interpretation of existing law two offices were invented—the one for dogmatic, the other for practical decisions, those of shekh [shaykh] el-Islam and the Great Mufti. This closing of doctrinal inquiry by the Ottoman sultans, and the removal of the seat of supreme spiritual government from the Arabian atmosphere of Cairo to the Tartar atmosphere of the Bosphorus, was the direct and immediate cause of stagnation that Islam suffered from so conspicuously in the seventeenth and eighteenth centuries," *The Future of Islam*, 100.

35. Haim's tracing of al-Kawakibi's adaptation of Alfieri's diatribe against monotheistic religion in general to a critique of Islamic Sufism and corrupt exploitative ulama is substantiated by the extreme rhetoric and metaphors that do not easily fit within the traditional Islamic critique of Sufism. The Western context that frames this condemnation is unmistakable. See Haim, "Alfieri and al-Kawakibi," 329–330.

36. Reflecting on the culmination of such sentiments, look at Osama bin Laden's ease at brushing away shari'a and its condemnation of his actions: "The fatwa of any official Aalim has no value for me. History is full of such *Ulema* who justify *Riba* [usury], who justify the occupation of Palestine by the Jews, who justify the presence of American troops around Harmain Sharifain. These people support the infidels for their personal gain. The true *ulema* support the Jihad against America." The distinction between false and true ulama is thus based on their position versus the justification of jihad against politically designated "infidels" and not on their religious learning or their legal body of evidence. Again, Albertini's thesis seems relevant here: "One needs to pay attention to the eminent danger coming from leading fundamentalists who are aiming at disabling entirely the Islamic scholarly tradition, realizing all too well the threat that this tradition represents to fundamentalism's violent anti-Western ideology and generally to its attempt at controlling and manipulating Muslim societies," 456.

37. *The Future of Islam*, 85.

38. The study of Olivier Roy on globalized Islam is pertinent to the understanding of the appeal of Islamism to the full spectrum of Westernized Muslim youth and the inculcation of the values of "no hierarchy, no order of knowledge, no gradation" in their diverse movements. See "The Loss of Religious Authority and the 'Objectification of Isalm,'" and "The Crisis of Authority and Religious Knowledge," in *Globalised Islam: The Search for a New Ummah* (London: Hurst, 2004), 151–156, 158–171.

39. We even can see how it had shaped Sayyid Qutb years before his "radicalization/Islamization." His childhood autobiography's, *A Child from the Village*, opening chapters expose the imposture *sufi madhjub* (enraptured mystic who is "drawn" to the highest divine realms without his own striving) and the pompous ignorant *'alim* and the ineffectual *kuttab*, the religious madrassa. On the other hand, the book extols the modern secular school in which, as he recalls, he spent his happiest times. Qutb pointedly informs us that he, as a child, could replace the religious educational curricula of the *kuttab* with his own self-styled learning of the Qu'ran, proving the formal religious madrassa redundant. A look at Osama bin Laden's childhood schooling shows an uncanny correspondence; see, Steve Coll, "Young Osama: How He Learned Radicalism, and May Have Seen America," *New Yorker*, December 12, 2005.

40. Look up, for example, the debate between Mahmud Shukri al-Alusi (1857–1924) and Yusuf al-Nabahani (1849–1932) in defense of *ijtihad*: Mahmud Shukri al-Alusi, "*Ijtihad* and the Refutation of Nabahani" in *Modernist Islam 1840–1940: A Sourcebook*, ed. Charles Kurzman (Oxford University Press, 2002), 158–170.

41. Olivier Roy notes: "What is often called the 'Wahhabisation' of the Is-

lamic curriculum (namely reducing the corpus to only the Koran and Hadith, literally interpreted) does not mean that Wahhabi doctrine is replacing more traditional teachings. What it does involve is a diminution of the curriculum in terms of content and length of studies." *Globalised Islam*, 170.

42. Muslim jurists qualified to interpret the law and generate *ijtihad*.

43. Reference is to Ahmad Khan ibn al-Sayyid Taqiyy Khan (1817–1898), Tahhan, 323.

44. In the *al-Manar* edition of *Umm al-qura* al-Kawakibi notes that this hadith material is compiled by the scholar al-Imam al-Shawkani al-Yemeni (1759–1834), Tahhan, 337. Tahhan proposes that al-Kawakibi might have meant the commentary by Shawkani on *Kitab Muntaqa al-Akhbar* (n. 326). Interestingly, al-Shawkani, the Zaydi Shi'a who converted to Sunni Islam, became the proponent of the necessity of *ijtihad* for ulama and rejection of the principle of *taqlid* (imitation in legal matters) and was possibly an inspiration for al-Kawakibi's Yemeni character.

45. Baber Johansen, "The Constitution and the Principles of Islamic Normativity against the Rules of *Fiqh*," in *Dispensing Justice in Islam*, ed. Muhammad Masud, Rudolph Peters, and David Powers (Leiden: Brill, 2006), 168–193.

46. See Roy, "The Religious Market and the Sociology of Islamic Actors," 171–175.

47. One has to remember in this context that Sayyid Qutb's *Ma'alim fi'l-Tariq* also addresses a vanguard that will accomplish the next uprising.

48. Outlined through the works of, for example, Olivier Roy and Gilles Kepel.

PART II

Enver Pasha in uniform, 1911, by Nicola Perscheid.

General Enver Pasha on the cover of *Sport and Salon* magazine, 1917, by Carl Pietzner.

CHAPTER 6

Revisiting Networks and Narratives:
Enver Pasha's Pan-Islamic and Pan-Turkic Quest

ŞUHNAZ YILMAZ

As profound changes are currently taking place in the Muslim world, intersecting trajectories of numerous subversives and mavericks once again transform the social and political landscape of the Mediterranean. The rise of Enver started a century ago in the Balkans and along the shores of Tripoli, and his fall, which mirrored the fate of the Ottoman Empire, ended with his death fighting along the Basmachi tribes in Bukhara. He often had to navigate in uncharted waters at a time of drastic political change and turmoil, and the intricate networks he operated in often facilitated this arduous journey.

While Enver's activities as a part of the triumvirate of the Committee of Union and Progress (CUP) or his role during World War I is much better known, the earlier period gave way to his rapid rise. However, his struggles after the war and the fall of the Ottoman Empire have received very little attention. Ultimately, his pan-Islamic and pan-Turkic agenda led to his death fighting in Bukhara, but as a result of his failure, these later chapters in his life are not part of the better-known narrative of the collapse of the Ottoman Empire and the rise of modern Turkey. Nevertheless, his life reflects the drastic change and turmoil at the end of empire and the multilayered networks in which he navigated. While these networks were originally based in the Balkans and the Mediterranean, during his earlier career, in the later period after 1918 they were directed toward the East. Eventually, Enver got entangled in the struggle to control Central Asia, amid the Russian civil war and the emergence of the Soviet Union. This transition, where ultimately the Muslim Mediterranean drops out of the picture, in many ways reflects the realities of a changing geopolitical landscape as well.

With the fall of the Ottoman Empire at the end of World War I, Enver was forced to give up his political and military position and to escape abroad. This study aims to shed light on the intricate web of networks that he formed during his émigré years (1918–1922) extending all the way from Anatolia to the Caucasus and to Central Asia. First, he attempted to collaborate with the Bolsheviks and tried to resume a leading role in the nationalist struggle in Anatolia. Failing to achieve this goal, he pursued pan-Islamic and pan-Turkic ideals and joined the Basmachi movement in Central Asia. In this period, Enver utilized a number of old and new networks, while navigating in unfamiliar territory and cultures. This study aims to provide a critical analysis of Enver's motives, role, and impact in an intricate web of networks in this eventful final chapter of his life.

Enver's Rise: Activities and Networks in the Mediterranean

Enver is one of the most controversial figures in Turkish history. On different occasions, he has been labeled as a subversive, hero, or maverick. Hence, it is extremely interesting to revisit the networks he operated in and narratives of history concerning Enver. There are few people in Turkish history whose rise and fall have been as influential and dramatic as that of Enver Pasha. This young graduate of the Imperial War College was only in his mid-twenties when he became the "hero of freedom" after the Young Turk Revolution of 1908. Thus, his rapid rise within the military ranks started.

In 1909, Enver became a military attaché in Berlin, where he formed personal contacts with some high level German government officials and even the Kaiser himself. In this period, he developed a lifelong admiration for German culture and military power. During April 1909, Enver returned to Istanbul to join the Action Army (*Hareket Ordusu*) in the suppression of a conservative counterrevolution against the constitutional government. This incident resulted in the consolidation of the power of the CUP, leading to the overthrow of Abdülhamid II and his replacement by his brother Mehmet V. After the revolution of 1908, Enver (together with Cemal Bey) had an increasingly significant role in army committee relations as well.

Enver increased his fame further at Tripoli of Barbary. In the autumn of 1911, he volunteered to fight in the Libyan war against the Italians, during which he successfully organized Arab tribes in resistance. He fought with such distinction that he earned a double promotion to the rank of a lieutenant colonel. Particularly, the defense of Benghazi (Cyrenaica) enabled Enver to display his organizational skills by forming effective defensive units from Arab tribes. In this period, Enver wrote a series of letters to the sister of Hans Humann, the German naval attaché in Istanbul, which reveal detailed information about his ideas and activities in Tripoli.[1] On the one hand, Enver despised the European attempts to dismember the Ottoman Empire, while, on the other hand, he admired European civilization and culture. For instance, in one of his letters he reveals this dilemma by saying "your civilization is a poison, but a poison that awakens people."[2] When Enver's frustration with the lack of supplies and money grew worse, he started to express stronger resentment toward the European powers, especially at the Italians and the British. Eventually, he stopped reading European newspapers and built himself a "palace" like "an oriental general's tent" having neither windows nor a door because of the lack of glass and wood.[3] Moreover, Enver even printed paper money bearing the signature of the "New Saviour of Tripoli of Barbary, Enver Bey."[4] Enver's aspirations, however, could not be confined to ruling a distant land of the Ottoman Empire. Hence, when the developments in the Balkans and the First Balkan War shifted the attention of the Ottoman Empire to a much closer threat, Enver left Benghazi to defend the crumbling empire, as well as to fulfill his aim for greater power.

Enver strongly criticized the government's passive policies throughout the Balkan Wars. He particularly opposed the plans to cede Edirne as a part of a peace settlement. Edirne had a strategic importance, as well as a symbolic significance as the former capital (1365–1453) of the Ottoman Empire. He accused the influential senior bureaucrats for "signing the will of the fatherland with their shaking hands."[5] On January 23, 1913, Enver led an attack by a small group of Unionist officers on the sublime porte. The grand vizier was forced to abdicate at gunpoint and the minister of war was killed. They stated the goal of this coup d'état, known as the "Sublime Porte Incident," as an energetic resumption of the Balkan War to avoid further territorial losses. However, ultimately the complete loss of Macedonia, most of Thrace, and even Edirne would indicate how distant they were from achieving their aims. On the domestic scene, the coup resulted in the establishment of a Union and Progress Party cabinet with Mahmud Şevket Pasha as the grand vizier. After the assassination of Mahmud Şevket on June 11, 1913, the triumvirate formed by Enver, Talat, and Cemal Pasha started ruling the country. Thus, the power was transferred from the constitutional monarchy of 1908 to the rule of a Committee of Union and Progress triumvirate, which would last until 1918.

Enver's eventual transformation from a young and ambitious hero of freedom, to a skillful organizer and dauntless warrior, into a virtual autocrat as a member of the ruling triumvirate of the CUP, was completed in 1913. As the CUP became increasingly penetrated by Turkist ideas, a shift emerged from the convenient ambiguity of all-encompassing Ottomanism and relatively more inclusive pan-Islamism to pan-Turkism. This caused the non-Turkish subjects of the empire to feel less and less comfortable. As the reactions in the periphery hardened, the attraction of alternative ethnonationalist organizations grew accordingly. Greek, Bulgarian, and Armenian nationalism, which also had external support, was already quite strong. Under the CUP, Albanian and Arab nationalism became significant movements as well.[6] The unraveling process of the empire had already started.

Since Enver served a major role in the restoration of the parliament and the constitution in 1908 as the "hero of freedom," such a transformation might seem surprising. However, as Hanioğlu highlights, "Except for its value as a 'modern' symbol and a mechanism for preventing Great Powers' intervention, 'parliament' as well as 'representative' government meant little to the Young Turks and their adherence to Le Bon's theories viewing assemblies as 'a type of mob' potentially hazardous to society, shaped their attitude toward parliament as an institution."[7] Thus, despite their claims of establishing a parliamentary system as their primary goal, their underlying motives were marked by a desire to limit the absolute powers of the sultan and to pursue a more active and militaristic approach in response to the dismemberment of the Ottoman Empire. Following this strategy, during the Second Balkan War Enver led the troops, which recaptured Edirne. This victory once again greatly enhanced his power and prestige. Reflecting his excessive self-confidence, he wrote, "I am as happy as a child, not because the entire Islamic world admires me, but because I am pleased with myself. I was the only person who could enter Edirne in a single night."[8]

In the following two years, Enver had a meteoric rise from the rank of a lieutenant-general to deputy commander-in-chief and ultimately to minister of war. He further consolidated his power in 1914, when he married an Ottoman princess, Nacive Sultan, joining the royal family and becoming the son-in-law of the caliph. Thus, at the outset of World War I, Enver emerged as a very powerful political and military figure. Enver Pasha had a decisive influence in leading the Ottoman Empire into the war as an ally of Germany. Consequently, as one of the most important Ottoman political and military leaders, he played a key role in determining the fate of a truncated empire, which, in turn, shaped his own destiny.

Émigré Years: Networks in Anatolia and the Caucasus

After the signing of the Mundros Armistice on October 30, 1918, marking the Ottoman defeat at the end of World War I, Enver, Talat, Cemal, and other leading Unionists left Istanbul on November 2, 1918, aboard a German vessel. In the meantime, in Istanbul court-martial proceedings issued death sentences in-absentia for the fugitive Committee of Union and Progress leaders. Talat Pasha then concluded, "Our political life is over."[9] Enver, however, had no intentions of leaving neither the political nor the military arena. He considered the Ottoman defeat only as a temporary setback. Thus, in the last meeting of the CUP leaders before their flight, Enver voiced his strong desire to fight "the second phase of the war." He optimistically emphasized that the Ottomans also won the Balkan War in its second phase.[10] Enver initially planned to go directly to the Caucasus as a new base for his struggle. He stated, "We lost the war. In accordance with the Armistice, the British will be coming to Istanbul. Rather than seeing the British in Istanbul like this, I am determined to go to the Caucasus to serve Islam."[11]

Even before World War I, during the September–October 1913 annual meeting of the CUP, formation of clandestine networks with Muslim and Turkic groups abroad became an official policy.[12] The Committee dispatched several special agents to Russia, Iran, India, and Afghanistan to carry out propaganda and clandestine activities, such as establishing secret branches of the CUP in the Caucasus and Turkestan.[13] With a substantial Turkic and Muslim population under tsarist rule, pan-Turkism and pan-Islamism became dominant themes in the Ottoman and German propaganda campaign against Russia during the war. Russian sources indicate that Turkish agents had actively crisscrossed Transcaucasia.[14] Before the Ottoman surrender in 1918, Enver Pasha had already established a military force in the Caucasus under the command of his brother Nuri and uncle Halil Pasha.[15]

Illness and his failure to reach the Caucasus forced Enver to postpone his plans to resume the fighting.[16] In the meantime, he received the news of the disbanding of the military unit in the Caucasus and the arrest of his relatives in command. These unexpected developments led Enver to join other fugitive CUP leaders in Germany.[17] During the winter of 1918–1919, Enver attempted to contact the British agents in Berlin for a settlement.[18] When he realized that these efforts were futile, he turned his attention once again to the East. His most important contact in this period was to visit the Bolshevik Comintern Secretary Karl Radek in prison to propose a Muslim–Soviet alliance against the British. Enver also played a role in the release of Radek by the Germans.[19]

In the meantime, Enver's persistent efforts to reach Russia were obstructed by a series of catastrophes. In one of his letters to Mustafa Kemal, Enver wrote, "With the realization that the aid for Anatolia would be provided only by the Russians, I agreed with the people here [meaning the CUP leaders in Germany] to leave for Russia accompanied by Bahaeddin Şakir Bey. However, during the course of one year, I was detained twice and spent five months in prison. I survived six plane crashes."[20] When Enver finally reached Moscow in early 1920, he established contacts with the Soviet foreign office and with Lenin. At the same time, he was in touch with the Turkish nationalist delegation, led by Bekir Sami, which was visiting Moscow.[21] In this period, Enver emerged as a significant intermediary in forming the initial networks between the nationalists in Anatolia and the Soviets in Moscow.

Representatives of the Ankara government initialed a friendship treaty with the Bolsheviks. The diplomatic bargaining for financial and military assistance, however, was deadlocked because of the Soviet insistence on the cession of the Van and Mush districts to Armenia.[22] At this point, Enver entered the diplomatic scene. In the end, the Soviets gave up their demands and agreed to provide the Turkish mission with a substantial amount of weapons and ammunition.[23] Although the nature and scope of Enver's contribution to the negotiations are unclear, after this meeting he wrote a letter to Mustafa Kemal enthusiastically informing him about his meeting with Chicherin accompanying the representatives from Ankara, boasting that the successful conclusion of negotiations was mostly due to his timely intervention.[24]

Mustafa Kemal, however, was quite skeptical about Enver's intentions while acting as an intermediary and trying to present himself as a representative of Turkish nationalists. Moreover, Mustafa Kemal was concerned that an overemphasis on pan-Islam by Enver might alienate the antireligious communists from the nationalist struggle in Anatolia. He wanted to emphasize, instead, the anti-British nature of the Turco–Soviet alliance and to present their aim as a struggle against British oppression, "which tries to lower all the Muslim and non-Muslim peoples of the East to the level of farm animals."[25]

The Soviets were not concerned about Enver's pan-Islamic motives at this stage. On the contrary, they thought that his networks and influence in the Islamic world could be manipulated in two major ways. First, Enver could assist in facilitating the unity of the Muslim peoples of the former Russian Empire under Soviet rule. In this period, during the Russian Civil War, the Soviet rule was under serious challenge in the Caucasus and, especially, in Central Asia. Second, Enver could instigate resistance against British imperialism in the Islamic world in general.[26] Hence, with the encouragement of the Soviets, Enver Pasha proclaimed the formation of a "Union of Islamic Revolutionary Societies" (İslam Cemiyetleri İttihadı) that was intended to be a Muslim Revolutionary International. This party's Turkish affiliate, the "People's Councils Party" (Halk Şuraları Fırkası), was also founded.[27] The Young Turk émigrés envisioned a division of labor among themselves in promoting anti-imperialist revolutionary networks in different parts of the Muslim world. Enver Pasha was to be in charge of Turkestan, Cemal Pasha of Afghanistan and India, and Halil Pasha of Iran.[28]

Enver participated at the communist-sponsored "Congress of the Peoples of the East" held in Baku September 1–9, 1920. He was not a part of the Kemalist Turkish delegation. Instead, Enver had a special status as representative of "the Union of the Revolutionary Organizations of Morocco, Algeria, Tunisia, Tripoli, Egypt, Arabia, and India," apparently in order to emphasize Enver's networks with the Muslim leaders of numerous local movements. Those ties, however, often had been limited to having conversations with them in Berlin. At the congress, Enver's speech juxtaposed communist terminology with Unionist ideas, often referring to the struggle against capitalism and imperialism, oppressed peoples, and national self-determination. He also attempted to justify the Ottoman entry into World War I on the side of imperial Germany as choosing a lesser evil that, at least, accepted the Ottoman Empire's "right to survival." He claimed that he had always fought against imperialist powers and his only goal was to preserve the independence of his country.[29]

Nevertheless, there was not much in the Unionist record that projected them as champions of either oppressed nations or the proletariat. Enver's enthusiasm for the Ottoman entry into World War I as an ally of the Germans and his role in the decision for Armenian deportations and massacres aroused further suspicions regarding the sincerity of his claims. Yamauchi emphasizes that, "At the Baku Congress, Enver was mistrusted by the majority of the communist deputies, especially those who were principally composed of non-Muslims, and they undoubtedly did not offer him a platform for further political ventures. It appears that the objectives of his Bolshevik sponsors, Zinoviev and Radek, were entirely defeated."[30] Moreover, the delegates from the Kokand and Gandje districts, who were not permitted to conclude their speeches, were spreading the news about the misdeeds of the Bolsheviks and the massacres of Muslims.[31]

During his stay in Baku, Enver established contacts with various Muslim groups, most significantly with the Volga Tatars and Mir-Said Sultan Galiev. He seems to have been greatly influenced by the ideas of the "Muslim National Communists" Sultan Galiev, Ryskulov, and Khodzhaev, who propagated support for all revolutionary movements in the colonial world and for communism with a nationalistic and Islamic undertone.[32] Tatar leader Sultan Galiev actually built on Lenin's ideas in *Imperialism, the Highest Stage of Capitalism*, arguing that the class struggle was now taking place on an international scale and the Europeans were exploiting colonized nations in the most advanced and brutal form through imperialism. He claimed that this exploitation has also permeated the Muslim world, naturally bringing along with it seeds of national liberation movements and revolution. Sultan Galiev argued, "All Muslim colonized peoples are proletarian peoples and as almost all classes in Muslim societies have been oppressed by the colonialists, all classes have the right to be called 'proletarians' . . . . Therefore it's legitimate to say that the national liberation movement in Muslim countries has the character of a socialist revolution."[33] As a result of these interactions, Enver combined his preexisting pan-Islamic and pan-Turkic inclinations with some communist ideas and terminology to produce the unique blend of communism, nationalism, and Islam reflected in Enver's political program entitled Mesai (Labor).

By the end of the Baku Congress, however, the Soviets realized that it had failed to meet their expectations. Zinoviev even sent a telegram to Lenin expressing his disillusionment with the results. In fact, Enver's personal contacts with a number of Muslim delegates, especially with those from Turkestan, were making the Russians quite apprehensive. The general opinion in Baku was that "he was 'advised' by the Soviet authorities to return to Moscow at his earliest convenience."[34] Thus the Baku Congress, which was supposed to be the highest point of Enver's collaboration with the Bolsheviks, led both sides to a realization of their conflicting interests and diverging paths.

Enver returned to Europe from October 1920 to February 1921 in an attempt to inaugurate the Islamic Revolutionary Societies. During this period, he established contacts with the Germans and the Italians for arms and ammunition sales to Moscow. In the meantime, he also tried to maintain an uneasy balance between acting as a loyal supporter of the Turkish nationalist cause and attempting to persuade the Bolsheviks to provide support for a military expedition to Anatolia.[35] He strove to present himself as a better leftist alternative for the Soviets than the nationalist government of Ankara.[36] Enver was very eager to regain his lost leadership position, which he believed that Mustafa Kemal had "usurped."[37] He had several meetings with the first ambassador of the Ankara government to Moscow, Ali Fuat Cebesoy, who tried to deter him from interfering in Anatolian affairs.[38] Bekir Sami Bey also tried to persuade Enver that he should fight for his fatherland and for Islam outside Anatolia in the East.[39] In response to these appeals, Enver wrote a long letter to Mustafa Kemal expressing his loyalty and his contentment to support the nationalist movement from abroad. However, when the Kemalists arrested Major Naim Cevad, whom Enver had sent from Russia to Anatolia with large amounts of propaganda material for the People's Councils Party, it was revealed that Enver had no intention of abandoning his former plans.[40]

Enver's scheme of initiating a national guerrilla resistance movement based in Anatolia dates back to 1915 and was instigated by the fears of an Allied breakthrough at the Dardanelles.[41] The key actor for implementing these plans, both during and after World War I, was the "Special Organization" (Teşkilât-ı Mahsusa) established by Enver in 1914. The Ottoman version of a military secret service, combining intelligence and propaganda activities with a guerrilla organization,[42] Teşkilât-ı Mahsusa initially propagated pan-Islamic themes and later increasingly pan-Turkic ones. Its activities were complemented by the formation, in 1918, of another organization, the Guard (Karakol), which sheltered former Unionists. Karakol significantly benefited from the resources and expertise of Teşkilât-ı Mahsusa and played an important role in the national resistance by smuggling men and materials to Anatolia and by establishing clandestine resistance cells. The nationalists also made extensive use of the secret depots of arms and ammunition established by Teşkilât-ı Mahsusa.[43] These organizations and a group of former Unionists in Anatolia still supported Enver, and he tried to utilize these networks to regain control in Anatolia.

During the early stages of the nationalist struggle, Mustafa Kemal's position was not totally secure. Reports indicated that "Baku, the

Unionist stronghold, at the center of the Oriental intrigue" was becoming "the rival of Angora."[44] The British even considered Enver and his followers to pose a more serious threat than the Kemalists. According to them, there were "two parties in Anatolia, not only one. The weaker is that of Mustafa Kemal and the Nationalists. . . . They have failed and their adherents are going over to the other far more dangerous party, that of Enver, Talat, and the C.U.P.—Jewish-German-Bolshevik combination."[45] Enver, eagerly striving to capture the leadership of the nationalist movement, had been gaining strength.

In this period, when the ultimate victor of the leadership battle in Anatolia was still unclear, the Soviets provided support for both sides. On the one hand, the nationalist delegations were visiting Moscow,[46] and Mustafa Kemal was corresponding with the Soviet Foreign Commissar Chicherin.[47] On the other hand, the Soviets were also financing the Unionist campaign.[48] Mustafa Kemal was seriously concerned about the challenge posed by Enver. The Turkish Grand National Assembly issued a decree on March 12, 1921, prohibiting Enver and Halil Pasha's return to Anatolia "since this would be detrimental to the internal politics and external relations" of the Ankara government.[49] On July 16, 1921, Enver wrote to Mustafa Kemal, "By the news, which you have been sending through my friends, I understand that you do not want us to return. . . . For the time being since we are being helpful to our motherland in Moscow, we are not coming back. . . . However, when we start to feel that . . . our staying abroad becomes useless and even dangerous for Turkey . . . and the Islamic world, we will return to Anatolia.[50]

Enver's efforts and expectations to regain control of Anatolia reached their peak during the Greek offensive against Ankara. The nationalists began withdrawing and even considered temporarily moving the Turkish Grand National Assembly to another city further away from the war zone.[51] Just two weeks after writing to Mustafa Kemal, on July 30, 1921, Enver arrived at Batumi. He met with a number of other Unionists and started to wait for an opportunity to return to Anatolia. It is noteworthy that the Congress of the People's Councils Party, meeting in Batumi on September 5, 1921, revived the name "Union and Progress Party." It also demanded that the Ankara government abandon its hostility toward the émigré Unionists. According to Aydemir, Enver Pasha had even requested his uniform, sword, and decorations from Istanbul in preparation for his Anatolian expedition.[52]

In this period, Enver maintained his support among the émigré Unionists and was also closely linked with a number of influential fig-

ures in Anatolia, posing a serious challenge to Mustafa Kemal. As Rustow states, "The Trabzon Defense of Rights Society was openly sup-
porting Enver, and in the Ankara Assembly a group of about forty
ex-Unionists are said to have been working secretly to replace Kemal
with Enver."[53] Mustafa Kemal's decisive victory at the Sakarya battle of
September 2–13, however, consolidated his position, marking the end of
the Anatolian dreams of Enver and his supporters.

Last Battle among the Basmachi: Networks in Central Asia

In the wake of the battle of Sakarya, the Soviets shifted their support
wholeheartedly to Mustafa Kemal. Thus, Enver had to give up his plans
to regain power in Anatolia. This development ended his collaboration with the Bolsheviks. Moreover, events in Russian Turkestan had
already started to indicate Soviet designs for control over Central Asia
and forced Enver to realize the gloomy prospects of his hybrid ideology
of Bolshevism being compatible with Islam.

At the time of the Baku Congress, the new reformist government of
the Young Bukharans (*Yash Bukharalılar*) overthrew the Bukharan Emir
Alim Khan with the help of the Red Army, which stormed Bukhara
City.[54] The Young Bukharans constituted the political branch of the Reformist movement Jadidism in Turkestan. The Jadid movement had begun with a strong focus on education and targeted the improvement of
the traditional schools and madrassas (pl. mudaris). The movement assumed a political character in response to the oppressive policies of the
emir, who was perceived as a puppet of Tsarist Russia and its representatives in Bukhara. First, the 1916 uprising in Turkestan and then the 1917
October Revolution inspired the Young Bukharans to plan the overthrow of the emir.[55] Lacking any substantial military power, however,
they had to seek the assistance of the Soviet Commissariat in Tashkent
and the Red Army.

Following the deposition of the emirate in Bukhara, Mirza Rahim
Khan became the head of the interim government, Fayzullah Khoja
served as the president of the ministerial council, and Osman Khoja became the minister of finance on August 29, 1920. The Young Bukharans
who had replaced the emir, in collaboration with the Bolsheviks, proclaimed a People's Soviet Republic on September 2, 1920. Osman Khoja
served as the first and last president of the ephemeral Bukharan Republic between 1921 and 1922.[56]

Although the Young Bukharans anticipated that Bukhara would be at least semi-independent, they were soon greatly disillusioned. The pressure from the Red Army, the removal of the state treasury, and the increasing Russian control were clearly signs reflecting the genuine Soviet intentions. In the meantime, the fugitive emir still struggled to hold out in Eastern Bukhara with the support of a sporadic Muslim resistance movement, the Basmachi.[57] When Alim Khan's situation became totally untenable in Turkestan, he fled to Afghanistan in February 1921 and continued to support the Basmachi movement across the border. These disunited partisan bands contested Soviet rule over Turkestan in a period during the Russian Civil War following the October Revolution, when this region was cut off from European Russia by White armies. The partisans often came from different social classes and frequently fought under different leaders for different goals. What united the traditionalist and reformist Muslims, however, was their belief that Bolshevik policies posed a grave threat to Islam and their independence. Hence, eventually even a major part of the Young Bukharans would become active supporters of the Basmachi resistance against Soviet domination in 1922.

When the Soviets sent Enver Pasha to Central Asia in November 1921, they had three main motives. First, Enver would be prevented from intervening in Anatolian affairs. Second, his popularity among the Muslims could be exploited by the Soviets in order to curtail the support for the Basmachi. Finally, Enver could be useful in counteracting a possible attempt by the Afghans (with British support) to interfere in Central Asian affairs under the banner of Islam and pan-Islamic ideas. However, Enver had rather different motives of his own, which took their final shape during his visit to Bukhara.[58]

Enver's goal was to lead a pan-Islamic and pan-Turkic battle in Turkestan. He dreamed that a successful struggle in Turkestan would form the base for an international pan-Turkic state with a pan-Islamic undertone. Although he had received some news about the developments in this region through the Muslim delegates he met during the Baku Congress, he had very scarce knowledge about Central Asian realities. In his memoirs, the prominent Bashkir leader Zeki Velidi Togan describes his secret meetings with Enver in Bukhara. Togan acknowledged that Enver was "an idealist out of touch with real life and incidents. He has not read any of the European or Russian publications concerning the geography or statistics of Turkestan. Without any doubt he decided on what he was going to do in Turkestan during his stay in Bukhara."[59] The distorted information, most of which Enver received from Hacı Sami, sounded very tantalizing. Hacı Sami claimed, "In 1916, as a simple and unassuming Turk I raised all of Kirgizistan against the Russians. Given your [Enver Pasha's] great fame and popularity nothing can stand in our way in Turkestan."[60]

In addition to his pan-Turkic and pan-Islamic ideals, there were significant (and frequently overlooked) practical considerations shaping Enver's decision to abandon his communist allies. Ever since it had become evident that Enver could no longer play an important role in Anatolia, his relations with the Soviets had grown more ambivalent. There was also an increasing degree of mutual distrust. Enver was very alarmed when the Bolsheviks did not allow Cemal Pasha to visit Bukhara upon his return from Afghanistan to meet him. When he asked the Russian Consul Jurinev about the date of Cemal's return to Afghanistan, Jurinev replied, "The return of Cemal Pasha to these areas? Forget about it. We are also well aware of the kinds of activities you are engaged in here."[61] Togan argues that Enver perceived this bold remark as an outright threat and was considering that the Russians would eventually kill both Cemal Pasha and himself.[62]

Togan warned Enver numerous times during their secret meetings about the problems associated with his decision to join the Basmachis. He also cautioned Enver against any overt collaboration with them and the traditionally minded ex-emir. Togan also opposed the idea of a direct military confrontation with the Bolsheviks and advised Enver to support the movement from Afghanistan.[63] In this period, Enver even briefly considered returning to Berlin via Moscow to rejoin his beloved wife Naciye Sultan.[64] However, even his love for her and the birth of their youngest son were not enough to make him leave the battlefields. In the end, Enver's Central Asian dreams and idealistic motives prevailed. Only twenty-three days after his arrival in Bukhara, Enver used the pretext of going on a "hunting expedition" to defect to the Basmachis.

After Enver's defection, there was a radical change in how the Soviets depicted him. They blamed their disloyal partner as "an adventurist, to whom Turkey and afterward Bukhara were indebted for some of the most tragic and bloody pages of their history."[65] In fact, this Ottoman warrior, now unwanted in Anatolia, was seeking a new home that could form the base for his future glory.

The initial response of the Basmachis to Enver Pasha was far from cordial. Enver sent word to the fugitive emir in Afghanistan that he was willing to fight on his side. He also tried to meet with Ibrahim Laqay, a loyal supporter of Alim Khan and one of the major leaders of the Bas-machi movement in Turkestan in the ex-emir's absence. When Enver and his companions entered Laqay tribal territory under Ibrahim's con-trol, they were immediately disarmed, since they were distrusted as pre-vious Bolsheviks. In the following three months, Enver reported that he was a virtual prisoner in the hands of Ibrahim in numerous letters scrib-bled on tiny pieces of paper that Enver sent to his wife.[66] Gaining a bet-ter understanding of the movement into which he had rushed with very little knowledge, Enver soon became aware of the bigotry of many of the Basmachi bands. He wrote in despair to his wife: "After the morn-ing prayer in Göktaş, I cried while burning the photographs of you and our children. The people of this area are extremely conservative. There is constant propaganda against me. In order to destroy everything that would get a reaction from these bigots, I also had to burn the books that I had with me."[67] In the end, Enver acknowledged that it was a big illu-sion for an outsider like himself to think that he could accomplish some-thing with these people.[68] Ibrahim Bey released Enver after receiving a letter from Alim Khan granting Enver the title of "ghazi" and ordering that Enver should be allowed to fight for the cause of Islam as the son-in-law of the former sultan-caliph.[69] In addition, the intervention of Os-man Khoja was another important factor expediting Enver's release.[70] Finally, Enver was ready to fight.

As the paths of Enver and the Soviets diverged, relations between the Kemalists and the Bolsheviks rapidly improved.[71] In September 1921, Mustafa Kemal ordered the allocation of 40 percent of the production in the Black Sea region for the famine-struck Soviet Union as a gesture of Turkish support and goodwill.[72] Following the Turkish victory at Sa-karya, the Soviets resumed providing the Turks with financial aid, some arms, and ammunition. Although the Soviets never acknowledged it, Os-man Khoja has argued that the funds for this Soviet assistance had actu-ally been provided through financial support from the Young Bukharan government in Turkestan, which, in turn, was very supportive of the na-tionalist struggle in Anatolia.[73] On December 19, 1921, General Frunze, the Commander of the Ukrainian Red Army and a member of the ex-ecutive committee of the Communist Party in Ukraine, visited Ankara to sign a treaty of friendship between the Turkish nationalists and his government.[74] This was the same General Frunze who had led the Red Army into Turkestan and overthrown the emir of Bukhara in collabo-ration with the Young Bukharans. On another occasion, while Enver was fighting against the Bolsheviks in Eastern Bukhara during the early days of March 1922, Comrade Aralov, the new Russian Ambassador in Anatolia, was praising the strong bond of friendship between Ankara and Moscow.[75] Despite a degree of suspicion and mistrust, through their international isolation and respective struggles the bonds between the Turkish nationalists and the Bolsheviks grew stronger. In contrast, by this time Moscow had completely severed its ties to Enver.

The day after his release, Enver issued a declaration inviting the separate Basmachi bands to unite against Moscow under his command.[76] But the Basmachi often fought under different leaders for different aims. Enver Pasha struggled, without much success, to unite all the rebel leaders under his command. In the meantime, he had some considerable military achievements to his credit. In this period, the Young Bukharans' leader Osman Khoja started to become wary of the oppressive Soviet policies. He not only established close contacts with Enver Pasha, but even employed Turkish officers who had escaped from the Russian war prison camps in Krasnoyarsk while forming the Bukharan militia that would constitute the core of the future army of the republic.[77] By mid-spring 1922, at the peak of their power, Enver's forces controlled all of the eastern part of Bukhara. The Soviet authorities consequently attempted to negotiate with Enver in April 1922, but Enver's response was too demanding.

Enver refused to negotiate a truce with Moscow. Moreover, on May 19, 1922, he also sent an "ultimatum" through his friend Nariman Narimanov, the chairman of the government of Soviet Azerbaijan, giving the Soviets two weeks to withdraw their troops from Turkestan.[78] In response, the Soviets declared Enver an agent of the British and dispatched Red Army units to this region. Meanwhile, Enver had to struggle with a variety of additional problems, besides fighting the Russians. Basmachi bands of different ethnic origins were at times busier fighting each other than the Soviets.[79] There were especially deep animosities between Turkmens and Uzbeks and between Kirghiz and Uzbeks. In addition, Enver was still an "outsider" for many of the Basmachi leaders because of his pan-Islamic and Turanian ideas and history of collaboration with the Soviets. Ibrahim Bey, in particular, was a constant source of trouble for Enver from the outset. Enver even had to dispatch some forces to fight against him in July 1922.[80] About 16,000 rebels were operating in Eastern Bukhara. Yet, at most 3,000 were loyal to Enver.[81]

Enver, the self-proclaimed "Commander in Chief of all Islamic troops, son-in-law of the Caliph and the Representative of the Prophet," started issuing decrees on civil life in Bukhara. These bold moves made the ex-emir quite anxious and he began to withhold his support to En-ver. Since Enver counted on receiving significant military assistance via Afghanistan, he was deeply disappointed. He desperately attempted to produce his own ammunition at Baysun, but the results were highly dis-couraging.[82] Moreover, Enver often engaged in Ottoman-army-style open battles against the Soviets. However, the Basmachis were much more experienced and successful with guerilla tactics. Consequently, Enver's already weak forces started to diminish rapidly. Brief successes were increasingly followed by defeats and heavy losses. Nevertheless, Enver did not give up fighting until he was killed by machine-gun fire while leading a cavalry countercharge against a superior Russian force on August 4, 1922.[83]

After Enver's death the Basmachi resistance did not withstand the Soviet strategy of combining repression with a degree of appeasement (particularly on sensitive religious issues). Hence, although the Bolshe-viks aimed to carve up Central Asian republics within a federal system, which brought the ephemeral Bukharan experiment to an end, they also revived many of imperial Russia's Islamic institutions.[84] Thus, the So-viets withdrew their support from the Islamic reformists, whose insis-tence on independence was quite a nuisance for the Bolsheviks. At the same time, they restored *Waqf* land to mosques and reopened Quranic schools and Shari'a courts. Consequently, during the second half of 1922, popular support for the resistance movement sharply declined. Deprived of mass support, Basmachis were reduced to dispersed bands confined to mountainous areas. The resistance movement, however, would emerge once again during the Stalin era as a reaction to the com-pulsory collectivization of agriculture.[85]

As Enver was joining the Basmachi movement, he had said, "It is nec-essary to struggle for Turkestan. If you are afraid of the death that you deserve, you are doomed to live like a dog. You would be cursed by the past and future generations. However, if we are ready to die for indepen-dence, we can provide those who are following us with free and happy lives."[86] Enver failed to realize his grand dreams in Turkestan. Yet, at least he managed to achieve this last wish, to die on the battlefield just like the Ottoman Empire.

Conclusion

There are only a few political figures in Turkish history whose rise and fall have been as dramatic and controversial as that of Enver Pasha.[87]

When the Ottoman Empire lost World War I, he had to give up his position of military and political leadership. Although Enver left his country, he definitely did not leave the political scene. Consequently, Enver's émigré years provide significant insight into the formative stage of Turco–Soviet relations. Enver also presented a challenge to Mustafa Kemal's leadership of the nationalist struggle, which was mostly shaped around Unionist organizations. Enver's networks with the former Unionists in Anatolia and with the Bolsheviks abroad enhanced his determination to assume the leadership of the nationalist struggle. He had to forfeit this goal, however, after Mustafa Kemal's decisive victory against the Greeks in Sakarya.

The collaboration between the Bolsheviks and a group of émigré Unionists led by Enver did not last long. The shift of Soviet support to the Kemalists in Anatolia and Soviet designs for establishing control over Central Asia sealed the end of Enver's honeymoon with the Bolsheviks. These turns of events also inspired Enver to fight on the side of the anti-Soviet Basmachi resistance in Central Asia. During this last phase of Enver's life, his pan-Islamic and pan-Turkic ideas gained ascendance. Throughout his struggle in Central Asia, he strove to rally the support of the masses to his pan-Islamic and pan-Turkic ideals. He tried to achieve this goal by approaching local networks and leading an indigenous struggle against Moscow with limited resources and even less insight.

Enver's quest in Central Asia was laden with a number of problems from the outset. First, Enver had very limited knowledge of the realities of Turkestan and the Basmachi movement. Second, Enver tried to impose his pan-Islamic and Turanian ideals on an indigenous movement. Yet, the Basmachis had neither the intention nor the power to serve as a springboard for the formation of a pan-Islamic empire. They were just fighting against the Russian oppression. Finally, Enver lacked a realistic assessment of his capabilities and limits. His uneasy relations with the ex-emir, his bold ultimatum to Moscow, and his frequent engagement in open warfare rather than partisan resistance were just a few examples of this major weakness.

In assessing Enver's networks and activities in the Caucasus and Central Asia, it is crucial to understand the historical context and to revisit and challenge the existing narratives of history. Enver and his contemporaries were deeply traumatized by the rapid disintegration and the ultimate collapse of the Ottoman Empire. Yet, the Russian Revolution created new opportunities and challenges for them. Not only Enver, but also a number of his colleagues, perceived the rise of communist power and the prevalent revolutionary atmosphere as a golden opportunity to meet the challenge of the West. Thus, an analysis of their initial collaboration with Moscow and their subsequent promotion of pan-Islamic and pan-Turkic ideas should take into account these momentous changes in the international arena as well. Enver's émigré years were the final episode of a life-long quest for imperial and personal glory at a time of drastic change, marked by an intricate web of networks and rapidly shifting alliances.

Notes

The author conducted parts of the research for this article at the Center for Russian, East European, and Eurasian Studies (CREEES), Stanford University. The author gratefully acknowledges the support of the Center for her research. Moreover, the author also benefitted from TUBA-GEBİP and TUBİTAK-BİDEB grants in support of her academic research.

1. Şükrü Hanioğlu, *Kendi Mektuplarında Enver Paşa* (Istanbul: Derin Yayınları, 1989), 73–211.

2. Charles Haley, "The Desperate Ottoman: Enver Pasha and the German Empire–I," *Middle Eastern Studies* 30, no. 1 (January 1994): 13.

3. Şevket Süreyya Aydemir, *Makedonya'dan Orta Asya'ya Enver Paşa*, vol. 2 (Istanbul: Remzi Kitabevi, 1970), 234.

4. Haley, "The Desperate Ottoman," 11.

5. Hanioğlu, *Kendi Mektuplarında Enver Paşa*, 222.

6. Şükrü Hanioğlu, *A Brief History of the Late Ottoman Empire* (Princeton: Princeton University Press, 2008), 166–167.

7. Şükrü Hanioğlu, *Young Turks in Opposition* (New York: Oxford University Press, 1995), 31–32.

8. Hanioğlu, *Kendi Mektuplarında Enver Paşa*, 29.

9. Şevket Süreyya Aydemir, *Makedonya'dan Ortaasya'ya Enver Paşa*, vol. 3 (Istanbul: Remzi Kitabevi, 1970), 497.

10. Masayuki Yamauchi, *The Green Crescent under the Red Star: Enver Pasha in Soviet Russia 1919–1922* (Tokyo: Institute for the Study of Languages and Cultures of Asia and Africa, 1991), 9. In this book, Yamauchi publishes numerous documents from the Turkish Historical Association Archives, which hereafter will be indicated as THAA.

11. Letter from Enver Pasha (in Crimea) to his uncle Kamil Bey dated November 12, 1918 (THAA Klasör 2/ Fihrist 732), in Yamauchi, *The Green Crescent under the Red Star*, 79.

12. Jakob Landau, *Pan-Turkism: From Irredentism to Cooperation*, 2nd rev. ed. (Bloomington: Indiana University Press, 1995), 49.

13. Ibid., 50–52.

14. Y. K. Sarkisyan, *Ekspansionistkaya politika Osmanskoy Impyerii v Zakavkaz'ya*, chapter 2.

15. Halil Pasha, *Bitmeyen Savaş: Kütülmare Kahramanı Halil Paşa'nın Anıları*, M. T. Sorgun (Istanbul: 7 Gün Yayınları, 1972), 247–248.

16. Hüseyin Cahid Yalçın, "Tanıdıklarım: Enver Pasha," *Yedigün*, no. 150 (March 1936), 32.

17. Halil Pasha, *Bitmeyen Savaş*, 267–277.

18. Yamauchi, *The Green Crescent under the Red Star*, 13.

19. Erik Jan Zürcher, *Milli Mücadelede Ittihatçılık* (Istanbul: Bağlam Yayıncılık, 1987), 217.

20. Enver's letter from Moscow to Mustafa Kemal (Ankara), c. May 21 (THAA Klasör 7, Mustafa Kemal Dosyası, Fihrist 5), in Yamauchi, *The Green Crescent under the Red Star*, 229; "Haksız ve Lüzumsuz bir Ta'riz," *Liva-el Islam* 12 (September 1921): 1.

21. Dan Rustow, "Enver Pasha," *The Encyclopaedia of Islam*, 700.

22. Turkish Parliamentary Library (T. B. M. M. Kütüphanesi), *Minutes of Meetings of the Turkish Grand National Assembly*, "Reports and Discussions on the Relations with the Russian Bolshevik Republic," I.84, C.3, 10.16.1920; I.85, C.1, 10. *Gizli Oturumlarında Sorunlar ve Görüşler* 17.1920. Also, see Mustafa Kemal, *Türkiye Büyük Millet Meclisi, 1920–1923* (Problems and Opinions in the Confidential Meetings of the Turkish Grand National Assembly), ed. Raşit Metel (Ankara, 1990), 141–155.

23. The Soviets promised to deliver 15,000 Austrian rifles with 2,000 cartridges each, French guns for three batteries with 1,000 shells each, and one million cartridges. Yamauchi, *The Green Crescent under the Red Star*, 120.

24. Kazım Karabekir, *İstiklal Harbimizde Enver Paşa ve İttihat ve Terakki Erkanı* (Istanbul: Menteş Matbaası, 1967), 21.

25. Letter from Mustafa Kemal to Enver dated October 4, 1920, in Ali Fuat Cebesoy, *Moskova Hatıraları* (Istanbul: Vatan Neşriyatı, 1955), 56.

26. Şuhnaz Yılmaz, "An Ottoman Warrior Abroad: Enver Pasha as an Expatriate," *Middle Eastern Studies* 35, no. 4 (October, 1999), 49.

27. Dan Rustow, "Enver Pasha," *The Encyclopaedia of Islam*, 700.

28. Kazım Karabekir, *İstiklal Harbimizde*, 10–17.

29. Ibid.

30. Yamauchi, *The Green Crescent under the Red Star*, 33.

31. On the Baku Congress and Enver's role in it, also see Şuhnaz Yılmaz, "An Ottoman Warrior Abroad: Enver Pasha as an Expatriate," 50–51.

32. For further information on this issue, see Richard Pipes, *The Formation of the Soviet Union: Communism and Nationalism* (Cambridge, MA: Harvard University Research Center, 1968), 260–262.

33. Geoffrey Hosking, *The First Socialist Society: A History of the Soviet Union from Within*, 2nd ed. (Cambridge, MA: Harvard University Press, 1993), 110–111.

34. PRO FO 371/ 5178 (E 13412/345/44).

35. Yamauchi, *The Green Crescent under the Red Star*, 33–34.

36. Eric Jan Zürcher, *Milli Mücadelede İttihatçılık* (Istanbul: İletişim Yayınları, 1987), 227.

37. For a detailed account of the conflict and competition between Enver Pasha and Mustafa Kemal during this period, see Salahi Sonyel, "Mustafa Kemal and Enver in Conflict, 1919–1922," *Middle Eastern Studies* 25, no. 4 (October 1989): 506–515. For a psycho-biographical account of Enver's troubled relations with Mustafa Kemal, also see Norman Itzkowitz and Vamik Volkan,

The Immortal Atatürk: A Psychobiography (Chicago: University of Chicago Press, 1984), 76, 82–83, 93, 105.

38. Dan Rustow, "Enver Pasha," *The Encyclopaedia of Islam*, 700.

39. Bekir Sami Bey (Moscow) to Enver Pasha (Berlin), November 1920 (THAA Klasor 28/Fihrist 439), in Yamauchi, *The Green Crescent under the Red Star*, 125.

40. Dan Rustow, "Enver Pasha," *The Encyclopaedia of Islam*, 700.

41. Eric Jan Zürcher, *The Unionist Factor: The Role of the Committee of Union and Progress in the Turkish National Movement 1905-1926* (Leiden: Brill, 1984), 169. At that time, even leaving Ankara and establishing a base in Konya or Eskişehir was under consideration.

42. For additional information, see Ergun Hiçyılmaz, *Belgelerle Teşkilat-ı Mahsusa* (Istanbul: Ünsal Kitabevi, 1979); Philip Hendrich Stoddard, "The Ottoman Government and the Arabs, 1911-1918: A Preliminary Study of the Teşkilat-ı Mahsusa" (PhD diss., Princeton University, 1963).

43. Eric Jan Zürcher, *The Unionist Factor*, 168.

44. *Political Report on the Caucasus*, Constantinople, 7 September 1920 (confidential) PRO FO 371/5178 (E 14638/345/44).

45. S.I.S., September 2, 1920, no. 110/ 676/5, PRO FO 371/5178 (E 11702/ 345/44).

46. Turkish Parliamentary Library (T. B. M. M. Kütüphanesi), *Minutes of Meetings of Turkish Grand National Assembly*, "Reports and Discussions on the Relations with the Russian Bolshevik Republic," I.84, C.3, 10.16.1920.

47. Robeck to Curzon, June 12, 1920, no. 695, PRO FO 371/ 5178 (E 6346/345/44). See also attached article, "Tchicherine et Mustapha Kemal Pasha," in *La Cause Commune*, the Russian weekly newspaper published in Paris, sent by the British Embassy in Paris.

48. S.I.S., September 2, 1920, no. 110/ 676/5, PRO FO 371/5178 (E 11702/ 345/44).

49. Turkish Republican Archives, Decree of the Parliament concerning Enver and Halil Pasha, 3.12.1921, no. 731/ 385.

50. Turkish Republican Archives, Decree of the Parliament concerning Enver and Halil Pasha, 46–47; A. F. Cebesoy, *Moskova Hatıraları*, 231.

51. K. Gürün, *Türk-Sovyet İlişkileri (1920–1953)* (Ankara: TTK Yayınları, 1991), 46.

52. Aydemir, *Makedonya'dan Orta Asya'ya Enver Paşa*, vol. 3, 586.

53. Dan Rustow, "Enver Pasha," *The Encyclopaedia of Islam*, 700.

54. Edward Allworth, ed., *Central Asia: 130 Years of Russian Dominance, A Historical Overview*, 3rd ed. (Durham, NC: Duke University Press, 1994), 244–246.

55. For an Uzbek historian's detailed study of this period based on archival documents, see Hamid Ziyaev, *Turkistanda Rossiya Tajavuzi va Hukmranliga Qarshi Kurash* (Tashkent: Şark Naşriyet, 1998), 400–430.

56. Timur Kocaoğlu, "Osman Khoja (Kocaoğlu) between Reform Movements and Revolutions," in *Reform Movements and Revolutions in Turkistan: 1900–1924, Studies in Honour of Osman Khoja*, ed. Timur Kocaoğlu (Haarlem: SOTA, 2001), 31–48. This revealing study sheds light on a critical pe-

riod eclipsed by Soviet historiography regarding the Reformist Movement (Jadidism) in Turkestan and the activities of one of the leading members of its political branch of the Young Bukharans, Osman Khoja. After Osman Khoja came to Turkey, he adopted the last name Kocaoğlu.

57. In Richard Pipes, *Formation of the Soviet Union: Communism and Nationalism (1917–1923)* (Cambridge, MA: Harvard University Research Center, 1968), 178, there is a discussion on the obscure origins of the word *basmachi*. Pipes states that Zeki Velidi Togan traces the word from "basmak" meaning "to press" and *"basmachi"* being "the oppressed." According to Hosking, the term *basmachi* (brigands) was fastened on the various guerrilla groups by their opponents, while they referred to themselves as "freemen." Geoffrey Hosking, *The First Socialist Society*, 113. For a comprehensive account of the awakening of national consciousness among the various Turkic Peoples of Russia and different resistance movements, see Nadir Devlet, *Rusya Türkleri'nin Milli Mücadele Tarihi (1905–1917)* (Ankara: Türk Kültürünü Araştırma Enstitüsü, 1985).

58. Timur Kocaoğlu, "Osman Khoja (Kocaoğlu) between Reform Movements and Revolutions," in *Reform Movements and Revolutions in Turkistan: 1900–1924*, 40.

59. Zeki Velidi Togan, *Hatıralar: Türkistan ve Diğer Müslüman Dostu Türkleri'nin Milli Varlık ve Kültür Mücadeleleri* (Istanbul: Tan Matbaası, 1969), 392. Zeki Velidi Togan was a well-known and highly respected figure in Turanian circles and played a leading role in the Bashkirian struggle for independence.

60. Togan, *Hatıralar*, 390. These claims of Haci Sami were, of course, greatly exaggerated.

61. Aydemir, *Makedonya'dan Orta Asya'ya Enver Paşa*, vol. 3, 633.

62. Togan, *Hatıralar*, 391.

63. Togan, *Hatıralar*, 387–389.

64. Arı Inan, ed., *Enver Paşa'nın Özel Mektupları* (Ankara: İmge Yayınları, 1997). This book is a collection of the private letters of Enver Pasha written to his wife Naciye Sultan and Halil Pasha. The frequent letters of Enver Pasha (written almost on a daily basis) to Naciye Sultan usually have a very romantic and emotional tone.

65. Soloveichik, "Revoliutsionnaia Bukhara," *Novyi Vostok*, no. 22 (1922): 281.

66. Aydemir, *Makedonya'dan Orta Asya'ya Enver Paşa*, vol. 3, 641–658.

67. Ibid., 652.

68. Ibid., 658.

69. Said Alim Khan, *La Voix de la Boukharie Opprime* (Paris: Maisonneuve Frères, 1929), 36–37.

70. "Bukhara'nın Ilk ve Son Cumhurbaşkanı Osman Hoca Anlatıyor: Enver Paşa'yı Nasıl Kurtardım," *Yakın Tarihimiz* 1, 403–405.

71. Rumbold to Curzon, January 24, 1922, no. 95, Foreign Office Confidential Print (E 1107/27/44), vol. 3, 36.

72. Mustafa Kemal to Turkish Embassy in Moscow (letter to be presented to Chicherin), September 3, 1921, no. 2705, in Turkish Ministry of Culture, ed., *Atatürk'ün Milli Dış Politikası: Milli Mücadele Dönemine Ait 100 Belge (1919–1923)*, vol. 1 (Ankara: Kültür Bakanlığı, 1981), 353.

73. Osman Kocaoğlu, "Rus Yardımının İç Yüzü," *Yakın Tarihimiz*, vol. 1, 292–93; Mehmet Saray, *Atatürk'ün Sovyet Politikası*, (Istanbul: Veli Yayinlan, 1990), 76–78.

74. Kamuran Gürün, 76. The Treaty of Friendship was January 1922.

75. Rumbold to Curzon, Constantinople, March 7, 1922, no. 229 (confidential), Foreign Office Confidential Print 2755/5/44, vol. 3, 47.

76. Mehmet Saray, "Bukhara Cumhuriyeti'nin Türkiye'ye Yardımı," in *Reform Movements and Revolutions in Turkistan: 1900–1924* (Haarlem: SOTA, 2001), 345.

77. Raci Çakıröz and Timur Kocaoğlu, "Türkistan'da Türk Subayları (1914–1923)," *Türk Dünyası Tarih Dergisi*, no. 1–11 (1987), 40.

78. Joseph Castagn, *Les Basmachis* (Paris: Ernest Leroux, 1925), 49–50; Glenda Fraser, "Basmachi-II," *Central Asian Survey* 6, no. 2 (1987): 37–38.

79. Richard Pipes, *Formation of the Soviet Union: Communism and Nationalism*, 257.

80. Glenda Fraser, "Basmachi-I," *Central Asian Survey* 6, no. 1 (1987): 61.

81. K. Vasilevskii, "Fazy Basmacheskovo dvizheniia v Srednei Azii," *Novyi Vostok*, no. 29 (1930): 134.

82. Glenda Fraser, "Enver Pasha's Bid for Turkestan, 1920–1922," *Canadian Journal of History* 22 (1988): 207.

83. For a detailed account of Enver's death, see S. Aydemir, vol. 3, 683–686; and E. Kozlovskiy, Krasnaya Armiya, and Srdeney Azii (Tashkent: Publications of Political Administration, 1928), 37. In his book published by the Turkish Historical Association, Baymirza Hayit, however, gives the date of Enver's death as August 5, 1922. Baymirza Hayit, *Türkistan Devletlerinin Milli Mücadeleleri Tarihi* (Ankara: Türk Tarih Kurumu, 1995), 283.

84. Robert Crews, *For Prophet and Tsar: Islam and Empire in Russia and Central Asia*, first paperback ed. (Cambridge, MA: Harvard University Press, 2009), 365.

85. Geoffrey Hosking, *The First Socialist Society*, 113–114.

86. Vakit Muhittin Bey, 11.25.1923, quoted in Togan, *Hatıralar*, 395.

87. For a first hand account of the early years and rapid rise of Enver, see Enver Paşa, *Enver Paşa'nın Anıları (1881–1908)*, ed. Halil Erdoğan Cengiz (Istanbul: İşbankası Kültür Yayınları, 1991); Şükrü Hanioğlu, *Kendi Mektuplarında Enver Paşa*.

Bibliography

Aydemir, Şevket Süreyya. *Makedonya'dan Ortaasya'ya Enver Paşa*, vol. 3. Istanbul: Remzi Kitabevi, 1970.

Crews, Robert. *For Prophet and Tsar: Islam and Empire in Russia and Central Asia*. Cambridge, MA: Harvard University Press, 2009.

Devlet, Nadir Rusya. *Türkleri'nin Milli Mücadele Tarihi (1905–1917)*. Ankara: Türk Kültürünü Araştırma Enstitüsü, 1985.

Fraser, Glenda. "Basmachi-I." *Central Asian Survey* 6, no. 1 (1987): 61.

———. "Basmachi-II." *Central Asian Survey* 6, no. 2, (1987): 7-42.

―――. "Enver Pasha's Bid for Turkistan, 1920–1922." *Canadian Journal of History* 22 (1988): 207.

Gürün, K. *Türk-Sovyet İlişkileri (1920–1953)*. Ankara: Türk Tarih Kurumu Yayınları, 1991.

Haley, Charles. "The Desperate Ottoman: Enver Pasha and the German Empire," *Middle Eastern Studies* 30, no. 1 (January 1994): 13.

Hanioğlu, Şükrü. *Kendi Mektuplarında Enver Paşa*. Istanbul: Derin Yayınları, 1989.

―――. *Young Turks in Opposition*. New York: Oxford University Press, 1995.

―――. *A Brief History of the Late Ottoman Empire*. Princeton: Princeton University Press, 2008.

Hosking, Geoffrey. *The First Socialist Society: A History of the Soviet Union from Within*. 2nd ed. Cambridge, MA: Harvard University Press, 1992.

Inan, Arı, ed. *Enver Paşa'nın Özel Mektupları*. Ankara: İmge Yayınları, 1997.

Karabekir, Kazım. *İstiklal Harbimizde Enver Paşa ve İttihat ve Terakki Erkanı*. Istanbul: Menteş Matbaası, 1967.

Kocaoğlu, Timur. "Osman Khoja (Kocaoğlu): Between Reform Movements and Revolutions." In *Reform Movements and Revolutions in Turkistan: 1900–1924*. Haarlem: SOTA, 2001.

Landau, Jacob M. *Pan-Turkism: From Irredentism to Cooperation*. 2nd rev. ed. Bloomington: Indiana University Press, 1995.

Paşa, Halil. *Bitmeyen Savaş: Kütülmare Kahramanı Halil Paşa'nın Anıları*, M. T. Sorgun. Istanbul: 7 Gün Yayınları, 1972.

Pipes, Richard. *The Formation of the Soviet Union: Communism and Nationalism*. Cambridge, MA: Harvard University Research Center, 1968.

Yamauchi, Masayuki. *The Green Crescent under the Red Star: Enver Pasha in Soviet Russia 1919–1922*. Tokyo: Institute for the Study of Languages and Cultures of Asia and Africa, 1991.

Yılmaz, Şuhnaz. "An Ottoman Warrior Abroad: Enver Pasha as an Expatriate," *Middle Eastern Studies* 35, no. 4 (October 1999): 49.

Zürcher, Erik Jan. *The Unionist Factor*. Leiden: Brill, 1984.

―――. *Milli Mücadelede İttihatçılık*. Istanbul: İletişim Yayınları, 1987.

CHAPTER 7

Going to School: Women's Life Stories, Networks, and Education in Colonial North Africa, c. 1850–1962

JULIA CLANCY-SMITH

In 1943, as fierce military struggles over the future of North Africa, Europe, and the world raged in Tunisia, two young people secretly exchanged love letters by concealing them within the pages of dictionaries passed innocently back and forth. Tahar Darghouth, by then a mathematics instructor with diplomas from France and Algeria, wrote to his beloved Lilia (or Lili), who had attended the School for Muslim Girls in Tunis, the following:

> In order to more easily exchange correspondence, you can send me your letters by post addressed to Monsieur Darghouth, professor of mathematics at the Center of Secondary Studies, École primaire supérieure de Jeunes Filles à Rades. If you choose to do so, please send me your address.[1]

Thus, on the eve of the February 1943 Battle of Kasserine Pass, with Tunis still occupied by Axis troops, the lovers devised schemes to correspond by relying on trusted intermediaries (a cousin, Frida, Lili's Aunt Asma, and a host of others) who brought books and even novels back and forth. As bombs burst across the country, education continued for some students and passion eclipsed a world at war. But what is really telling is the networks that spun out from school, books and briefcases, family, servants, friends, and neighborhoods to permit Tahar and Lili to maintain contact—and eventually marry in July 1944. Later that same year, the couple relocated to Sfax, where Tahar accepted a post at the Lycée de Garçons. There he founded the first troop of "Scouts musulmans de Tunisie," whose members were his students, thus forging more circuits through schooling.[2]

Scholarship on girls' education in the late Ottoman Empire and precolonial or colonial Maghreb has expanded rapidly in the past decade as scholars pose new questions and deploy fresh approaches, notably gender theory, that are simultaneously institutional and biographical.[3] One question has yet to be explicitly raised: how did well-worn, novel, or concealed local and transnational connections shape opportunities for female education and thus the life trajectories of individuals and their social communities? This query opens up more questions: how did diverse states and, most importantly, colonial regimes, establish, redirect, or limit the range and density of networks? Even very current research emphasizing educational reforms and reformers neglects to explicitly trace the play of social conduits, particularly in debates regarding whether girls should be schooled. Indeed, one of the arguments marshaled against educating girls was that they would "be able to write letters to lovers, even while behind the veil."[4] Thus literacy itself expanded the reach of networks.

This was indeed what brought Tahar and Lilia together as a couple—writing ardent letters even though their families hailed from very different social milieus. In fact, their marriage was considered a *mésalliance* because Tahar's mother was the eldest daughter of the grand mufti of Tunis, Shaykh Belkhodja; his father's kin were notables as well. As for Lilia, her origins were more modest. Her father, Salah Djemaa, was a merchant from Djerba, and her mother came from the petty bourgeoisie of the capital city; they resided not in a splendid palace but in the *madina* near Place aux Moutons.[5] Indeed the move to Sfax by the newly wed Darghouth couple in 1944 was motivated by extended family discord in Tunis over their marriage, indirectly nurtured by schooling. Therefore, the kinds of social filaments generated by modern education were less amenable to scrupulous family management and engineering for successful marriage and household reproduction.

In addition, the changing nature of the state—in the case of Tahar and Lilia, the French Protectorate—can be teased out from their story. Originally established in 1900 by Protectorate officials with cooperation from some Muslim leaders to educate the girls of the Tunis notability, the School for Muslim Girls on Nahj Basha had become something else by the time that Lilia enrolled there for studies. The popular demand for education by Tunisians had outpaced and outwitted colonial efforts to restrict access to the classroom for both girls and boys. By the interwar period, this school attracted more diverse students, particularly from the petty bourgeoisie; it also educated many of the wives of Tunisian nationalist leaders.[6] Yet a comparative analysis of some places across France's empire reveals that male nationalist policies and discourse paradoxically muted women's voices, often for strategic political goals, while giving lip service to women's emancipation through schooling.

Inflected by gender norms, religious affiliation, generation, and class, schooling ensnared individuals and families in intricate relations that at times repositioned them in the local social order. Recent research defines networks as "phenomena that are similar to institutionalized social relations, such as tribal affiliations and political dynasties, but also distinct from them, because to be networked entails making a choice to be connected across recognized boundaries."[7] To the concept of some degree of choice can be added distinctions between homogeneous and heterogeneous networks, the latter more receptive to "new information and innovative behavior," which is critical for understanding shifting gender norms.[8] Conversational networks undergirded specific types of social communication, conferring an "insider" advantage about opportunities. Nevertheless, some kinds of networks are difficult to recuperate—for example, those undergirding secret political societies or organized illicit activities. For women's history, the challenge is even more daunting due to the matter of evidence and written source materials. Finally, individuals and their communities moved out of some social webs even as—or because—they engaged with new exchange circuits. That merits attention.

This chapter features the biographies of two North African women whose life stories are, however, intertwined with those of other women; they have been selected for several reasons. First, there is relatively abundant documentation on them. Second, their life stories, when juxtaposed, demonstrate how networks operated both in similar and different fashion within the larger context of families, households, and variant forms of French colonialism in the Maghreb.[9] From different generations, places, and social classes Fadhma Amrouche (1882–1967) and Tawhida Ben Shaykh (1909–2010) are relatively well known in North Africa, although they only appear episodically in conventional historical narratives.

My sources primarily consist of what these women said about themselves either in writing or during interviews as well as supplementary published or archival documentation.[10] Needless to say, the performative dimensions of life stories—including the critical factors of memory and audience—shape the record and thus the narrative. Moreover, each woman established different authorial relationships with her own story:

Amrouche initially composed an exclusively family memoir, while Ben Shaykh preferred that others write about her.[11] Nevertheless, a striking similarity emerges in these and other women's writings, which inevitably assume the guise of school memoirs. Indeed, Amrouche's first chapter is entitled "The Road to School." Thus I argue that by the mid-twentieth century, classroom remembrances constituted a new morally legitimate literary space for North African women's voices to be raised, heard, and committed to writing, and as such, represent a distinct, if unacknowledged, genre.[12] My methodology is to narrate each woman's story, pausing at strategic moments to analyze social fields yielding data on networks that in turn opened up possibilities, or conversely obstructed them, or somewhere in between.

There is nothing specifically North African or colonial about school memoirs, but gender I would argue is a key distinguishing element in the genre. In his last work, *Out of Place*, composed shortly before his death in 2003, Edward Said observed, "One of the things I tried to explore implicitly is the hold those very early school experiences had on me, why their hold persists, and why I still find them fascinating and interesting enough to write about for readers fifty years later."[13] In contrast, Albert Memmi, a Tunisian Jew born in 1920, expressed starkly unsentimental feelings about school in his *La Statue de Sel* (*The Pillar of Salt*) published in 1953: "How blind I was to what I really am, how naive it was of me to hope to overcome the fundamental rift in me, the contradiction that is the very basis of my life."[14] However, girls and women had a much more complicated relationship to learning and the schoolroom, which was conditioned not only by social class or colonial situation but also by local and familial gender norms, restrictions, and practices. As the Jewish-Tunisian lawyer and activist Gisèle Halimi (born 1927 in La Goulette) stated: "My studies and my readings gradually gave me the keys to defend myself . . . the *lycée* represented both a haven and a life for me where I learned, played, experimented, and read. In short, removed from the family foyer, I could be a young girl eager for knowledge and, despite all, happy to be alive."[15] And Halimi, from the same generation as Lilia Djemaa Darghouth, was a Jewish Tunisian student in Tunis during the Axis occupation and terrors of World War II.

Halimi's remark about the importance of physical distance or removal from her family household raises several issues. One is the historical processes that caused the older tradition of girls' moral/practical instruction, legitimated by religion, as locally received and centered in the home, to shift. Anthropologically, this represented a profound

The cover of a current edition of *Histoire de ma Vie.*

change—from a "house-based" society where the lineage oversaw the gendered transmission of knowledge for females, largely but not exclusively oral, to a society that accommodated, however unevenly or reluctantly, new ways of knowing and bodies of knowledge as well as new spaces of learning for women.[16]

Allowing female family members to attend colonial or foreign educational institutions, whether secular or missionary, entailed taking enormous social risks. Anbara Khalidi recalled that when she and her siblings were sent to the Saint Joseph Catholic school in Beirut just prior to World War I: "My brothers and I received a lot of criticism as we walked to and from school for our being enrolled in a foreign school, but most of the criticism was directed against my father."[17] Finally, the household as a site of scientific and cultural learning cannot be discounted. Both Khalidi and Hasiba Agha, elites to be sure, remembered vividly not only home-schooling in Arabic, the Qu'ran, and religious observances but also family gatherings with poetry recitals, readings, and musical performances.[18] Thus, we need to triangulate between three interrelated problematics: girls' education and schooling in general (which should not be conflated—indeed, they must be disaggregated); households as managers of social status and webs; and the bigger historical envelope of the state.

Albert Memmi's cultural humiliation and conflicted identities resonate in part with our first story—that of Fadhma Amrouche, thrice marginalized as a Berber, an illegitimate female child, and a convert. But Fadhma's positive schooling experiences also resemble those narrated by Halimi, demonstrating gender's decisive role, both in the classroom and without.

Fadhma Amrouche: From Kabylia to Tunis and Paris, 1882–1967

> I also recalled the day that the Minister of Education was supposed to visit the school (for girls). The older girls went out to pick branches of foliage in the ravine to make a triumphal arch to welcome him, but he never turned up. We went as far as Fort-National to meet him, wearing unmatched rope-soled sandals and we came back drenched.[19]

Fadhma Amrouche, a Muslim by birth, attended both secular and missionary schools, embraced Christianity, produced one of the first autobiographies, if not the first, written by an Algerian woman, became a naturalized French citizen, and raised numerous children, two of whom became well-know French literati—Marie-Louise-Taos Amrouche (1913–1976), a poet, singer, and novelist, and Jean Amrouche (1906–1962), a writer and poet. But the circumstances of her early life were unpromising at best because her mother had forged unconventional relationships in response to utmost adversity that would later prove significant.

Amrouche was born in 1882 in the remote village of Tizi-Hibel in the rugged mountains of Kabylia in northeastern Algeria.[20] Before Fadhma's birth, her mother Aïni Aït Mansour had been married very young to an old man from another village and tribe; when he died, she was only twenty-two with two small boys. As was the custom, Aïni's older brother demanded that she immediately return to her clan until she could remarry. Defiant, Fadhma's mother refused and was completely disowned: "My mother never saw her family's house again."[21] This meant that Aïni and her children were deprived of maternal familial networks, and above all, of male kin protection. Yet, the absence of these protective ties later led to Aïni's determination to send her daughter to school—not for an education per se but rather to shield her from harm. But before that transpired, Aïni had fallen in love, outside the bounds of marriage, which was how it all began.

According to village tradition, a woman pregnant out of wedlock was normally murdered to remove the moral stain of adultery. Yet by 1874, six years before Fadhma's birth, profound changes in the colonial legal system conferred upon French magistrates jurisdiction over Muslims in Kabylia. When it became apparent that the widowed Aïni was pregnant, and the father refused to acknowledge the child, the family of Aïni's deceased husband attempted to drive her out of the village and seize her sons and property. Fully cognizant of the danger to herself and her unborn child, plucky Aïni denounced her in-laws to colonial authorities, placing herself under their legal protection. In *Histoire de ma vie*, published many years later, Fadhma relates what her mother told her: "The (French) magistrates came to the village. The tribunal appointed a guardian and a deputy guardian . . . drew up an inventory of my mother's property and left with the decree that no one must harm the widow or orphans."[22]

Here is one of the glaring contradictions of colonialism, a striking example of the fact that women did not necessarily experience foreign rule in the same way that men did, and that a double patriarchy, French and indigenous, offered small spaces for women to exploit and maneuver. Moreover, the composition of Aïni's household was significant. Cut off from her own familial social universe, with no husband and two small sons—in addition to the "child born of sin"—Aïni was the breadwinner and protector, the head of household, which played an immensely important role in subsequent events—and the formation of her daughter's personality. What about other kinds of "non"-kin networks? We know that neighbors played a part in aiding the young widow, who also had to hire local laborers to help with the harvest. In addition, Fadhma's mother made decisions regarding her beloved daughter's future based upon her own desires and calculations about the possibilities and dangers "out there." But what was her experience with the French system of native justice, and how did she know about colonial social welfare institutions?—questions that directly engage networks.

Soon after Fadhma's birth, Aïni embarked on a three-year campaign with the public prosecutor to force her lover to publicly declare paternity. "All this time, through heat and cold, my mother returned to plead and harass the magistrates."[23] In one sense, she won because the presumed father was finally ordered to pay damages; but in another, she lost, as French law did not yet admit the legal establishment of paternity, which only came in 1912 but was applied differently in France's overseas territories. She must have come to know local colonial officials rather well since the magistrate's wife, herself childless, offered to adopt the little girl, an offer that was refused. Perhaps it was through these communication circuits that Aïni first learned of the White Sisters, although the order had run a mission in Tagmount, close to Fadhma's village, since 1894.

When it became apparent that Fadhma would be always persecuted and ostracized by fellow villagers, her mother entrusted the three-year old child to a nearby Catholic convent, known as "Ouadhias," so that her daughter might enjoy a better life, or at least survive. The presence of missionaries in the region is fundamental to Amrouche's story. Colonial proselytizing among the Muslim population increased with Charles Lavigerie's (1825–1892) appointment in 1867 as archbishop of Algiers. Lavigerie, founder of the Société des Missionaires d'Afrique, or "White Fathers," and later the "Sisters of Our Lady of African Missions," or "White Sisters," initiated an intense conversion campaign in the Kabylia. Amateur colonial ethnologists had put forth the notion that the Berbers retained elements of their ancient Christian faith and thus were more amenable to conversion from Islam.[24] The missionaries—both Catholic and Protestant—helped to stabilize France's military occupation of Algeria by providing health and social services to the army, European settlers, and indigenous population. In addition, they opposed organized prostitution, such as the military brothels, which recruited (or kidnapped) indigent Arab or Berber women as well as resident European women of humble status. During the terrible famine of 1867–1868, the missionaries took in thousands of orphaned girls who would have otherwise ended up as prostitutes, or so they argued.[25]

When missionary discipline proved too brutal, Fadhma's mother removed her daughter from the White Sisters' school in 1886 and took her back to the village. It was the village *qa'id* (French-appointed Muslim official) who informed Aïni of another girls' institution, a secular French boarding school near Fort National at Taddert-ou-Fella, and urged her to enroll Fadhma there for protection. In this period, Muslims serving the colonial regime were pressured to expand enrollments of indigenous children in primary schools. Indeed, the first "mixed" (for both boys and girls) secular school in Kabylia was founded in Aït Hichem in 1892 by the local *qa'id*, who sent his daughter there for education, both as a model for the Kabyles and surely to curry favor with the colonial hierarchy. The same dynamic can be detected in Fort National, where the French administrator Monsieur Sabatier made gestures to establish a girls' school.

He summoned all the *kaïds* [*sic*], cavalrymen and rural police in his area and asked them to ride through the *douars* [villages] and collect as many girls as possible. The *kaïds* and the horsemen set off, with the rural police, who set the example by bringing their own daughters. There were girls of all ages: some already adolescents and some still toddlers.[26]

Amrouche's school, which she came to cherish despite harsh living conditions, clearly illustrates the force of diverse, convergent, and often contradictory networks and their political agendas. First created around 1882 as an orphanage in Fort National, and then refashioned as a native girls' school in Taddert-ou-Fella just outside the city, it went through many stages that included periods of closure as warring factions in the debate over female education gained the upper hand. Fadhma spent ten years in residence at the school, from 1887 until 1897; but her mother had insisted on a personal interview with the commune's French administrator to whom she entrusted her daughter before enrolling her in school. However, the larger context for all schools during the early Third Republic was the passage of the 1881–1882 Ferry Laws, which made primary education free, secular, and compulsory; these laws were more or less applied in Algeria for indigenous male children.[27]

The school's director, Madame Malaval, tirelessly promoted girls' schooling, but her life story is important as well. She and her husband had come to Algeria from the Aveyron (Midi-Pyrénées region) after the phylloxera pest wiped out their vineyards, which suggests that they were not originally trained as teachers. However, the solidly bourgeois Mme. Malaval had attended a highly respected convent school in her native city of Rodez, maintaining contacts with the sisters even after she and her husband left for Algeria. The couple was hired to run the Fort National orphanage, but after Mr. Malaval died, along with their only child, Mme. Malaval was invited by French administrators to take over the new girls' school around 1884 as *directrice*. Catholic and extremely devout, she nevertheless resolutely obeyed the secular policies of the Ferry Laws in the classroom. Also significant for her career was that she herself was a widow, which paradoxically conferred on her greater liberty of action.[28]

In addition to overseeing the Taddert-ou-Fella institution, Malaval created several primary schools around 1893. But the Kabyle families only enrolled their sons by this period because it was compulsory for boys; fines were imposed for noncompliance, but not for girls. The impact of national educational changes in France on the colonies can be seen by the fact that Malaval served as inspector of these institutions; previously, women had been barred from this key post.[29] Nevertheless, it also demonstrates a pattern seen elsewhere—frequently the colonies offered more opportunity for French or European women than the imperial centers.

In 1892, Amrouche earned the coveted "certificate of study," one of few Kabyle girls to so do. The next year, the administrator of the Commune closed the girls' school, claiming that it was too expensive. Undaunted and well connected, Malaval ceaselessly petitioned members of the Chamber of Deputies in Paris and thereby kept the school running by mobilizing trans-Mediterranean influence. She had at her disposition a number of political entrées because the girls' school had turned into a colonial showcase: "We were visited by a succession of members of the French government, including Jules Ferry, and often tourists came simply out of curiosity, like the Grand Duke George of Russia."[30]

The institution was saved by reclassification as a "Normal School" in 1893, which meant that it was staffed by professional teachers, endowed with a library, and the students enjoyed decent food. Two years later, Fadhma and several other girls made the journey to Algiers to sit for an examination, the *brevet élémentaire*, which represented an enormous opportunity but also a dangerous gamble. Even though the girls had been well prepared for the exam, they all failed—or were failed on purpose. To make matters worse, that Kabyle girls dressed in "native" costume had gone to the capital provoked a scandal; the school was once again shut down for political reasons. Semiconcealed social circuits came to light when the school's closure was announced; some pupils wrote letters to the Methodist missions run by English teachers in the Kabylia, begging to pursue their studies there but to no avail. By this period, many colonial administrators opposed schooling for Muslim girls as a waste of money since it only produced women rejected by both societies at best; at worst, education bred native prostitutes, or so it was reasoned by male officials and their native allies.[31] Fadhma returned home for a while, only to be called back to the school, which struggled on for another two years, although its fortunes declined rapidly after Mme. Malaval was forced to resign. In 1897 it locked its doors for good.

Thus far we have seen that an unconventional household—female-headed—rejected by native society, and the presence of French magistrates as well as religious and secular educational missionaries came together to shape a life. Another factor at play was that, as part of their proselytizing program, Catholic missionaries created "Christian French families" by arranging marriages for converts and founding villages for them expressly to sever ties with extended family. Thus, they greatly interfered in the intimate realms of family and marriage, producing intractable fissures within Kabyle communities.

Devastated when her schooling had ended, Fadhma returned to the village, where she spent seven months laboring in the fields alongside her mother. Knowing, however, that acceptance would never be forthcoming—she was too educated and bore "an indelible mark" on her forehead as an illegitimate child—she used an informal, conversational contact to inquire about work with the White Sisters mission in Tagmount. In 1898, Fadhma was hired by the Saint Eugénie Hospital in Aïth Manegueleth to care for the sick, diseased, and dying, many of whom were converts and outcasts—beggars, orphans, and such. Clearly medicine, social welfare, and proselytizing were enmeshed; and Fadhma insisted at first upon her Muslim and Kabyle identity. Regarded with suspicion by the nuns due to her secular schooling in Taddert-ou-Fella and her faith, Fadhma, nevertheless, taught catechism because of her advanced learning.

But the atmosphere was stifling, and at times, hostile; several times Fadhma attempted to leave, even appealing to the Mother Superior to find her employment in France. Her plight must have been well known in the region, the product of both homogeneous and heterogeneous networks. She was offered work by a French administrator in Michelet, and several marriage proposals were made that she rejected.[32] Eventually an acceptable offer came, but only after Amrouche composed a letter to her suitor stating in writing her conditions for marriage. In 1899, she was baptized and wed to Antoine Belkacem-ou-Amrouche (ca. 1881–1959), a Kabyle convert himself.

Soon thereafter, the couple left for the Amrouche village. At first the couple resided with Belkacem's clan in their multigenerational household in Ighil-Ali, where a White Fathers mission, school, and Christian village for converts was established nearby. That they were Christians— *mturnis* or "renegades"—while the rest of the family remained Muslim, created intractable woes. Conversion deeply undermined "lineage-based identity," without totally breaking ties. Significantly, Belkacem's grandfather, the family patriarch named Hacène-ou-Amrouche, had sent his grandson to Catholic missionary schools for education. Why had Hacène taken such a decision? First, the patriarch was himself the son of a widow. He had enrolled in the French army in order to make a living, which was not unusual for the Kabyle males. Hacène fought in the Crimean War and survived the siege of Sebastopol (1854–1855) which, given the high mortality rates, was nothing short of miraculous, and he only returned to Algeria in 1871. This experience shaped his life trajectory, for he learned French and upon his return to the Kabylia was rewarded with a post as an interpreter, later that of *spahi*. He introduced French into his family circle, which betrayed his thinking on schooling provided by the "Rumis."[33] Here we see language acquisition as a force not only for physical migration but also status mobility through entrée to opportunity—for Hacène serving as an intermediary between ruler and ruled.

Another emerging trans-Mediterranean conduit was male labor emigration to the metropole just prior to World War I; indeed, one of Fadhma's half brothers departed for France in search of work. While the Kabyles had always had to abandon their hard scrabble mountain villages for the fields and cities of the plains below, this current of emigration was new and played a significant role in transforming local economies and spatially reconfiguring communication nodes.[34]

As their economic situation deteriorated in Algeria, the couple moved with their growing number of children to Tunis in 1908. This represented an older form of expatriation because many Algerians had fled the country after 1830 for the safety of Tunisia.[35] Belkacem found employment with the French railroads which not only provided steady income but also involvement in labor and syndicalist associations as well as other connections within a strange city. As an employee for the rail company linking Algeria with Tunisia, he and his family enjoyed free travel, which in turn meant that they could afford to send their sons back to the Catholic village in Kabylia for schooling. In addition, the Catholic Church had been present in precolonial Tunisia, so the couple was able to maintain homogenous networks with missionary orders there that offered social assistance. In 1913, the family was accorded French nationality, probably because of their Catholic faith, French language ability, and Belkacem's employment. But a year later, World War I broke out, and all French nationals in the colonies were mobilized; the family returned temporarily to Kabylia using their free rail travel.[36] Nevertheless, impecunious members of Belkacem's extended family imposed themselves upon the couple in Tunis whenever things went badly in Algeria, demonstrating the difficulty of dissolving kin ties.

Fadhma bore eight children in extremely trying circumstances; only one outlived her. In Tunis, their household differed because it was economically autonomous, and the spouses collaborated in all matters governing family life. Fadhma, who did not veil and spoke no Arabic, lived daily life as a cultural hyphen—belonging neither to local Tunisian society, nor to the culturally diverse communities of largely impoverished, but Catholic, subsistence migrants, Sicilians, Maltese, and Spanish, who called Tunis home. Yet they all shared one thing—deprivation that meant they cohabited the same urban spaces, whether houses, courtyards, or the streets, which created both social cooperation and conflict. Nevertheless, the fact that Fadhma was not only literate but also well versed in French set her apart from neighbors, associates, and kin. In their family, girls' and boys' schooling was a collective decision, although the couple drew heavily upon their missionary ties to meet the cost of education.

The nature of colonial rule in Tunisia shaped Fadhma's life trajectory from 1908 until 1953, when the couple briefly returned to Algeria, one year before the revolution erupted. The Protectorate did not merely superimpose the machinery of governance upon existing state and social structures but rather poached upon the modernizing reforms and institutions in place from Khayr al-Din's years as prime minister (1874–1878), if not before. These included significant advances in education, notably the establishment of the Sadiqi College in 1874, which produced a sophisticated, political class well on the way to nationalist sensibilities.[37]

In addition, the Amrouche family arrived at a key moment in thinking about indigenous female education. By 1900, many in Algeria and France viewed *l'Algérie française* as a moral parable for how not to govern other parts of the empire. In the eyes of Third Republic liberals, notably educators such as Louis Machuel, the most glaring failures lay in education for indigenous children, especially girls. Thus, Tunisia was imagined as a place where the wrongs of Algeria could be righted through more enlightened policies toward Islam and Muslims. In a public speech, the resident-general declared that: "The methods applied here in Tunisia [to rule] are superior to most of the French colonies."[38] More importantly, French advocates for native schooling at times allied with Tunisian reformers, but for different reasons.[39] From this confluence of interests came a new institution, the École Louise-Réne Millet, founded in 1900, in the Tunis *madina*, the first nonmissionary academic school for native girls where Tawhida Ben Shaykh first studied.

Fadhma actively oversaw her children's education both at home and at school. They attended missionary as well as secular institutions in Tunis and in Kabylia where some of the boys were sent as boarders. However, the most important dimension was that she herself served as an instructor on a number of occasions, preparing her son Paul for his secondary-school certificate using "a very old general course book, second-hand, in which all the exercises were explained."[40] In 1946 her son Jean, by then a recognized writer in France, asked Amrouche to compose her memoirs. For an entire month that year, she wrote feverishly recalling in ethnographic fashion all the details of her life in a stark autobiography, which, at that time, was destined only for her children's eyes.[41] In a note to Jean written upon the completion of her memoir, Fadhma stated:

> I bequeath you this story, which is the account of my life, for you to do what you like with, after my death. This story is true, not one episode has been invented, all that happened before my birth was told to me by my mother as soon as I was old enough to understand. I have written this story because I think it deserves to be known to all of you. . . . I wrote this story in memory of my beloved mother and of Madame Malaval who gave me my spiritual life i.e., the gift of reading, writing, and education.[42]

Out of respect for her husband, however, she would not consider publishing the intimately personal, and often painful, remembrances until after Belkacem's death in 1959. That year Amrouche moved to France to reside with her only daughter, Marie-Louise-Taos, who persuaded Fadhma to write the epilogue for the autobiography in 1962 when her beloved son Jean died. She ended her days in Brittany in 1967, still in exile; her memoirs were published posthumously the next year in Paris in a series edited by Albert Memmi—for an audience that Amrouche had probably never imagined.[43]

Amrouche was, and is today, celebrated as a precious repository of Kabyle songs, chants, legends, and lore, then in grave danger of disappearing. Indeed, it was Fadhma who instilled in her only daughter a love for, and ability to perform, traditional music and dance. Marie-Louise-Taos Amrouche (born in 1913 and also known as Marguerite Taos) was truly her mother's child. In 1934 she obtained the *brevet supérieur* in Tunis, which allowed her to pursue studies the next year in France at the prestigious École Normale in Sèvres for young women, founded in 1881. Upon her return to Tunis, Marie-Louise worked at a boarding school in Radès, a suburb where Fadhma and Belkacem eventually resided. In 1939, Marie-Louise performed at the Congrès de Chant in

Fez, where she was awarded a scholarship to study music in Spain; she eventually became a well-known singer in Europe and North Africa.

Starting in 1936, Fadhma, Jean, and Marie-Louise worked together to collect and commit Kabyle songs to writing; this collaboration eventually resulted in the translation and publication in 1966 of *Le grain magique*. In addition, Marie-Louise recorded several phonograph albums and produced programs for French radio where her brother had made a name for himself. One series of songs was entitled *Chants sauvés de l'oubli* (Songs Saved from Oblivion). Marie-Louise penned other works, including several realist novels. The earliest, published in 1947, *Jacinthe noire* (Black Hyacinth), draws in part upon Fadhma's life but is set within a Tunisian frame. Its heroine is a native girl sent to study in a French boarding school, where her cultural heritage renders her an outsider, eternally banished. A second novel, which appeared in 1960, was patently autobiographical; *Rue des Tambourins* narrates childhood memories of growing up in Tunis.[44]

From a Berber village in Algeria, to Tunisia, and then to France, Fadhma Amrouche's life odyssey constitutes a singular chapter in the history of female education, social and other kinds of mobilities, and translocal connectivities. It mirrors the harsh realities of native society as well as contradictions of French Algeria as lived, particularly for women. Nevertheless, the repressive armature of dual patriarchy was not invincible; some women exploited its soft spots to gain agency for themselves, but above all for their children. Yet this came with a price. Fadhma never lost her yearning for home. While much of her adult life was spent in Tunisia, those years are curiously enough characterized in Part III of her *Histoire* as "*L'exil de Tunis*." As she stated: "I always remained the 'Kabyle woman'; never, in spite of the forty years I have spent in Tunisia, in spite of my basically French education, never have I been able to become a close friend of any French people, nor of Arabs. I remain forever the eternal exile, the woman who has never felt at home anywhere."[45]

Amrouche clearly grasped the urgency of conserving a rich oral heritage endangered by the spread of modern schooling (and other factors) that she paradoxically celebrated so movingly.[46] Moreover, it is tempting to see these memoirs in their ethnographic density as an anomaly. Yet, it should be recalled that even seemingly remote places, such as Kabylia and the Aures, had since the 1920s hosted field research by female ethnographers—Mathéa Gaudry, Germaine Tillion, and Thérèse Rivière, to name only the best known. As originally conceived in Paris, these scientific missions aimed to document "the Berber" household and family, regarded as the unadulterated core of ancient cultural authenticity, immune from the outside world. Nevertheless, soon after her arrival in the Aures during the 1930s, Tillion realized that these peoples and regions had long been imbricated in translocal and transnational forces, much to their detriment.[47] In a sense, Tillion was "schooled" in field ethnography by the villagers of the Aures.

Now we travel to the *madina* of Tunis, to *Nahj Basha*, "the street of the pasha," where the Ben Shaykh (or Ben Cheikh) family resided in a *hawma*, or quarter, much preferred by city notables or *baldis*. Thus, from one point of view, the social circumstances surrounding the lives of Fadhma Amrouche and of Tawhida Ben Shaykh could scarcely have been more divergent; nevertheless, critical similarities can be discerned.

Dr. Tawhida Ben Shaykh (1909–2010): Women's Health Activist

A class photo taken of graduates from the Faculty of Medicine in Paris around 1936 shows a group of elegant young men whose poise betrays the status conferred by advanced education. In their midst sits the sole woman; wearing a hat and white dress, she seems slightly uncomfortable. Tawhida Ben Shaykh was, in 1936, the first North African Muslim woman to earn a French medical diploma. But identifying her only deepens the mystery. By the interwar period, feminists and nationalists condemned colonial education as a signal failure due to high illiteracy rates, especially among Muslim girls. Ben Shaykh's intellectual and social odyssey from the old city to the colonial city and then to Paris should be located in a transnational context of the early twentieth century, when education became central to the very practice of colonialism—to struggles over the nature and future of empire. The school photograph elicits a number of questions: What journeys brought this woman into the charmed circle of male graduates? How did she get from North Africa to France? What schools had she attended? And why had her family consented to studies so far from home?

I had the privilege of interviewing Dr. Ben Shaykh in her lovely residence in Tunis during the summer of 1998; by then she was eighty-nine years old and, while she could only move with the help of a walker, she was exuberant in mind and spirit. I asked her to narrate the events leading up to her medical studies in Paris during the interwar period. She recalled the pivotal role that her widowed mother, Halluma Ben Am-

Tawhida Ben Shaykh with her medical school class.

mar, played in her education from primary school on. "I come from a well-known Tunisian family. I never knew my father; we were four children, three girls and a boy. The son was born after my father's death. I was thus raised by my mother who was a most extraordinary woman."[48]

Here is another example of a widow who remained in her own home after her husband's death. Significant too was that Tawhida's only brother was younger; apparently there were no older male kin residing permanently within the household. She herself hinted during the interview that if an adult brother or uncle had been present to exert pressure on family decisions, perhaps her life story would have unfolded differently.[49]

Another critical element determined the story's evolution, a serendipitous event that reveals an essential, although unrecognized, dimension of female schooling—the issue of social space and networks. In 1909, the year of Tawhida's birth, a primary school, the School for Muslim Girls, was established close to her family residence on Rue du Pacha; it was originally located a few streets away but had been forced to move to more spacious quarters due to rising student demand. In 1918, Tawhida's mother enrolled her (and a sister) in this institution from which she obtained her *certificat d'études* in 1922.[50] The importance of the school's physical location—in close spatial proximity to her home— cannot be overemphasized in legitimating girls' schooling outside the home. Indeed, a comparative analysis of female-authored memoirs demonstrates that families preferred schools within the immediate neighborhood—often regarded by its denizens as an extension of domestic space. Moreover, as was true of Amrouche's institution at Taddert-ou-

Fella, the School for Muslim Girls had become a colonial educational showpiece, with many visitors and much fanfare in the international press.[51]

In 1922, the question of secondary education arose but there was no school near the family household in the *madina*. Halluma sent Tawhida and Zakiya to the Lycée Armand Fallières in the European quarter on Rue du Rome. Once again, the family strategy was directly inspired by spatial and moral concerns. This particular girls' lycée boasted an *internat*, boarding facilities, but only a few Muslim girls were enrolled. Tawhida and Zakiya boarded there, which avoided exposure to public streets and the socially awkward trip across town several times a day. Special arrangements were made so that the girls could observe religious duties, such as fasting during Ramadan; the staff awakened the girls for their last meal before sunrise. Tawhida spent six years at the *lycée* obtaining her *bac* (baccalauréat) in 1928.[52]

During the 1920s, the feminist movement took off and was marked by a watershed event in 1924: Manubiya Wartani, a young Tunisian woman, attended a public conference on the question of women's rights. Inspired by what she heard, Manubiya removed her veil and stood up in the crowd to make a speech in a manner reminiscent of Huda Sha'rawi's defiant public unveiling in the Cairo train station in 1923. In 1930, the Tunisian Tahar Haddad published the first call for women's emancipation, *Imra'tuna fi al-shari'a wa al-mujtama'* (*Notre femme dans la legislation islamique et la société*), which stirred up acrimonious debates. Finally, these years were marked by the emergence of well-organized Tunisian labor as well as nationalist movements.[53] During this time Tawhida had a chance encounter that utterly changed the course of her life—she made the acquaintance of a well-known researcher in microbiology, Etienne Burnet (1873–1960), and his Russian wife, Lydia, who resided in Tunis.

Burnet had come to Tunisia in 1919 somewhat by serendipity; he had contracted tuberculosis in Paris, which North Africa's warm sunny climate was said to heal. A school inspector's son, Burnet had achieved the coveted *aggregation* in philosophy prior to studies at the Medical School of Paris, beginning in 1899. His philosophical training and service during World War I in an ambulance corps on the French front convinced Burnet that nutrition played an important role in immunity from disease, an idea that had won him an international reputation among epidemiologists. In 1918, he married Lydia, who had been posted in a field ambulance in Salonika during the war. Upon his arrival in Tunis, Burnet was appointed health director from 1920–1928 and then deputy director at the Institut Pasteur of Tunis. Founded in 1893, the Institut was under Charles Nicolle's direction from 1903 to 1936; Nicolle was awarded a Nobel Prize for medicine in 1928. By this period, Tunisia was regarded as a premier laboratory for scientific studies of malaria, typhus, and other communicable diseases.[54]

Recalling that encounter seven decades later, Dr. Ben Shaykh stated in 1998: "I met Dr. Burnet here in Tunis quite by accident but first I made the acquaintance of Mme. Burnet." It seems that one of Tawhida's high school professors had introduced her intentionally to Lydia Burnet in order to encourage her to pursue advanced studies. When Lydia inquired about Tawhida's future plans after the *bac*, she responded, "I hope to engage in social welfare work and aid those who are needy."[55] The Russian woman promised to consult with her husband about opportunities and in the summer of 1928, Tawhida was invited to their home in the largely European quarter Belvédère where the Institut Pasteur was located. At the time, there was only one institution in North Africa that granted medical degrees, in Algiers. Neither Dr. Burnet nor Tawhida's family would entertain the notion of her enrolling there, perhaps because of colonial racism. Nevertheless, seeing her promise for medicine, Burnet offered to contact his numerous associates in Paris at the medical school as well as to help organize her student life in France.

For Tawhida's solidly bourgeois and socially conservative family, the idea of studying in France, even with the Burnets as mentors and chaperones, was unthinkable. Nevertheless, Tawhida had proved so gifted in secondary school that her professors from the Lycée Armand Fallières made a collective visit to Halluma, urging her assent to schooling far from home. One of the teachers observed that, "It would be a crime if she does not pursue her studies in Paris."[56] Her mother agreed.

Members of the extended family adamantly opposed the project, characterizing Halluma as "mad." Indeed, the day of Tawhida's scheduled departure in 1928, when she was packing her bags to take the boat to Marseille with Madame Burnet, and with a driver waiting at the door to take them to the port, a delegation of male relatives arrived at the house, including a shaykh, who characterized Paris as "*une ville de perdition*." However, Halluma stood firm, directing the shaykh to find a verse in the Qu'ran forbidding women's education. During the ensuing, and quite heated, discussion, Tawhida secretly sent word to the port for the ship to wait. And it did—she had never been outside of Tunis until then. Dr. Burnet had already left Tunis—the result of a falling out with Nicolle—to accept a post in Geneva at the League of Nations Health Organization. Together Tawhida and Lydia sailed across the Mediterranean.[57]

Few women attended the Faculty of Medicine at the time—a handful—and most were nationals. Since she was regarded as unusual—an Arab Muslim woman from the colonies, alone in the city without family, but enrolled at the prestigious school—many people desired to make her acquaintance. Tawhida spent eight years in the French capital, at first boarding at an international female students' *foyer*, funded by a wealthy American woman, and then residing within the Burnets' household. Through the well-connected couple, she mixed with "men of sciences, leading writers, and doctors of medicine." Thus the Burnets' mentoring increased the scope and diversity of networks available to Tawhida. But her intellect and hard work brought the coveted post of *externe* in Parisian hospitals; soon her younger brother arrived in Paris to study law, which demonstrates that individual educational migration often triggered familial displacements.[58] In 1931, Ben Shaykh joined the Association des étudiants musulmans d'Afrique du Nord en France, which brought her to the attention of other groups in the city. She was invited to lecture at the Congrès de l'Union des femmes françaises, where she provided a painful portrait of the circumstances of Muslim women in the French Empire.[59]

Medical diploma in hand, Dr. Ben Shaykh returned home in 1936, the same year that Burnet was named as director of the Institut Pasteur. She went into private practice near Bab al-Manara, specializing in women's reproductive health, frequently providing free medical services for poor women. But the decision was also motivated by a cruel paradox of colonialism: "I did not attempt to find a position in one of the colonial hospitals since they were controlled by the French. While there were several women doctors working in the Tunis hospitals, a Tunisian female physician had little chance of being accepted there."[60]

In her own fashion and on her own terms, she was active in the nationalist movement, which was inevitably intertwined with feminism, although in complex ways. Dr. Ben Shaykh collaborated with the women's journal *Leila* from 1937 on by writing articles signed with a *nom de plume*. An illustrated weekly published from 1936 to 1941, the journal was devoted to "l'évolution et l'émancipation de la femme musulmane nord-africaine."[61] In 1942 she married a Tunisian dentist trained in Paris, and the couple had three children. When the French army bombed a village in Cap Bon in 1952 with great loss of life, Tawhida investigated the scene of the massacre and wrote a detailed onsite report that she personally submitted to French authorities in protest. During the nation-

Tawhida Ben Shaykh during her awareness campaign for family planning in Tunisia. Courtesy of Helmoony, Wikimedia Commons.

alist struggles of the 1950s, she served as vice president of the Tunisian branch of the Croissant Rouge (Red Cross) and later established the first family planning clinic in 1963, playing a leading role in the Association Tunisienne pour le planning familial. However, her commitment to healing caused her to refuse a plum government post in 1970 offered by the prime minister: "I preferred to care for my patients and exercise my profession as a doctor."[62]

A reflection of her modesty, she declined to write her own life story—despite the urgings of family and friends to do so—but granted interviews to others. In 2000 a centenary celebration to commemorate the establishment of the School for Muslim Girls was organized in the capital. Following its well-calculated policy of promoting women's rights to deflect international criticism from its abysmal human rights record, the (recently defunct) Ben ʿAli regime attempted to highjack the festivities. On December 6, 2010, at the age of 101, Dr. Ben Shaykh died at her home in Tunis—as revolution broke out across the land.[63]

Conclusion

Unconventional households, webbed communication conduits, and divergent forms of colonialism converge in these biographies. Moreover, educating girls demanded risk-taking whose price could be quite heavy. Let's listen to another voice. Maherzia Amira-Bournaz was born in the Tunis *madina* in 1912 and from the same generation as Tawhida Ben Shaykh. In her memoirs, Bournaz states, "Alone, pitted against everyone, my mother insisted upon enrolling us in school, my sisters and me, during a period when educating girls was negatively viewed by society. Because of this, she had to endure interference from my father and sarcastic remarks from family and neighbors."[64] Yet it would be inaccurate to portray widows or mothers as the single most powerful force in education; fathers often braved public opprobrium when sending daughters or female kin outside the home to learn. Changes, small and large, in the nature and structure of households frequently exerted an immense impact on individual and collective life trajectories. The status of widowhood emerges as a key variable in girls' primary schooling under certain conditions. Widows often exerted de facto male authority in decisions about children's destinies.[65] And the desire to educate children sometimes meant that families relocated to distant towns or across the Mediterranean to seek schooling deemed more advantageous. Finally, the breaking of old molds and the fashioning of others was often the product of contingency—of chance or serendipity.

While male and female nationalists were in the streets protesting, another semiconcealed struggle was taking place within the domestic unit. Ultimately a seismic shift occurred when moralists, who a generation earlier opined that literacy would utterly compromise female virtue and morality, rendering girls unfit as wives and mothers, acknowledged that the "right" education acted as a moral shield for the mothers of the nation.[66] Nevertheless, it was families and households that defined modernity, principally with reference to female education. We might call this the "local household modern."

One of the paradoxes of the empire's demise was that the number of North Africans who travelled to the metropole for education increased. The movement of students from the Mediterranean's Muslim shores to Europe represented an older phenomenon dating back to the nineteenth-century Ottoman Empire. However, the participants in these earlier educational odysseys were all male and generally from elite families in Egypt or Istanbul. From the late nineteenth century onward, a select few Muslim (male) Arab or Berber students studied in Europe. After World War I, they engaged in anticolonial activities in solidarity with the more numerous and strident *Maghrebi* industrial laborers. The presence of women, such as Tawhida Ben Shaykh and Gisèle Halimi, in French institutions has scarcely been acknowledged, although their stories, replete with contradictions, illuminate unsuspected historical processes. As seen in Ben Shaykh's years in interwar Paris, North African university students there were highly politicized and well organized.

In their school memoirs, many women evoke the racism encountered in colonial schools in the Maghreb. Gladys ʿAdda, a Tunisian Jew, labor activist, and nationalist journalist born in Gabes in 1921, attended primary school with Muslim, Jewish, and European students; because native teachers were excluded from secondary education, all instructors were French or European. Undisguised racism on the part of the teaching staff awakened ʿAdda to the harsh realities of foreign rule and brought her into the radical labor movement. In similar fashion, Ben Shaykh founded her own medical practice in 1936 because of the exclusionary policies of colonial hospitals—and eventually launched the first successful family planning movement in North Africa (although the Ford Foundation usually receives the accolades for this).[67]

In Foucault's thinking, schooling represents a major forum for modern disciplining, something that male-authored memoirs poignantly show; for example, Jean Amrouche's *Notes pour une esquisse de l'état d'âme du colonisé.*[68] However, my years of interviewing North African women (and European expatriate women in teaching professions) schooled in diverse institutions uncovered processes that were less linear, much more complicated.[69] What struck me during these conversations now stretching well over a decade was that for girls, the school room represented a more ambiguous social space than Foucault's thinking admits. It offered liberation, however fleeting, from housework, caring for siblings, limitations on physical mobility—from the household itself. A number of women have mentioned to me that, when they received disciplinary citations for work or behavior deemed unacceptable, they were not displeased. For the punishment was to attend school for extra hours, when others did not. It got them out of the house.

Finally, associative life was incubated in these institutions that go to the very heart of networking. The Lycée de la rue du Pacha boasts a vibrant alumnae association and an illustrated journal, *Multaqa al-Ajyal,* which embody the enduring bonds forged in the classroom. Finally, analyzing girls' education and schooling from the viewpoint of individuals, families, and households, rather than a state-centered perspective, bestows a face and voice upon the local modern.

Notes

1. Aziza Darghouth Medimegh, "Introduction," *Lettres à Lili: Correspondance d'Amour à Tunis, 1943–1944* (Tunis: Les éditions Cartaginoiseries, 2007), quote p. 10, letter from Tahar to Lili, February 1943. This chapter draws upon

my in-progress monograph, tentatively entitled *From Household to Schoolroom to University: Women's Schooling in North Africa, c. 1840–1990*. A different version of this chapter appears in Patricia M. Lorcin and Todd Shepard, eds., *French Mediterraneans: Transnational and Imperial Histories* (Lincoln: University of Nebraska Press, 2014).

2. Aziza Darghouth Medimegh, "Introduction," *Lettres à Lili*, 160.

3. For examples, work by Rebecca Rogers, "Telling Stories about the Colonies: British and French Women in Algeria in the Nineteenth Century," *Gender & History* 21, no. 1 (April 2009): 39–59, and her *A Frenchwoman's Imperial Story: Madame Luce in Nineteenth-Century Algeria* (Palo Alto: Stanford University Press, 2012); see also Frances Malino, *Teaching Freedom: Jewish Sisters in Muslim Lands* (London: Palgrave Macmillan, 2008); and Julia A. Clancy-Smith, *Mediterraneans: North Africa and Europe in an Age of Migration, c. 1800–1900* (Berkeley: University of California Press, 2011), chapter 7. See also Spencer D. Segalla, *The Moroccan Soul: French Education, Colonial Ethnology, and Muslim Resistance, 1912–1956* (Lincoln: University of Nebraska Press, 2009); Beth Baron, *Egypt as a Woman: Nationalism, Gender, and Politics* (Berkeley: University of California Press, 2005); and Hamid Irbouh, *Art in the Service of Colonialism: French Art Education in Morocco, 1912–1956* (New York: St. Martin's Press, 2005).

4. Anbara Salam Khalidi, *Memoirs of an Early Arab Feminist: The Life and Activism of Anbara Salam Khalidi*, trans. Tarif Khalidi (London: Pluto Press, 2013), quote 13; Khalidi also notes that when her Muslim school for girls in Beirut was closed because of World War I, a respected local priest Father Yusuf al-Zahhar came to their household to instruct the family's children in science (57). See also Marilyn Booth's *May Her Likes Be Multiplied: Biography and Gender Politics in Egypt* (Berkeley: University of California Press, 2001); and Alice L. Conklin, *In the Museum of Man: Race, Anthropology, and Empire in France, 1850–1950* (Ithaca: Cornell University Press, 2013), whose work implicitly demonstrates the intricate branching out of school connections.

5. Medimegh, "Introduction," *Lettres à Lili*, 7.

6. Julia Clancy-Smith, "Éducation des jeunes filles Musulmanes en Tunisie: Missionaires religieux et laïques," in *Le pouvoir du genre: Laïcités et religions 1905–2005*, ed. Florence Rochefort (Toulouse: Presses Universitaires du Mirail, 2007), 127–143.

7. Miriam Cooke and Bruce B. Lawrence, *Muslim Networks from Hajj to Hip Hop* (Chapel Hill: University of North Carolina Press, 2005), 1.

8. Susan Cotts Watkins, "Social Networks and Social Science History," *Social Science History* 19, no. 3 (Fall 1995): 295–311.

9. Mary Hartman's *The Household and the Making of History: A Subversive View of the Western Past* (New York: Cambridge University Press, 2004) argues that studies of modernity should be centered within the household, which represents a major theoretical advance. Her principal thesis, however, revolves around the historical uniqueness of northwestern European household structures, with scant attention to other familial forms elsewhere. See also, Marilyn Booth, ed., *Harem Histories: Envisioning Places and Living Spaces* (Durham, NC: Duke University Press, 2010), on Muslim households in the *longue durée*.

10. *American Historical Review* 114, no. 3 (June 2009): 573–78, AHR Round-

table: Historians and Biography; see also Liat Kozma, "Moroccan Women's Narratives of Liberation: A Passive Revolution?" *Journal of North African Studies* 8, no. 1 (Spring 2003): 112–130.

11. Hélène Cixous and Mireille Calle-Gruber, *Rootprints: Memory and Life Writing* (New York: Routledge, 1997); see also Carolyn Duffey, "Berber Dreams, Colonialism, and Couscous: The Competing Autobiographical Narratives of Fadhma Amrouche's *Histoire de ma vie*," *Pacific Coast Philology* 30, no. 1 (1995): 68–81.

12. Habib Kazdaghli, ed., *Nisa' wa dhakira: tunisiyyat fil hayat al-'amma, 1920–1900* (Tunis: Édition Média, 1993); Maherzia Amira-Bournaz, *C'était Tunis 1920* (Tunis: Cérès, 1993); Maherzia Amira-Bournaz (1912–2002), *Maherzia se souvient: Tunis 1930 Récit* (Tunis: Cérès, 1999); and Effy Tselikas and Lina Hayoun, eds., *Les lycées français du soleil: Creusets cosmopolites du Maroc, de l'Algérie et de la Tunisie* (Paris: Autrement, 2004). There are numerous remembrances of school days written by Egyptian women, mainly in Arabic but also in French; for examples, Huda Sha'rawi, *Mudhakirrati* (Cairo: Dar al-Hilal, 1981); and Nabawiya Musa, *Tarikhi biqalami* (Cairo: Women and Memory Forum, 1999). The school memoirs of one of the first Turkish female writers, Halide Edib Adivar, *House with Wisteria: Memoirs of Turkey Old and New* (New Brunswick, NJ: Transaction, 2009), are particularly revealing of social networking and female education.

13. Edward Said, *Out of Place: A Memoir* (New York: Vintage, 1999), xii.

14. Albert Memmi, *La Statue de sel* (Paris: Gallimard, 1955); and Julia Clancy-Smith, "Albert Memmi and *The Pillar of Salt*," in *African Literature and Its Times*, ed. Joyce Moss (Los Angeles: Moss Publication Group, 2000), 337–346. Colonial schooling has also furnished the grist for Algerian novels; a noteworthy example is Mouloud Feraoun, *Le fils du pauvre: Menrad, instituteur Kabyle* (Le Puy: Les Cahiers du Nouvel Humanisme, 1950).

15. Gisèle Halimi, *Fritna* (Paris: Plon, 1999), quotes, 59, 165. In 1945, as Allied armies liberated Europe, Halimi obtained special permission with great difficulty to travel to Paris to pursue university studies there (163–64). See Natalie Edwards, *The Autobiographies of Julia Kristeva, Gisèle Halimi, Assia Djebar and Hélène Cixous: Beyond "I" versus "We"* (Evanston: Northwestern University Press, 2005).

16. Joëlle Bahloul, *The Architecture of Memory: A Jewish-Muslim Household in Colonial Algeria, 1937–1962* (Cambridge: Cambridge University Press, 1996), 51.

17. Khalidi, *Memoirs*, 40.

18. Author's interviews with Hasiba Agha, Carthage, 2009.

19. Amrouche, *My Life Story*, 26. See also Germaine Laoust-Chantréaux, *Kabylie côté femmes: La vie féminine à Aït Hichem, 1937–1939*, introduction by Camille Lacoste-Dujardin (Aix-en-Provence: Edisud, 1990); on p. 7, Laoust-Chantréaux quotes an French-Algerian newspaper from 1882: "The Kabyles are overly eager for schooling, they learn too well and too rapidly. It is terrifying to see so many acquiring an education; what will they become when they grow up?" (*L'Akhbar*).

20. Fadhma Amrouche, *My Life Story: The Autobiography of a Berber Woman*,

trans. and intro. by Dorothy S. Blair (New Brunswick: Rutgers University Press, 1989), first published as *Histoire de ma vie* (Paris: Maspero, 1968), and republished by Éditions La Découverte, 2000. Unless otherwise noted, references cited are to the 1989 edition.

21. Fadhma Amrouche, *My Life Story*, 4.

22. Ibid., 5.

23. Ibid., 6. See Jean Elisabeth Pedersen, *Legislating the French Family: Feminism, Theater, and Republican Politics, 1870–1920* (New Brunswick: Rutgers University Press, 2003), 139–161.

24. See Owen White and J. P. Daughton, eds., *In God's Empire: French Missionaries and the Modern World* (New York: Oxford University Press, 2012); Karima Direche-Slimani, *Chrétiens de Kabylie: Histoire d'une communauté sans histoire: Une action missionnaire de l'Algérie Coloniale* (Paris: Bouchène, 2004); and Patricia M. E. Lorcin, *Imperial Identities: Stereotyping, Prejudice and Race in Colonial Algeria* (London: I. B. Tauris, 1995).

25. Christelle Taraud, *La prostitution coloniale: Algérie, Tunisie, Maroc (1830–1962)* (Paris: Payot, 2003).

26. Amrouche, *My Life Story*, 10–11.

27. Sarah A. Curtis, *Educating the Faithful: Religion, Schooling, and Society in Nineteenth-Century France* (DeKalb: Northern Illinois University Press, 2000).

28. Amrouche, *My Life Story*, 10–29.

29. Christina de Bellaigue, *Educating Women: Schooling and Identity in England and France, 1800–1867* (Oxford: Oxford University Press, 2007); and Linda L. Clark, "Bringing Feminine Qualities into the Public Sphere: The Third Republic's Appointment of Women Inspectors," in *Gender and the Politics of Social Reform in France, 1870–1914*, ed. Elinor Accampo, Rachel G. Fuchs, and Mary Lynn Stewart (Baltimore: Johns Hopkins University Press, 1995), 128–156.

30. Amrouche, *My Life Story*, 15.

31. Rebecca Rogers, "Telling Stories about the Colonies: British and French Women in Algeria in the Nineteenth Century," *Gender & History* 21, no. 1 (April 2009): 39–59.

32. Amrouche, *My Life Story*, 44–55.

33. Jean-El Mouhoub Amrouche, *Journal (1928–1962)*, ed. and intro. Tassadit Yacine Titouh (Paris: Non Lieu, 2009), 9.

34. James McDougall, *History and the Culture of Nationalism in Algeria* (Cambridge: Cambridge University Press, 2005).

35. Julia Clancy-Smith, "Algeria as *mère-patrie*: Algerian Expatriates in Tunisia, c. 1830–1914," in *Identity, Memory and Nostalgia: France and Algeria, 1800–2000*, ed. Patricia Lorcin (Syracuse: Syracuse University Press, 2006), 3–17.

36. J. Amrouche, *Journal*, 10–11.

37. Julia Clancy-Smith, "Ruptures? Expatriates, Law, and Institutions in Colonial-Husaynid Tunisia, 1870–1914," in *Changes in Colonial and Post-Colonial Governance of Islam: Continuities and Ruptures*, ed. Veit Bader, Annelies Moors, and Marcel Maussen (Amsterdam: University of Amsterdam Press, 2011).

38. Versini, 1.

39. See the Archives Nationales de Tunisie, E Series, 271–274, *La Quinzaine*

Coloniale, July 10, 1907, for examples of debates on girls education: "Nothing can replace the nurturing of the mother; there is no influence as profound upon the children as hers." And "What a cause for decadence for a race to only have frivolous and ignorant mothers raising the children."

40. Amrouche, *My Life Story,* 129.

41. Jean Amrouche, *Chants Berbères de Kabylie* (Tunis: Monomotapa, 1939).

42. Amrouche, *My Life Story,* 193.

43. Albert Memmi, collection *Domaine maghrébin* (Paris: Maspero, 1968).

44. Taos Amrouche, *Jacinthe noire* (Paris: Maspero, 1972); *Le grain magique: contes, poèmes et proverbes berbères de Kabylie* (Paris: La Découverte, 1996); and *Rues des Tambourins* (Paris: Éditions Joëlle Losfeld, 1996).

45. Amrouche, *My Life Story,* 159; Charlotte H. Bruner, "Fadhma and Marguerite Amrouche of the Kabyle Mountains," in *The Word-Singers: The Makers and Making of Traditional Literatures,* special issue of *Pacific Quarterly Moana* 8, no. 4 (1984).

46. Amrouche is revered by Kabyle nationalists as a cherished mother because of her role in saving traditions of Berber cultural identity; in his preface to the *Histoire,* Kateb Yacine calls her *"la muse matriarchale,"* Introduction, 13; see also Judith Scheele, *Village Matters: Knowledge, Politics, and Community in Kabylia, Algeria* (Suffolk: James Currey, 2009).

47. Nancy Wood, *Germaine Tillion, une femme-mémoire: D'une Algérie à l'autre,* trans. Marie-Pierre Corrin (Paris: Éditions Autrement, 2003); and Julia Clancy-Smith, "La Question de la femme," in *Le siècle de Germaine Tillion,* ed. Todorov Tzvetan (Paris: Editions du Seuil, 2007), 239–250.

48. Perdita Huston, *Motherhood by Choice: Pioneers in Women's Health and Family Planning* (New York: Feminist Press, 1992), 96–98.

49. Author's interview, June 9, 1998.

50. Julia Clancy-Smith, "Envisioning Knowledge: Educating the Muslim Woman in Colonial North Africa, 1850–1918," in *Iran and Beyond: Essays in Middle Eastern History in Honor of Nikki Keddie,* ed. Beth Baron and Rudi Matthee (Los Angeles: Mazda Press, 2000), 99–118. On architecture and social space, see Zeynep Celik, *Empire, Architecture, and the City: French Ottoman Encounters, 1830–1914* (Seattle: University of Washington Press, 2008).

51. On the key importance of the *hawma,* see Isabelle Grangaud, "Masking and Unmasking the Historic Quarters of Algiers: The Reassessment of an Archive," in *Walls of Algiers: Narratives of the City through Text and Image,* ed. Zeynep Çelik, Julia Clancy-Smith, and Frances Terpak (Los Angeles and Seattle: The Getty Research Institute and the University of Washington Press, 2009), 179–192. Additional parallels emerge when comparing the life story of the director of the School for Muslim Girls, Charlotte Eigenschenck, who resembled Mme. Malaval in several ways. She was the widow of a colonial official as well as a formidable, but secular, educational missionary, exhorting her pupils to learn.

52. Clancy-Smith, "Envisioning Knowledge"; Clancy-Smith, "Éducation"; and author's interview.

53. Kenneth J. Perkins, *A History of Modern Tunisia* (Cambridge: Cambridge University Press, 2004), 73–104; Nadia Mamelouk, "Anxiety in the Border

Zone: Transgressing Boundaries," in *Leila: Revue illustree de la femme* (Tunis, 1936–1940); and in *Leila: Hebdomadaire Tunisien Independent* (Tunis, 1940–1941) (PhD diss., University of Virginia, 2007); and Kazdaghli, *Nisa' wa dhakira*.

54. Service des Archives de l'Institut Pasteur, biographie, "Etienne Burnet (1873–1960)," http://www.pasteur.fr/infosci/archives/e_bur0.html; and Kim Pelis, *Charles Nicolle: Pasteur's Imperial Missionary, Typhus and Tunisia* (Rochester: University of Rochester Press, 2006).

55. Kazdaghli, *Nisa' wa dhakira*, 23–24.

56. Author's interview, 1998.

57. Kazdaghli, *Nisa' wa dhakira*, 24–26; and author's interview, 1998.

58. Author's interview, 1998; and Kazdaghli, *Nisa' wa dhakira*, 26. Another Tunisian was studying psychiatry in Paris during the 1920s—Salem ben Ahmad Esch-Chadely—who earned his diploma in 1929 and subsequently returned to practice in La Manouba psychiatric hospital outside Tunis.

59. Biographie, *Tawhida ben Cheikh*, March 2, 2011, http://www.african success.org/visuFiche.php?id=981&lang=fr.

60. Kazdaghli, *Nisa' wa dhakira*, 27.

61. On the history of Tunisian women's literature, see Lorna Lunt, "*Mosaïque et mémoire: Paradigmes identitaires dans le roman feminin tunisien*" (PhD diss., McGill University, 2000).

62. Kazdaghli, *Nisa'wa dhakira*, 28; and Huston, *Motherhood by Choice*.

63. Jamila Bahri Benous, et. al., *Dar El Bacha: Reflet d'un siècle, 1900–2000* (Tunis: Éditions Caractère, 2000); and Tahar Melligi, "Tunisie: Tawhida Ben Cheikh, première femme médecin de Tunisie," *La Presse* (Tunis), December 20, 2010.

64. Amira-Bournaz, *C'était Tunis 1920*, 39.

65. Willy Jansen, *Women without Men: Gender and Marginality in an Algerian Town* (Leiden: E. J. Brill, 1987), 238–239.

66. One important question is: Why have these household struggles, so significant to North Africa's evolution, been so rarely evoked in the literature? Perhaps because educated women, a problematic category to be sure, were not necessarily in agreement with nationalist leaders regarding the nation's postcolonial social order—in other words, with the nature of the state.

67. Julia Clancy-Smith, "Gladys Adda," in *Oxford Encyclopedia of African Biography* (New York: Oxford University Press, 2011). When I asked the Tunisian writer Dorra Bouzid (1936–), who studied at the School of Pharmacy in Paris during the 1950s, about her cultural and emotional relationship to France, she replied, "We were opposed to racism and colonialism, not to Europe or the West." Author's interview with Dorra Bouzid, La Marsa, 2009.

68. Jean Amrouche, in *Etudes méditerranéennes* 11 (June 1963): 76–77.

69. On the problems of interviewing, see Brinkley Messick, "Subordinate Discourse: Women, Weaving, and Gender Relations in North Africa," *American Ethnologist* 14, no. 2 (1987): 210–225.

CHAPTER 8

Mukhtar Al-Ayari, a Radical Tunisian in the 1920s and His Place in Labor History

STUART SCHAAR

Al-Ayari served in France as a soldier during World War I and after. On many occasions he got into trouble with his officers and after return- ing to Tunisia boasted about his insubordination while in the ranks. He returned to Tunisia as a committed Leftist and found work as a tram- way employee. He quickly became one of the rare native leaders of the French labor union and the newly formed Communist Party. His ora- torical abilities, indefatigable energy, and intelligence attracted the at- tention of French Leftists in Tunis. His independent spirit clashed with his European superiors at the tramway company, who fired him after he had a dispute with a Jewish passenger. The French union thereafter em- ployed him full-time as an organizer and scores of French police reports demonstrate that he attended most Communist Party and union meet- ings where he spoke frequently. When the CGTT formed at the end of 1924 Al-Ayari left the Communist Party and the French-dominated union and became a major organizer and leader of the new formation along with the better known M'Hammad 'Ali and Tahar Haddad. He and M'Hammad 'Ali were exiled from Tunisia on November 26, 1925, after which he worked on a Cairo trolley. He died in Paris, never to re- turn to his native land. Because he was a communist he has received lit- tle attention from Tunisian professional historians of nationalist per- suasion, who have mostly ignored his contributions. Even communist historians give him scarce attention, mentioning that he was important, but adding little detail about his activities. This chapter explains his im- portant role as a mass leader and places him in his rightful place in the forefront of early twentieth-century Tunisian history.

In 2000 I attended a conference in Tunisia organized by the history department of the University of Manouba dealing with the 1920s in Tunisia. I delivered a paper on the relationship between the local economic crisis caused by repeated drought and the development of the nationalist movement.[1] I was surprised that one of the participants in the conference, a Tunisian history professor, repeatedly attacked one of the iconic figures of that period, Al-Tahîr al-Haddad, popularly known as Tahar Haddad. He, along with M'Hammed 'Ali[2] and Al-Ayari, the subject of this chapter, with the backing of the Old Destour Party founded the first indigenous trade union, the CGTT, at the end of 1924. It was the second oldest native labor union established in Africa after that of South Africa.

For a brief period in 1925, Haddad served as the general secretary of the union after the arrest and forced exile of his two collaborators. A Left-leaning intellectual who read European authors in Arabic translation, Haddad soon thereafter wrote an amazing book in Arabic on Tunisian workers and the labor movement, which was fifty years ahead of its time and filled with astute sociological analyses.[3] In 1930 he published another book, which caused a great stir, on women and the need to aid in their liberation.[4] At the time he was attacked by prominent ulama and his enemies in the Destour Party as punishment for attempting to split the Old Destour and form a new party four years before Habib Bourguiba founded the New Destour party. I was in the uncomfortable position of being the only one at the conference willing to take on this professor and come to Haddad's defense. I had written an article about Haddad in 1996 and recognized his importance as a courageous public intellectual at the beginning of the twentieth century.[5] As often happens under dictatorships, the audience at this conference must have been cowed by the presumed presence of thought police. It became clear to me that this hero of Tunisian feminists, after whom the major woman's center in Tunis is named, had fallen out of favor with the Ben 'Ali regime because of his Leftist politics. By the new millennium—before the Arab Citizens' Revolt began in December 2010—the Left had a diminished place in Tunisian collective memory.

Historians understand only too well that evaluations of heroes and heroines change as political winds change. It should have come as no surprise that Haddad would come under attack in the conservative and stultified intellectual space created by Ben 'Ali's policies. Nevertheless, I was taken aback by the vehemence of the professor's attacks against one of the major figures of modern Tunisian history.

This was not new in Tunisia. For example, while Habib Bourguiba ruled, no serious scholarship could be published in the country on the founder of the old Destour Party Shaykh 'Abd al-'Azîz al-Tha'albî, Bourguiba's arch enemy and intellectual equal. On three occasions, Bourguiba's police searched for al-Tha'albî's voluminous correspondence that Dr. Ahmed Ben Milad had purchased from the shaykh's family. Luckily Ben Milad had hidden the archive outside of his home, thereby preserving valuable documents, which he used to write a major book about this man.[6]

So it is that one of the leaders of the CGTT, Mukhtar Al-Ayari, has mostly been forgotten in the historiography of postcolonial Tunisia. The exceptions include acknowledgment of his importance as a communist and labor union leader by Habib Kazdaghli in his Arabic volume, *Tatawwar al-harakat al-shuyu'ya bi Tunis* (*The Development of the Communist Movement in Tunisia: 1919-1943*).[7] Kazdaghli, the leading expert on the history of the Tunisian Communist Party, repeatedly states that Mukhtar Al-Ayari was an important figure in the early communist movement in Tunisia,[8] but, unfortunately, gives scant details about his daily involvement in Party and labor union organizing and debates. He does list six articles that Al-Ayari wrote in the newspapers that he edited for the Communist Party, *Habīb al-Umma* and *Habīb al-Sh'ab*, without giving details about their content.[9]

Unfortunately, the communist press rarely contained signed articles, out of fear that the police would arrest authors for their radical ideas and writings. In addition, there are several amateur compilations written by aging trade unionists or former communists who have assembled documents to tell the story of the creation of the CGTT and the trial and exile of its leaders. Despite their reproduction of valuable archives, these works lack analysis, portray their heroes as saints, rarely cite documents that show erratic or violent sides to their subjects, never deal with shortcomings, and provide no broader contexts.[10]

As a leading figure in the new Communist Party in Tunisia and an outspoken participant in party and labor union meetings, Al-Ayari played a key role in Leftist and trade union politics in the country. We know a great deal about his speeches and activities between 1922 and 1925 when the French police in Tunisia filled Old Destour, communist, and labor union meetings with their spies, who reported daily on what transpired during those gatherings. The metropolitan French and Protectorate authorities exaggerated the importance of the Communist Party, but since the Old Destour had allied itself with the communists for a short period in the 1920s, the French found it convenient to attack the nationalists for their communist sympathies. By doing so, the Protectorate administration hoped to discredit the nationalists and divide the Tunisian bourgeoisie, since many of its most important members, mainly landowners, clearly favored capitalism. Al-Tha'albî was attacked on many occasions from within his party for this Left alliance. But he had spent months in Paris during which time only the French Communist parliamentarians gave unflinching support to the Young Tunisians and the fledgling Destour Party. His tasks were made more difficult as a result of the French socialists' refusal to back the nationalist program of independence. The communists, on the other hand, gave their full support. The conservative French press, some of the Arab press representing wealthy Tunisians, as well as socialist newspapers condemned the Destour repeatedly for its alliance with the Communist Party. These attacks weakened al-Tha'albî's control of his party and was a contributory factor leading to his own exile from the country between 1923 and 1937.

At Communist Party and French labor union meetings Al-Ayari spoke often since his oratorical gifts and genuine working class credentials made him a crucial asset for the French Left. Nevertheless, he is largely ignored in later accounts of the period. There are many books and articles written about Haddad and M'Hammad 'Ali in Arabic and French, but Al-Ayari's communist affiliation made him a pariah for most nationalist historians. This can be explained by the fact that while the Communist Party supported Tunisian nationalism in the 1920s, by the 1940s and 1950s, on the eve of independence, as was the case throughout North Africa, some individual communists may have supported nationalism, but the Party as an institution showed little enthusiasm for North African independence. Most nationalist historians therefore underplayed the contributions of communists when writing their modern histories.

However, Al-Ayari is especially appealing as a subject of investigation since, after some initial hesitation, he broke with the Communist Party and the French labor movement and joined the new trade union without sacrificing his radicalism. By contrast, his contemporary Dr. Ahmed Ben Milad remained an internationalist throughout his long life and therefore was neutral on the issue of creating an indigenous trade union. Al-Ayari paid for his choice by being banished from his country in November 1925 and died in exile in Paris without ever returning home.

His Life

We know very little about Al-Ayari's early life. What we do know comes from scattered brief biographical notices, his declarations during public meetings as reported on by police spies, and correspondence about him exchanged between French officials. The French historian Juliette Bessis tells us that he was born in 1897 and volunteered for military service during World War I. She also relates that he was wounded in action and received a war medal.[11] The records of the Tunisian tribunal that tried and exiled the labor union leaders, as reported in the Tunisian press, differs from Bessis, telling us that he born in 1889, making him thirty-six years old in 1925, and that he was literate in French and Arabic. This source also mentions that he was married and the father of four children.[12] In a telegram sent by the French Resident General to the Civil Controller of Kairouan in 1922 warning the latter that Al-Ayari was on his way to his city to spread propaganda and raise funds for the Communist Party, he is described as nearly 5 feet 6 inches tall, with black wooly hair, a large nose, olive colored skin, dressed as a European, and wearing a *chechia*—a black nationalist cap. He wore on his jacket lapel a pin showing Vladamir Lenin's face.[13] His archival photo shows a man wearing a necktie with a pudgy attentive face.[14]

A police note early in 1921 informs us that he attended the Franco-Arab school at Bab Sadoun in Tunis, where he learned to express himself in French. He was not as fluent a speaker as the better educated M'Hammed Ali, but his passion compensated for his shortcomings, and he had no complexes whatsoever about speaking extemporaneously at public meetings before thousands of workers. In fact, his working class style of delivery added authenticity to his persona and made him more valuable.

According to the same document, he first worked as a hairdresser and then as a messenger for the police. Early on he tried to become a police officer, but because of "his bad behavior" his request was refused. The report also claimed that he was violent, giving an example from 1909 when he had a heated confrontation with a police officer. The note added in a disparaging tone that he was a frequent visitor to the red light district of Tunis.[15] We learn from another police record from 1922, reporting on a speech that Al-Ayari delivered, that he served in the French military for eight years. His literacy, he claimed, did not help him gain a military rank. He remained a simple soldier, he lamented, because if they promoted him to sergeant, he told his audience, he would not have made any distinctions between French and Muslim soldiers, something the French would not have tolerated. Instead, he continued, they promoted simple-minded Bedouins who, out of fear, always favored the French soldiers over the Muslims. These Bedouin officers, he added, often maltreated their coreligionists.[16] French police officer

Paul Clapier reported in spring 1922 that Al-Ayari spoke at a Communist Party meeting about being punished frequently while he served in the French army because he refused to do his chores and pushed his comrades in arms to revolt against their officers.[17]

His violent language and unruly behavior, according to these police reports, continued while he was employed by the Tramway Company of Tunis after the war, as well as when he served as a labor union leader. We learn that while Al-Ayari served as secretary general of the French tramway union, he was suspended from his job following a complaint lodged against him by a Jewish Tunisian rider who claimed that Mukhtar slapped him when he asked the price of a ticket. Following an inquiry initiated by the company, he was fired. One hundred tramway workers met on the night of March 23, 1921, at the Labor Exchange to hear Mukhtar, who told them that the Jewish passenger had retracted his complaint, but the company, wanting to make an example of him, fired him anyway. A delegation was sent to the French resident general to demand Mukhtar's reintegration.[18] All this happened before the founding of the Communist Party when Mukhtar was affiliated with the socialist SFIO union. Its head, Joachim Durel, decided to allow him to remain secretary general of the Tramway Union despite his having been fired by the company. Durel also named him as a propagandist for the socialist labor union charged with travelling through Tunisia, especially in the mining centers and other work places, as a propagandist. Although his fellow tramway workers wanted to strike over his being fired, Dural opposed the idea and carried the union with him.[19] In his new position every Friday, on payday, Mukhtar collected 4 francs from the Tunis tramway workers for union dues and 50 centimes for himself.[20] Several European leaders of the socialist labor union clashed with Mukhtar over his mixing extremist politics with union affairs and wanted him dismissed as a union official. But the top leaders such as Durel understood his importance and wanted him to stay.[21]

Most existing secondary accounts of Al-Ayari's role in labor union and Communist Party politics leave out police notes reporting the provocative language he used in his speeches. The archives are filled with his violent verbiage, which disturbed Protectorate authorities and provided them with voluminous files with which they built a case for his being exiled. By using such language, he drew attention to himself and led the authorities to record his nearly daily speeches and movements in and out of Tunis. For example, at a meeting of the native section of the Communist Party of February 24, 1922, he warned anyone in the audience who was a police spy that they risked their lives by working as undercover agents for the French. In the same meeting he told the workers that the Party's tasks were not easy and that to succeed they might have to take up arms. He then insulted the Protectorate government and its administrators.[22] A week later at another meeting of the Party, he laid out a plan of action in response to government attacks against the Communist Party, including police raids of members' homes, closing of Party newspapers, and general harassment. He suggested mounting a propaganda campaign calling on people to stop paying their taxes, breaking gas burners for lighting up the thoroughfares of Tunis, destroying electric street lamps, and attacking other public property.[23] A few weeks later, at another meeting of the Communist Party, he called on his comrades not to fear the police since going to prison was not such a bad thing and if they died for the Communist cause that would be an honorable death. He added that they were working to get rid of the colonial state and ended his speech by crying long live Communism and down with the evil government.[24]

In early April 1922, Shaykh al-Tha'albî had convinced Nasir, the ruling bey, to abdicate, thereby creating a constitutional crisis. (See chapter 4, which deals with Kmar Bayya's role in pushing Nasir Bey to adopt nationalist positions.) The Arab press announced the abdication, and the Destour and Communist Parties began mobilizing the population in support of the ruler. It seemed to French officials as if the institutions of the Protectorate were unwinding. Only forceful intervention of the highest Protectorate administrators and military officers, and a French show of military force, convinced the bey to reverse his decision and remain in power. Al-Tha'albi was sent into exile most likely as a result of his role in this failed abdication attempt, and the country was placed on military alert making any subversive and violent language uttered at public meetings ever more suspect and viewed as dangerous for public order.[25] Police commissioner Paul Clapier reported that on April 5, the moment of the attempted abdication, Al-Ayari woke up at 4 a.m. to organize a work stoppage of the tramway workers in solidarity with the bey. The militant then went to the central market in downtown Tunis to invite native traders to close their shops, which they did. He then went to the Destour Party headquarters on England Street where he found a large crowd, which he addressed. In his speech he invited them to take to the streets and march calmly without disturbing foreigners and Jews. He grabbed hold of a Tunisian flag and led them toward a larger demonstration already going on in support of the bey. On the way, he was stopped frequently by French police officers who interrogated him. The Director of the Police, he had heard, had offered an award of 1,000 francs to anyone who brought Al-Ayari to the central police station for questioning.[26] At this critical moment of heightened tension, the same Clapier reported that Al-Ayari announced at a meeting of the native section of the Communist Party that if the Tunisians revolted one day to win their independence, the first thing that he would do was to find the director of the police in order to break his neck in retaliation for his directive promising a 1,000-franc award for anyone who brought him to the central precinct.[27] During this period, filled with mass demonstrations in favor of the bey, Al-Tha'albî recruited Al-Ayari as a Destour Party organizer.[28] The shaykh, himself a workaholic, appreciated Al-Ayari's vitality, forcefulness, and organizational skills.

By April 15, 1922, at another Communist Party meeting, Al-Ayari called on his comrades to spread the word to their friends and relatives to boycott Mr. Alexandre Millerand, the French president, scheduled to visit Tunisia. Al-Ayari called for the closing of shops and people staying home a week before the president arrived. He ended his speech with the slogan "Long live Communism" and "Down with French Tunisia."[29] Al-Tha'albî supported this position but was forced by the Old Destour leadership, under pressure from the resident general, to break ranks with the communists and call off all demonstrations against the president's presence in the country.

At the same meeting, Al-Ayari raised the ante and called on the Communist Party to propagandize seriously and spread insubordination among soldiers stationed in the country, calling such a campaign "primordial for the Communists." He went on to claim that such action could produce valuable auxiliaries for the Party.[30] The French Communist Party in the early 1920s had made antimilitarism into a pillar of its colonial program.[31]

The principal subject of agitation for communist youth in the colonies should be antimilitarism, the program read. This antimilitarism should take the same form of agitation as in France. It is a struggle that the youth should enthusiastically participate in by attacking the racism inherent in the relationship between French and colonial soldiers. French capitalism and militarism upholds that racism.

Al-Ayari, having spent eight years as a soldier, understood the potential for organizing military insubordination and even revolt. French authorities in Paris even expected a revolutionary eruption to break out by summer 1922 and warned the resident general about French, Italian, and Spanish communists propagandizing in North Africa to this end.[32] The more Al-Ayari spoke his mind in public meetings, the more the French police followed his every move and recorded his speeches.

In early 1922 the French Protectorate authorities had begun formulating policies for expelling Tunisian radicals. Over the next few years they exiled major nationalist and Leftist leaders, such as Al-Ayari, who incited fellow Tunisians to act against the Protectorate. Several leaders of the CGTT were tried and banished from the country at the end of 1925 for between five to ten years. Al-Ayari received a ten-year sentence and died in exile. Although this policy removed valuable activists from the Tunisian scene, given the mass nature of nationalism others quickly took their place, and one generation later forced the French to leave the country completely. Fearless militants such as Al-Ayari might have been criticized as provocateurs, as everything they said in public meetings was reported back to French officials by police spies, but more than most leaders they imbued their fellow union members and political leaders with extraordinary courage, something that once again became the hallmark of the Tunisian revolt of 2010–2011.

Notes

1. My paper, "Economy and Politics in Tunisia, 1920–1925," was published in *La Tunisie dans les années 20*, ed. Al-Hadi Jallab (Tunis: Université de Manouba, 2000). Also see Stuart Schaar, "Mukhtar al-Ayari, A Radical Tunisian in the 1920s, and his Place in Labour History," *Maghreb Review* 36, no. 1 (2011), 40–48, © *Maghreb Review* 2011. Used with permission.

2. See Eqbal Ahmad and Stuart Schaar, "M'Hammad Ali: Tunisian Labor Organizer," in Edmund Burke III and David N. Yaghoubian, eds., *Struggle and Survival in the Middle East*, 2nd ed. (Berkeley: University of California Press, 2006), 164–177.

3. Tahar Haddad, *Al-ummal al-tunisiyun wa zuhur al haraka al-inqabiya* (Tunis: *al-maṭba'ah al-fannīyah*, 1927).

4. Tahar Haddad, *Imra'atuna fi al-sharia wa al-majtama'a* (Tunis: *al-maṭba'ah al-fannīyah*, 1930).

5. Eqbal Ahmad and Stuart Schaar, "Tahar Haddad: A Tunisian Activist Intellectual," *Maghreb Review* (London) 21, no. 3–4 (1996): 240–255.

6. See my article, "'Abd al-'Azîz al-Tha'albî: An Early Bridge between Indian, Middle Eastern and North African Islam," *Maghreb Review* 30, no. 1 (2005): 98–129. In the 1980s, I became friends with Dr. Ben Milad and visited him often at his Bardo home. On one occasion he told me about the unsuccessful searches to find al-Tha'albî's archive. Ben Milad with Muhammad M. Driss used these documents to write their book *Shaykh'Abd al-'Azîz al-Tha'albî wa al-haraka al-wataniya 1892–1940* (Carthage: National Foundation of Carthage, 1991).

7. Tunis: University of Tunis, Faculty of Letters, 1988.

8. See Kazdaghli, *Tatawwur al-harakat al-shuyu'ya*, 77, 84 n. 183, 89 n. 194, 93, 95, 99.

9. Kazdaghli, *Tatawwur al-harakat al-shuyu'ya*, 77. The communists probably used Al-Ayari's name on the masthead of its Arabic newspapers because he was one of the few Muslims playing a prominent role in the Party. Although he could speak and write French, Al-Ayari had no advanced education allowing him to edit a complex publication such as the Party's newspaper.

10. For a major example of this type of useful memoir, which integrates Mukhtar Al-Ayari as an important labor leader, see Khémais El Abed, *Mohammed Ali El Hammi et la France: La naissance de la CGT tunisienne (1924–1925)* (Tunis: Centre de Publication Universitaire, 2004).

11. Juliette Bessis, *LES FONDATEURS: Index biographique des cadres syndicales de la Tunisie coloniale (1920–1956)* (Paris: Éditions Harmattan, 1985), 68–69.

12. *La Depêche Tunisien*, March 13, 1926.

13. Nantes, 1st deposit, Tunisia, no. 1542 (2) 6, folios 511 and 512, telegram no. 8, Resident General to Civil Controller Kairouan, April 24, 1922. The Lenin pin is mentioned in Police Note No. 306, signed [Paul] Clapier in Nantes, 1st deposit, no. 1700 (2) 1, folio 455, March 25, 1922.

14. See Khémais El Abeid, *Mohammed Ali el Hammi et la France*, 94.

15. Archives Générales, Archives de Premier Ministre (Tunis), série Histoire du mouvement national, February 12, 1921, carton 15, dossier 1–13.

16. Nantes, 1st deposit, Tunisie no. 1700 (2)-1, folio 50, January 21, 1922.

17. Nantes, 1st deposit, Tunisie no. 1697–2, folio 444 recto, police note signed Clapier, April 8, 1922.

18. Tunis, Archives du Premier Ministère, série histoire de mouvement national, carton 15, dossier 1, folio 9, no. 107, note, March 24, 1921.

19. Tunis, Archives du Premier Ministère, série histoire de mouvement national, carton 15, dossier 1, folio 11, no. 342, March 31, 1921.

20. Tunis, Archives du Premier Ministère, série histoire de mouvement national, carton 15, dossier 1, folio 24, no. 355, April 2, 1921.

21. Tunis, Archives du Premier Ministère, série histoire de mouvement national, carton 15, dossier 1, folio 26–1, May 6, 1921.

22. Nantes, 1st deposit, Tunisia, no. 1697–2, folio 303, note by police commissioner Paul Clapier, February 25, 1922.

23. Nantes, 1st deposit, Tunisia, no. 1697–2, folio 320, report by police commissioner Farfal, March 6, 1922.

24. Nantes, 1st deposit, Tunisia, no. 1700 (2) 1, folio 455, report by police commissioner Paul Clapier, March 25, 1922.

25. The best description of events surrounding Nasir Bey's attempted abdication and al-Tha'albî's role in instigating this action is in Ahmed Ben Milad and Muhammad M. Driss, *Shaykh 'Abd al-'Azîz al-Th'albî wa al-haraka al-wataniya*, 240–246.

26. Nantes, 1st deposit, Tunisia, no. 1697–2, folio 438, note no. 414, April 6, 1922.

27. Nantes, 1st deposit, Tunisia, no. 1697–2, folio 445, note no. 442, April 8, 1922.

28. *La Tunisie française*, April 9, 1922.
29. Nantes, 1st deposit, Tunisia, note 584, no. 1697, folio 491, April 15, 1922, 2.
30. Nantes, 1st deposit, Tunisia, no. 1697–2, folio 495, April 15, 1922.
31. Nantes, 1st deposit, Tunisia, no. 1701–3, folio 395–401, "Programme Colonial," n.d., with documents from August 23, 1924, 4.
32. Nantes, 1st deposit, Tunisia, no. 1700 (2), Minister of Foreign Affairs to the Resident General Lucien Saint, May 20, 1922, folio 119.

Bibliography

Ahmad, Eqbal, and Stuart Schaar. "Tahar Haddad: A Tunisian Intellectual [1920's]," *Maghreb Review* (London) 21, no. 3–4 (1996), 240–255.
———. "M'Hammad Ali: Tunisian Labor Organizer." In *Struggle and Survival in the Middle East*, edited by Edmund Burke III and David N. Yaghoubian, 164–177. 2nd ed. Berkeley: University of California Press, 2006.
Al-Hadi, Jallab, ed. *La Tunisie dans les années 20*. Tunis: Université de Manouba, 2000.
Haddad, Tahar. *The Tunisian Workers and the Birth of the Trade Union Movement (al-'ummâl a-ltûniiyün wa dhuhûr al-harakah al-niqâbiyah)*. 1st ed. Tunis: Arab Printers, 1927. French translation by Abderrazak Halioui. *Les travailleurs tunisiens et l'Emergence du mouvement syndical*. Tunis: Maison Arabe du Livre, 1985.
———. *Our Women in Islamic Law and Society (imra' atuâ fi al-shari' ah wa al-mujtama')*. 1st ed. Tunis: Artistic Printers, 1930 (repub., Tunis: Maison tunisienne de l'Édition, 1978). This book has been partially translated into French by M. Mutafarrij in *Revue des études islamiques 3* (1935): 201–230; and completely republished in a less adequate translation as *Notre femme, la législation islamique et la société*. 1st ed. Tunis: Maison Tunisienne d'Édition, 1978.

Index

www.ingramcontent.com/pod-product-compliance
Lightning Source LLC
Chambersburg PA
CBHW020531270326
41927CB00006B/526